Everett Lee Millard

FREEDOM IN A FEDERAL WORLD

How we can learn to live in peace
and liberty by means of world law

Oceana Publications, Inc.
New York

Library of Congress Catalog Card Number 59-8609

CONTENTS

Preface *by* Stewart Boal 7

THE QUESTION

1. A World Safe for Democracy 11

   *Law as a democratic method — A democratic source
   of law — The role of geographic security — In unity
   is freedom*

2. The Peril of Our Time 24

   *The Platonic Fallacy — Autocracy in modern dress —
   How anxiety invites tyranny — It is happening
   here — You pay the bill — Power never balances*

3. Can Freedom Survive? 39

   *Is planning futile? — The muddling approach —
   Revolution or evolution — Where there is a way,
   there is a will*

THE PROPOSAL

4. A Parliament of Man 54

   *A compromise in representation — Economic
   and educational weighting — Weighting on a
   graduated scale — Logic of a bicameral Assembly
   — Democracy bores from wtihin — How democracy
   defends itself*

5. Life, Law and Liberty 72

   *A World Development Authority — Atoms for peace-
   keeping — Making use of the Trusteeship Council —
   Strategic areas — NeptUNO rules the seas — Man in
   the realm of space — Powers we do not need —
   Selection of an executive — Sources of finance —
   World law in everyday life*

6. E Pluribus UNum 94

   *Cutting the veto down to size — Areas of world
   federal sovereignty — Where persuasion is better
   than force — What is a minimum government? —
   Policeman on a world beat*

THE EVIDENCE

7. Europe First 111

*Growth of the Pan-European concept — Germany as
an asset to peace — The British contribution to
world order — Europeans seek security*

8. The Russians: Are They Human? 125

*The dream and the reality — Exploiting the Com-
munist weakness — When doctrine bows to
circumstance — Security is a two-way street — People
to people*

9. The Meek Shall Inherit... 142

*Every man may love liberty — The new voter —
Neutrals want world law — The debate on revision*

10. Appraisal of Americans 158

*From colony to colonial power — A conflict of
interests — The American mission — The Charter and
the Constitution — Yankee initiative — Economic
co-existence — Learning to live with the world*

THE CONCLUSION

11. The Search for Solutions 175

*A Peoples' Constitutional Convention — Federal
Union among democracies — The Charter revision
approach — Putting the people in the UN*

12. Govern unto Others... 192

*The obstacles to overcome — Education for survival
— How government sets us free*

The Conference 207

Libraries 224

"Where there is no vision,

the people perish . . ."

Proverbs XXIX, 18

PREFACE

An area of government is an area of peace. You are familiar with the keeping of peace in the areas of your city, your state and your nation. A world government is obviously the path to world peace—if government is somehow possible over so great an area.

World peace does not require a world super-government: it needs an international federal government, with direct relation to the individual citizen, but acting in fields largely outside the sovereignty of established nations. A federal government at the world level will mean an international "buffer state", limited to a few specific jurisdictions which are necessary and effective in keeping the peace, and leaving to the nations all other powers.

The alternative is not pleasant to think about. "The world may be destroyed, all or most of the people of the world killed, civilization brought to an end," warns Dr. Linus Pauling, Nobel Prize winning scientist, commenting on the material in this book. "The United States is in greater danger than ever before in its history. Next year, or the year after that, the whole of the United States might be a radioactive waste, with every American dead; and, of course, with Russia a radioactive waste, every Russian dead, and devastation spread over all or most of the world."

No one knows how long the present truce may last. A peace based on fear of retaliation may or may not give men enough time to seek permanent solutions. All we can be sure is that we must lose no time in seeking progress toward solutions which promise an enduring peace.

There are already enough books to prove "why" the only workable solution to the world's desperate peril is the creation of a world law. What humanity needs now is a practical strategy for action toward its establishment. This is not a book which argues "why": it is a book which studies "how".

7

It seeks to visualize who will make world law, and what powers it is desirable that a proposed world legislature shall wield.

Obviously any plan to gain world peace which fails to assure the growth of world freedom would be inadequate. Equally plain is the fact that a plan which strengthens freedom in part of the world but fails to assure peace in all of it would be insufficient. It is the goal of this book that we may learn how to gain peace with freedom.

The difficulties of such a course are formidable. But men may, if they will, look fate in the eye. This pilot study of ways and means toward world law will, we may hope, lead to wider discussions and to more thorough studies of the complex undertaking which this book must, of necessity, oversimplify.

This book has, in a real sense, not one author but nearly four hundred authors. It reports a five-year conference among students of world affairs possessing many varied backgrounds of belief and experience. Participants in the Conference Upon Research and Education in world government ("CURE") include scientists, lawyers and legislators, churchmen and educators and writers, businessmen and sociologists and leaders of world federalist organizations.

Everett Lee Millard, who describes the discussions he has organized and led, is Executive Director of CURE and Editor of its discussion bulletin *One World*. As an officer of the United States Navy during World War II, Mr. Millard designed gunsights which aimed a half-billion dollars' worth of anti-aircraft guns. On behalf of the World Veterans Federation, he has conducted a forum on United Nations Charter revision among leaders of twenty million war veterans.

Contributors to CURE's discussions are united by the traditions of free men. Two-thirds of American participants are descendants of Revolutionary soldiers. Half of the American male correspondents are members or veterans of the United States armed forces. A Dutch conferee was a member of the wartime underground Resistance. A contributor from India served time in British political prisons. A British member flew in the Battle of Britain to save a bastion of human freedom. All of the participants in CURE's debates have in common a purpose to help make the world safe for democracy.

CURE's debates are informal. Conferees each month contribute their varied views to a letter of discussion published for the Conference under the auspices of an Illinois Non-Profit Corporation and supported by subscriptions and gifts. Essays, debates and votes serve to "boil down" the participants' opinions to form a consensus, an area of majority opinion. This book tells, sometimes in votes or in the words of consultants, sometimes with the addition of background material or of editorial commentary by Mr. Millard, the gist of CURE's inquiries.

Today every man's peace and happiness hang by a thread. Enormous events take place uncontrolled by any processes of government. No one is in charge. The designers of the United States Constitution did not intend that the office of the Presidency should be responsible for running the international affairs of the world. Heads of other states are equally helpless.

The world scene has nightmare elements. Russia and America circle each other warily, like two dogs each unwilling to mind its own business, each afraid it may have to fight unless some one intervenes. The stage is set for a war no one wants.

The study of world law is a subject which most of us would willingly leave to philosophers and statesmen. Yet statesmen themselves have confessed their need of guidance by citizens and philosophers. In 1953 the State Department of the United States and the Committee on Foreign Relations of the United States Senate asked the advice of all Americans on the question of revising and strengthening the Charter of the United Nations. It was in this atmosphere of a search for paths to peace that the inquiries of CURE developed.

By 1955 CURE's studies became the only proposals from any source — individual, organizational or governmental — cited in the General Assembly of the United Nations during a week-long debate on revision of the United Nations Charter. At the conclusion of this debate, the General Assembly voted to prepare a Conference for the purpose of reviewing the United Nations Charter. Like the work of "Committees of Correspondence" in Revolutionary times which prepared for the birth of the American republic, the studies of CURE illuminate the task of the proposed Conference, and, we may hope, may even play a part in making the existence of such a Conference possible.

Freedom in a Federal World presents CURE's discussions for the first time to the public.

A key democratic initiative in world politics, these discussions suggest, is the creation of an Assembly of Peoples in addition to the present chamber of governments in the General Assembly of the United Nations. In support of this concept, the report presents evidence that an improved system of representation will enable the United Nations to assume greater and more decisive responsibilities for the keeping of world peace.

The book explains why disarmament can follow logically as a result of a more effective world legislature. It predicts that this evolution will offer greater, rather than less, individual freedom to the world's citizens. CURE's conferees point out that the jurisdictions most necessary to a peaceful government of international affairs will be those which interfere least with the domestic sovereignties of nations.

The study identifies as the chief political obstacle to world law not Russian obstructionism, but a confusion of goals among the world's free peoples. Probing into contemporary psychology, CURE's consultants hint that the mental hazard to peace is not so much public indifference as its opposite: excessive public anxiety. *Freedom in a Federal World* concludes that understanding the aims of world democracy is a first step toward lessening the war worries of the atom age.

Though the book presents a set of proposals, its real intent is to serve as an outline or introduction to the meaning of world law. Its approach seeks the reasonable attitude. It begins by defining democracy and tyranny in such terms that we may usefully operate with them to construct the rationale of a free and ordered world. It uses specific proposals to test the general validity of planning, rather than in the manner of an exclusive revelation. And, finally, this study summarizes what citizens and leaders are doing and can do to achieve the governed world which is a generally accepted but elusive goal of modern political thought.

Stewart Boal, President
Conference Upon Research
and Education
in world government

Chapter 1.

A World Safe for Democracy

"Democracy is the natural condition of human relationships," declares conferee Philip Isely, Lakewood, Colorado, Secretary of the Committee on Elections of the North American Council for a Peoples' World Constitutional Convention.

There is some truth in Philip Isely's remark. Facing the cave bear, a man was on his own. In a primitive society, the right to have an opinion is not for everyone, but it is shared by more than a few. But democracy in a higher culture is a challenge to its citizens' skills, in initiative of the individual, in constructing a system of law, in the development of a representative form of government, and in the organization of these political institutions over a united and secure geographic area.

At all levels, a democratic society seeks to make the highest use of its members' individual capacities.

In an argument, as we defend our ideas, we may become conscious that the other fellow can make a pretty good case too. Modern education teaches modern youngsters that there are two sides to a lot of questions — so much so, that many of us modern people are quite willing to take either side of an argument if we can find someone to oppose us on the other.

"The peculiar evil of silencing the expression of an opinion is that it is robbing the human race; posterity as well as the existing generation; those who dissent from the opinion, still more than those who hold it. If the opinion is right, they are deprived of the opportunity of exchanging error for truth; if wrong, they lose, what is almost as great a benefit, the clear perception and livelier impression of truth, produced by

11

its collision with error," wrote John Stuart Mill in his essay *On Liberty.*

"The only way in which a human being can make some approach to knowing the whole of a subject," Mill added, "is by hearing what can be said about it by every variety of opinion. No wise man ever acquired his wisdom in any mode but this."

Just as a sound exists only when there is someone to hear it, an idea exists only when there is someone to dispute it, or something for it to change.

"Controversy is as vital to an organization as oxygen to an organism," declares Dr. Vernon Nash, Santa Barbara, California, lecturer, author of *The World Must Be Governed* and a founder of United World Federalists.

Freedom to differ stimulates and fertilizes the human mind. Where there is no problem there is no progress.

"Every science, philosophy, art and technology in the world has been developed by reciprocal criticism among protagonists," states Alfredo Rodrigues Brent, Bergen, The Netherlands, author of *Federatie van de Wereld* and a veteran of the World War II underground Dutch Resistance. "No know-it-all group has ever contributed to human advance. The vanguard of a movement is no place for people who need their backs slapped to keep their knees straight. Unity means unity of purpose; it is not spelled uniformity."

When man unlocks the secrets of the universe, he finds at the center the electron and the proton, tiny opposing polarities of the atom. There is enough energy in the atoms of a glass of water, if fully utilized, to propel a steamship across the Atlantic Ocean; and its molecules are so many that if you pour out the contents and allow them time to disperse uniformly about the earth, a fresh glassful of water dipped anywhere from a river or an ocean will contain a couple of molecules from the original glassful. The infinitesmal conflicts within the atom, infinitely repeated, constitute all matter and energy, from the glassful of water to the sun a half-million times the earth's mass, remultiplied by the million suns of our galaxy which we see as the Milky Way, and further remultiplied by a hundred thousand million other galaxies in the vast reaches of space.

Conflict is basic not only to the matter and energy of the universe, but to the daily life of mankind.

All of us come from the Chinese principles of yin and yang, the male and the female. The biology of nature all about us combines opposites to form new life.

Man's religions, originating in Jerusalem, Arabia, Persia, India and China, endeavor to guide his behavior by placing moral insights opposite mere existence.

The dramas of the Japanese theater portray the struggle of human will against fate. Japanese decorative art draws vitality from draftsmanship which dwells lovingly upon the reverse or "S" curve, whose linear contrast conveys a sense of motion to the static scene.

European polyphonal music such as that of Palestrina and Bach weaves its voices in a counterpoint which derives its strength from its occasional dissonances, and its nobility from the logic with which the dissonances occur.

Western philosophy with its emphasis on dualistic and dialectic systems of thought, Western medicine with its lore of antibodies, the elaborate commercial network of the West neatly balancing its credits and debits, all harness the clash of opposing forces by methods with which we are familiar.

Among the discoveries of Western culture is the psychology of human motivation which has developed from theories of Austrian analysts. The causes and cures of man's neuroses are still controversial. It seems clear, however, that disturbances of personality in man, insofar as they are not merely physical in origin, are in general self-destructive. The suicide, the drunkard, the accident-prone driver, the divorce-prone spouse, the juvenile delinquent, the prostitute, the dope addict, the criminal, the gambler, the psychotic—even the martyr in religion and the compulsive hero in war—are all personalities whom psychiatrists see as inviting, either in reality or symbolically, the destruction of their own selves.

As techniques of therapy, psychologists try to direct aggressive impulses away from one's own self, and toward more useful exterior outlets. In this way psychiatry seeks to replace a death urge by a life urge.

Modern man realizes, additionally, that aggressions turned away from one's own self to injure other men are, in a larger sense, pathological too, because they are destructive of human

13

society as a whole. In this interpretation, war represents the death urge on a mass scale. A good proof of the validity of these concepts of modern psychology is that they turn out to be a newer and less mystical way of thinking about old truths.

The institutions of government express the life urge of a culture. A healthy society makes constructive use of its citizens' aggressions. A desirable relationship among humans is one which directs a major part of its citizens' energies toward the conquest of environment, not merely in a physical sense but also in an intellectual sense. The citizen, in this relationship, finds his personal satisfaction in a consciousness of his value to the community.

One of democracy's most necessary skills is the utilization of the self-respect of the individual.

Law As a Democratic Method

A second of democracy's skills is law.

Government exists to limit the expression of citizens' hostilities toward each other, and to organize their energies for useful purposes. Laws, equally, limit and control the actions of the government.

"The American constitutional system is in the great tradition which places the fundamental law above the will of the government," Chief Justice Earl Warren of the United States Supreme Court has declared: "The people of Israel governed themselves as a federation of tribes, without any central government, under a constitution."

Citing this statement by the American Chief Justice, Alfredo Rodrigues Brent comments that "for a very long time this Jewish constitution was passed from generation to generation by word of mouth only. Some 400 years B.C., this constitution was written down. By that time a permanent conference on application of the various articles of law to current events and circumstances had developed. The minutes of the conference meetings were kept in writing and this compilation of minutes covering the meetings of several centuries, together with the original constitution and moral law, form what is today known as the Talmud."

"These were written instruments in the Swiss Confederation beginning with 1293," adds Quincy Wright, Chicago, Illinois,

14

Professor Emeritus of Political Science at the University of Chicago and author of A *Study of War* and other books.

Political science is as complex as the mathematics of radar, the chemistry of nuclear fission or the dynamics of a rocket. And the laws by which men can govern themselves in peace may prove more lastingly essential to man's existence than the newer skills of radar, atomry or rocketry.

In a democracy, a Bill of Rights is the cornerstone of freedom. A Bill of Rights guarantees that free speech, trial by jury and the secret ballot are legal truths, not a ruler's whim.

"Maybe more important than a Bill of Rights would be the simple Biblical phrase, 'Do unto others as you would have them do unto you'," remarks Anne P. Dennis, Califon, New Jersey, past Chairman of the Oldwick, N. J., Chapter of United World Federalists.

The Golden Rule, which many of us know from the Christian Bible, is also a tenet of Taoism, Buddhism, Judaism and other beliefs. It appears no less than fourteen times among the analects written down by the disciples of Confucius. Like the prophets of Communism, Confucius would have liked to abolish all governments; but no workable form of government ever has been able to rely entirely upon the self-restraint of its citizens. The moral principle of the Golden Rule finds practical expression in the laws of a democratic society.

Government under law in a nation is comparable to a well-adjusted personality in the individual: each provides a sense of values. A rule of law provides security to the individual, in the sense that every citizen knows the rules which govern his conduct and protect him against the misconduct of others. Laws are not only a restraint, but also a charter, for the liberties of the individual.

A Democratic Source of Law

A third skill necessary to a modern definition of democracy is the making of laws through a representative form of government.

Many shades of meaning become associated with the word "democracy". It is common to hear someone speak of an acquaintance as "democratic", suggesting that the person is not a snob. A churchman may assert that men need only return to

15

piety in order to live in democratic brotherhood with each other. Communists believe that state ownership of property is the realization of democracy, even if the state is a dictatorship which also owns the consciences of its people.

"I was born a Southern Democrat and still am, and I want democracy to win," says Mrs. Clyde Tiele-Raney, The Hague, The Netherlands, a former citizen of the United States. Yet the name of Mrs. Tiele-Raney's party in the American South has long stood for a denial to Negroes of their right to vote; and the term "democratic" used in a world sense is very different in meaning from its use with a capital "D" as in Dixie.

None of these suggested definitions is what we mean by a political democracy.

The original meaning of the word, in ancient Greek, is a state in which the people are the source of power. As monarchy is the rule of a single man, and aristocracy or oligarchy is the rule of a class or group, so democracy is a self-rule of and by the people.

Even this definition is vague, and over the years it has been subject to all sorts of interpretations.

In Athens, where only freemen could be citizens, it meant a direct democracy, an assemblage of the free populace.

When the United States became a federal government in 1789, its lawmakers were representatives of the people and of the states; but neither the Declaration of Independence nor the Constitution of the United States spoke of "democracy". Instead, Article IV, Section 4 of the Constitution guaranteed to each state a "republican" form of government. Only citizens who owned substantial property, determined by qualifications varying from state to state, and averaging about one-tenth of the adult male population, had the privilege of voting for their representatives in the legislature of the nation.

Not until the election of Andrew Jackson in 1928 could substantial numbers of citizens vote without owning property. Legal devices to discriminate against the poor, the uneducated, and colored voters have waned gradually in the United States during the course of its history. Today there are a few states of the American South where, as a century and a half ago, the voters still number only one-tenth of the adult citizens.

Snobs like to say that unlimited voting in a representative democracy is folly because it equates the vote of a peasant with the vote of a philosopher. This criticism, however, over-looks the essential purpose of popular elections in a representative system. A representative democracy assumes that persons of superior ability are by nature candidates for leadership, not only politically but economically and socially. Elections are the means by which common citizens choose their leaders and protect themselves from exploitation. Voting expresses the power of the plain man.

It is a common notion in the United States that Republicans are the party of money, and Democrats are the party of people. This is not so untrue as the Republicans claim, nor so evil as the Democrats make out. Money is one path to leadership. When a party abuses the power of wealth or the power of popularity, the people may reject its candidacy for a continued tenure of office.

Under a representative form of government, with free nominations, general suffrage and a secret ballot, the ordinary man possesses a sovereign power of review over the affairs of the democratic state.

The Role of Geographic Security

A fourth essential to democracy is the skill to organize a secure geographical area under united political institutions.

Security from aggression, according to 97% of participants in a vote of CURE's forum, is vital to the existence of democratic government. The historical significance of this simple thesis appears to have escaped the notice of political analysts. A look at the map is enough to show us, however, that successful democracies are, in general, located in relatively isolated areas where they seldom face hostile challenges from neighbors. Many examples suggest that democracy is a vigorous flower of civilization which thrives best under a united government relatively safe from trespass.

The world's oldest parliament meets to govern the fishing settlements of remote, sea-girt Iceland.

British democracy arose in an island kingdom able to resist invasion for nearly a thousand years.

On the North American continent dwell two nations which are descendants of the British tradition, Canada secure in the shelter of the more powerful United States.

17

The peninsulas of Europe offer to their inhabitants a relative measure of insulation from frictions with other peoples. The concept of democracy first appeared in the radiant dawn of the Athenian mind, nurtured on the Greek Peloponnesus. The Roman law grew to maturity on the peninsula of Italy. Two millennia later, during the Second World War, the only democracies remaining untouched in Europe were Sweden, on the Scandinavian Peninsula, and Switzerland in her Alpine nest.

Sociologists point out that democracy can exist only in a society possessing a well-developed middle class, able to mediate between the rulers and the relatively submerged handworkers.

Another sociological principle is that democracy works best under conditions which afford good contact and communications between citizens. Such units as the Greek city-state, the Swiss canton, or the New England town meeting are small enough to fulfill this requirement. When larger units are involved, democracy can work only if its citizens possess means of organization and communications independent of the government. These conditions, too, are associated with a society whose middle class is large and active.

The existence of a middle class, with its communications and organizations independent of the state, is characteristic of such stable democracies as those of England, the United States and Canada, Switzerland and the Scandinavian nations. But a middle class cannot sustain democracy under adverse geographic circumstances. Middle classes are nowhere more vigorous than among the many nations of the European mainland. Yet, among the European nations, democratic institutions have been, at best, shaky.

Why do some democratic governments operate with a two-party system, while others are divided into a dozen parties, their cabinets changing every little while? No two-party system is written into a constitution. You will look in vain for a concealed clause which can secure two-party rule in some cases, or frustrate it in other instances. The two-party system flourishes best in stable and secure nations. We may speculate that multi-party setups are a danger signal in republics whose areas are inadequate for their safety.

France, lacking a natural security of geographic location, has fought vigorously for the self-respect of the individual. But

18

France within living memory has three times suffered invasion. France owes the successes of her democracy to the French spirit and her failures largely to the disadvantages of French geography. The relative instability of parliamentary democracies in France, Germany and Italy is largely due to the insufficient political organization of Europe in its entirety.

A little of democracy, like a little knowledge, is a dangerous thing.

It seems logical to believe that, in due course, a regional federation among the nations which will constitute a United States of Europe can help to stabilize the democratic freedoms of their citizens.

Political unity cannot by itself, of course, guarantee the rise of democratic practices.

Until World War II, isolated Japan had never sustained a major military defeat. Villages of the Japanese countryside had developed rudimentary forms of democracy comparable to the town meeting. Her national government, despite the rising importance of a middle class, clung to a feudal tradition. Japan resembled England in a geographical environment favoring the development of law and parliamentary government. The relatively more powerful role of the British parliament was a measure of the Western nations' accomplishment in the organization of liberty.

In the West, too, favorably situated nations sometimes lagged. On the peninsula of Spain, as in Japan, social organization remained in a relatively feudal stage. In history and in social and political organization, there is more than a passing kinship between the Spanish state and the neighboring Arab civilizations on the opposite shore of the Mediterranean Sea. Largely lacking a middle class, Spain made less advance in parliamentary institutions than her European neighbors. The feudal structure of Spanish society, rather than geography, appears to have determined its political configuration.

Immigrants from the Iberian Peninsula colonized the southern half of the Americas, abandoning the feudal mold of their European antecedents, but bringing with them little habit of self-government. Despite the development of a middle class, the liberties of the New World Spanish and Portuguese still suffer from political hangovers of autocracy and of geographical disunity. Here, too, perhaps, there is need of a greater

19

scope of government. It seems likely that the eventual emergence of a United States of South America will aid in stabilizing its citizens' freedoms.

Anyone who doubts this might consider what the plight of the United States of America would be if its states lacked a national federal government. Would a dozen or four dozen independent North American countries remain free and at peace?

If we consult history we remember that there were many border disputes, several trade embargoes and even a few minor wars among the early states. And if we study American state governorships and legislatures we may conclude, as did the authors who wrote *Our Sovereign State* under the editorship of Robert B. Allen, that state governments are often more vulnerable to political corruption than is the national government. A disunited America would be but a flimsy shelter for its citizens' liberties.

A successful "institutionalization of democracy", as sociologists call it, appears to require both a diversification of social structure and an integration of geographic area.

With each passing year, the barriers of the sea or of the mountains are less effective for the protection of a democratic society. Today the shape of security is no longer to be found in a peninsula, an island or a continent. The world itself is the final challenge to the organizational skills of democracy. The only remaining shape of security is now a sphere.

In Unity Is Freedom

"Politics is a little like French dressing: three parts power and one part passion," quips John Holt, Boston, Massachusetts, schoolteacher and a former Executive Director of the New York State Branch of United World Federalists.

One of CURE's conferees close to politics is Hiram Sibley, Chicago, Illinois, planning consultant with the American Hospital Association and a former United Nations Relief and Rehabilitation Administration official in Greece.

"In a popular government when the size has increased so that the government can no longer be near the people, it becomes a matter of pressure," writes Mr. Sibley. "A careful analysis of our state and federal governments will indicate that

20

the things that get done happen because the pressure is greatest. A wise leader will direct these pressures, and that is the principle I follow whenever I have an opportunity to guide our state legislature or administration."

Such pressures are not necessarily democratic.

"Ask a thoughtful American what he thinks democracy is, and he will say, more or less, that it is government by the people. I do not know whether the people of Athens ever had such a government. I do know that we do not have it, have never had it, and are not in the imaginable future going to get it," John Holt observes. "Democracy, throughout the history of our country and of all the countries we think of as democratic, is government of the many by the few—the few who have had the will, energy and talent to get political power, and to hold onto it.

"Democracy is a struggle for political power, not a sort of perpetual referendum.

"The difference between what we call democracies and what we call dictatorships is not that in one a government is by the many and in the other by the few. It is by the few in both cases. The difference is that in a democracy the roads to political power are relatively open, so that the man at the top is continually subject to challenge by others further down the political ladder."

Citizens in a democracy have a power of review or a right of rejection over their government; but this power is in several respects imperfect.

Every Jew, every Negro, Indian, Mexican or Filipino, every Chinese-American or Nisei knows that American political practices fall short of the theoretical equality promised by the Constitution.

In many American state legislatures, antiquated systems of representation allow the votes of sparsely settled country districts to dominate the affairs of teeming city populations.

Most members of city, state and national legislative bodies are dependent upon election contributions from interests which seek, in return, to win privileges in legislation at the expense of ordinary voters.

Tens of millions of citizens disfranchise themselves by failing to vote in elections, accepting a second-class citizenship by reason of their apathy.

Despite such limitations, the power of a democratic people is mighty. Throughout the world, in an increasing number of nations, and to a growing degree, citizens have come to control their governments. Today's world grants powers of self-government to larger populations than the prophets of past centuries ever envisioned.

What, then, of doleful prophecies of a "1984" in which thought control, hidden persuaders and "big brother" techniques will make "other-directed" automatons of us all? Of such stuff, in this age of anxiety, are the nightmares of intellectuals made. Will world government be world dictatorship, and all our days be regimented?

To see what might conceivably happen in such circumstances, let us imagine that a single dictatorial power somehow gains control over the whole of the earth. Let us assume that its unopposed rulers become secure from most major menaces except those invented by the feverish brains of space fiction writers. If our reasoning is correct, the consequences are easy to foresee. A single dictatorial world government would have no foreign conflicts to fear. An army with nothing to do but bully civilians will soon take on the character not of a military but of a police force. Scientists, technicians and administrators, freed from the unquestioning loyalty which they would owe to an imperilled government, will ask an increasing share of rights and benefits. Rank-and-file citizens, released from the dread of destruction, will seek a growing measure of personal dignities—and they will know how to get what they want. The pretexts for authoritarian discipline will have vanished.

Though not every nation, in the past, has developed the practices of democracy, most peoples are familiar with democratic methods at least at the local level in their shop or in their community. A government of world scope will include among its citizens hundreds of millions who have had a taste of political self-reliance, and who possess a measure of experience in self-government. Citizens of any world government whatever are sure to have the will and the skill which are necessary to the establishment of freedom.

By such reckoning, the attraction of democratic political institutions will beckon the people of any imaginable united world. Quizzed on this hypothesis, 73% of CUREspondents venture to believe that citizens of a single, secure world civilization will not permit themselves to be governed by a tyranny.

Can we follow this logic another step? Could the free world surrender to Communism and, like a clever jiu-jitsu warrior, accomplish the defeat of tyranny by seeming to yield to its strength? Would an undisputed world capital at Moscow become, within a generation or two, an effective fount of world freedom and justice?

Certainly logic would say so — if annihilation were the certain alternative. But the principal objection to such a capitulation would not be the loss of wealth, the rape of womenfolk, or the purges of capitalists and "bourgeois" and intellectuals which Westerners might fear during such a strategy of self-abnegation. Annihilation is not the only alternative. The real sin in a logic of meekness would be its surrender of initiative by those skilled in democratic government to those unskilled. Moscow's primitive satrapy cannot govern well what it now controls: to entrust liberty into the hands of those who know least about it would be a relinquishment of responsibility almost as abject as would be our fatalistic acceptance of an atomic holocaust. Liberties are to share, not to sacrifice.

A period of autocracy does not seem a necessary stage in man's progress toward world unity. Free men possess assets of social understanding and constitutional experience which they can use to construct a democratic world law directly upon the foundation of present liberties. The federal principle of association between states for a government of their common affairs is adaptable to the larger purpose of world security. We can blame no one but ourselves if we neglect to explore the potentialities of these democratic skills in government as an answer to the challenge of our time.

It seems evident that the success of human civilization is inseparably linked to the institutions of political democracy.

Chapter 2.

The Peril of Our Time

Every people has a right to choose its own form of government. In the opinion of 72% of participants in the Conference Upon Research and Education in world government, a people's choice of governments may extend even to tyranny, if they want it. But one nation's choice affects everyone, many conferees believe: tyranny in one nation is a matter of concern to all.

"Erection of an authoritarian government, by any means, in any country, must be a matter of grave interest to all other peoples of the earth," writes Col. R. Frazier Potts, Miami, Florida, Commander of the 9187th Air Reserve Group, United States Air Force and a founder of Federal Union. "Our concept of freedom does not allow a householder to do whatever he chooses with his property (as, for example, using it as a house of prostitution) in disregard of the welfare of his neighbors and of the community. Our recent and present experiences have shown only too clearly that every authoritarian power is a nuisance and a menace in the world community."

A people's choice of tyranny is a relinquishment of any right to further choice. If a people "choose" Communism or fascism, if they "elect" to abandon elections, what choice or election remains for new citizens when they come of age? Does liberty include the "freedom" to become slaves?

Thomas Jefferson, who was not afraid of revolutions, urged that Americans should overthrow their government every twenty years, in order to keep it healthy.

"While it seems to be doubted today, American history cannot other than sustain the right to revolt against any government as an equal right in time or rank with a right to choose a government," says Kenneth R. Kurtz, Weston, West Virginia, news broadcaster and past Chairman of the student Federalist organization WORLD.

"I see these rights as antecedent to, and existing independent of any government order—therefore always available to be drawn on by a people; rights which do not disappear when tyranny takes over," he goes on. "And if you think this is impractical, consider the history of revolutions, and how this position has been drawn on in all successful revolutions. Nothing could be more practical."

The somewhat cautious consensus of CUREspondents is that revolution is far from finished as a relief valve against tyranny, even in the face of possible annihilation by modern weapons. In the opinion of 63%, revolt is still today a practical way to overthrow tyranny.

But the emphasis may shift, many conferees think, away from armed revolution and toward mass slowdown or passive resistance as a peoples' veto of abuse by authority.

The Platonic Fallacy

More than two thousand years ago the Greek philosopher Plato pictured in *The Republic* what he considered an ideal state. In Plato's republic, each citizen was to do the work to which he was best suited by birth or ability. There would be laborers, artists, merchants and administrators, and the ablest men would choose other able men to succeed them as leaders.

Plato took for granted the world of aristocrats and slaves in which he lived. He suggested what he thought would be an ideal state: but he did not describe what we should now think a practical way to attain it. Nowhere did Plato mention any elections, parliament or other means by which the people might control their leaders. In Plato's day, when Athenian freemen met to discuss affairs of state before a temple, democracy was in its most rudimentary form, an early stage in the long evolution of political institutions. It would be unjust to expect Plato to have invented democracy as we know it.

The personal charm and the moral insights of Plato's writings have made him one of the great teachers of following ages. But it is obvious that his political prescription can be stretched

25

to cover a multitude of sins. His republic was a model for James Madison; and it was also a model for Karl Marx.

The primitive Platonic republic, without the democratic improvements developed by later ages, offers a precedent for modern tyrants who assert that men should be ruled for their own good, but without their own consent. The judgment of good and evil, in the totalitarian ideal, rests within the consciences of men who win their way to leadership.

But modern democratic peoples know that the conscience of an ambitious man is a dangerously frail substance.

Autocracy in Modern Dress

The germ of totalitarianism lies dormant in every society, ready to run a fever when the body politic becomes unhealthy.

The serious student of mankind must reckon with the attraction which authoritarianism holds forth, even to idealistic and decent men, in societies which lack security. The promise of a firm authority, the assurance of a state-guaranteed job, the protection of military discipline offer magnetic attraction to citizens who are apprehensive of hard times or of hostile attack. The paternal state appears to offer order and safety to men in retreat from danger. Co-operative action is an instinctive behavior of imperilled groups.

Mussolini made many a dejected Italian street loafer into a self-respecting worker whose leisure was occupied with sailing the Adriatic Sea or tracking the ski slopes of the Dolomite Mountains. Count Albert Apponyi, chief Hungarian envoy to the League of Nations, upon returning to his homeland from Italy in 1933 deplored "the collapse and misery whose proofs meet us here in Hungary at every step" and told his countrymen that the Italians accepted "with determination and joy the discipline and hard work" which Fascism asked of them.

Hemmed in by the vengeful Allies of World War I, Germans came to feel that the democratic Weimar Constitution sapped the valor which their nation needed for the recovery of its pride. Hitler's government disciplined the German state into a fighting force. To many Germans, Naziism became patriotism.

Stalin's stubbornness, ruthlessness and nationalism helped give the Russian people unity and fortitude to survive through World War II and into a precarious peace.

In some countries totalitarianism may assert a claim to economic necessity. A nation possessing little private capital may seek to raise itself by the bootstraps. It may undertake to form public capital by means of state regimentation, using one five-year plan after another to build up heavy industry and to develop natural resources. Who can ask China to industrialize herself by floating bond issues among her citizens? Instead, she "shanghais" their labor and their lives; and her excuse is that the urgencies and perils of the epoch permit no alternative. Dams and mines, harbors and airfields, smelters and looms bring the warlike posture to a totalitarian society, while the full belly remains a dream.

A people accepts tyranny through intimidation or fear. Totalitarianism is not necessarily contrary to the wishes of the governed. In many societies, from Plato's time to the present, a boss's program has won support of a popular majority. All too often the people ask for it.

"Freedom is a heavy burden to most people," declares John Holt, "and if they can find someone they reasonably trust to relieve them of it, they will be happy to turn it over to him."

Whether or not the people want it, authoritarianism most easily takes command in the environment of an "atomized" or "mass" society. The government of a mass society has a monopoly of the means of communication. Individuals who may wish to oppose the government lack the communications and the independent political organizations through which to make their opposition effective.

An ancient tyranny or a feudal oligarchy was a mass society by definition. It lacked the middle class, the communications and the non-governmental organizations which were to accompany the later rise of democratic practices. A modern totalitarian leader, on the other hand, must undertake to create a mass society by "atomizing" his citizenry. He must monopolize communications and destroy independent groupings. Today's totalitarian must turn back the clock. He must suppress the skills of self-government which have become available to modern populations.

One stage in the process of "atomization" which facilitates the rise of a despot is the fracturing of an organized opposition party into many splinter groups. When a two-party system gives place to a multi-party situation, we are observing a trend

27

toward a mass society vulnerable to the authoritarian leader.

The case history of authoritarianism points to a background of economic, moral and social ills. Whatever the immediate cause, always in one form or another, like a lowered state of resistance in the political organism, insecurity is present. Tyranny is a political disease. Its germ is fear. Its symptoms are various forms of authoritarian discipline. And its mortal end is, all too often, war.

How Anxiety Invites Tyranny

The search for security, like the effort to find happiness, is not an end in itself. Anyone who puts his own happiness ahead of other people's is likely to end up supremely unhappy; and the person who sets his security above his self-respect is a fair bet to wind up someone else's slave.

"A welfare state that 'does everything' is a great threat to liberty," declares John Logue, New York, N. Y., of the Department of Political Philosophy of Fordham University.

But individualism, like conformity, has its excess. Security is a matter of degree. Only the most aboriginal of capitalists would lump together all social welfare, all socialist economy, and all autocratic government. Real life is more complicated than that.

There can be democratic nations with socialism, like the Scandinavian countries. And there can be autocracies with capitalism, such as Portugal and Spain.

A capitalist nation, like any other, contains the seeds of authoritarianism. The business world is full of conformists, as David Riesman points out in *The Lonely Crowd*. German steel barons backed Hitler. Certain American oillionaires supported Senator Joseph McCarthy. Some capitalists who talk loudly against socialism are really expressing their distaste for democracy.

The efficiency of raw capitalism is greatest in an expanding frontier economy, where new developments stir a yeasty ferment of enterprise and rivalry. The high achievement level of rugged individualism is bought at the expense of social hostility, personal insecurity, status rivalry and other psychological discomforts which impel the individual to get ahead and to defeat others. Some of the pioneer's psychological traits have

28

become less useful in the atomic age. Today an increasing number of able men see their goal as a better human society, and fewer see their goal as individual wealth and power.

"The personality of modern man has not caught up with him yet," declares Dr. Abram Kardiner in *The Psychological Frontiers of Society*, blaming the obsolete patterns which persist in our growth system and the insecurity of our social order. As long as these continue, he says, "we must expect the continuation of all those defenses which mutual hostility and envy create, the most destructive of which is our 'class' system in which everybody is obliged to guard his self-esteem by having social relations only with those who can act as mirrors to his effective self. This seems to be the motive for exclusiveness, snobbishness, cliques, clubs, neighborhoods, race hatreds, and the like.

"In the structure of the personality of modern man are very explosive elements which can lead to mutual destruction."

The statistics of crime and juvenile delinquency, of automobile slaughter, of divorce and drunkenness, and of mental breakdown offer obvious illustrations of Dr. Kardiner's thesis.

Civilized man gambles away each year astronomical sums of money. During the Second World War, Americans gambled away more of their money than they invested in war bonds. The outlet which people find in gambling transfers some of the uncertainty and risk of their personal lives to an inanimate sacrifice of wealth.

Others among us prefer living sacrifices. Many of our favorite "sports" are spectacles where paid performers risk injury or death: a bull-fight, a rodeo, boxing, wrestling, football, an air show or an auto race.

Murders are among the commonest fare of our daily metropolitan papers. Modern man's endless appetite for books and shows and news of gunplay, crime, terror and mystery expresses his aggressive impulses. Self-identification with violence is our vicarious and socially acceptable form of hostility.

The desire which we call "love", as Freud's pupil Dr. Theodor Reik points out in his *Psychology of Sex Relations*, is often a response to the apparent self-assurance of another person which is lacking in oneself. In the Western legend an all-too-familiar type of "romantic" love is a hopeless love: for someone dead or unobtainable, for an unresponsive partner, for an irresponsible neurotic or for a drunkard. Many people in an individualistic society lack enough self-assurance to enjoy fully what they possess; the insecure lover's self-doubt too easily taints the possession of the beloved. Frustration and frigidity, hangovers from the Victorian age, still inhabit millions of our homes. The dissatisfied wife, the desperate husband are familiar figures in the divorce courts of Paris or Podunk, of Munich or Minneapolis.

"We measure success in terms of material wealth, power and privilege. The price paid by those who succeed all too often is such as to destroy their happiness," comments Erwin H. Klaus, Fresno, California, Chairman of the Special United Nations Subcommittee of the American Veterans Committee. "All too often it consists of mental and physical indigestion, inability to assimilate gains for such fruitful purpose as leading a wholesome family life, regret for the loss of ideals, lack of identification with and therefore lack of acceptance by one's fellowmen."

Psychological discontent is a spur which drives many individuals to excel. But it also preoccupies large portions of Western populations with ego gratification and status struggles. It submerges the Golden Rule. Its heavy content of guilt and resentment invites mobilization by a "big brother" who "knows best".

Under the individual stresses of a highly competitive society, the weakest personalities tend to break down. Torn by the group stresses of a disunited world, the morale of a nation may break down. Goaded past reason, each people will break down in its own way. Every society has its own lines of stress, its points of fracture. The most capitalist of Western nations, as we have seen, can also be the most hysterical about enemy spies. No one is immune. World insecurity imperils the psychological health of individuals and nations alike.

It Is Happening Here

The age of isolation is past. Americans learned in 1950 that Russia, too, had perfected an atom bomb. Frustration and anger welled up in a wave of Congressional investigations and loyalty oaths. Behind the flag-waving, it was easy to sense fear.

Geographic isolation, when it existed, gave Americans security. The psychological hangovers of isolation cannot stay the tide of physical events. New arms have destroyed security for all nations; more new arms cannot restore anyone's safety. A military deadlock is a posture of peril.

"The hopelessness of winning a war has been by no means in all cases a deterrent to starting it," observes Quincy Wright, "as witness Spain in 1898 or Japan in 1941. According to Roosevelt in 1938, the Axis world included 10% of the world's population and resources, the rest of the world 90%; but the 90% didn't prevent the 10% from starting war."

With arms grow fears, and vanish freedoms.

The power and productivity of the United States, the long mental conditioning of Americans in democratic procedures, all combine to resist the loss of liberty. It is the opinion of 78% among CURE's contributors that democratic institutions in the United States can survive a cold war. But peril lies latent. An 80% consensus of correspondents find elements of totalitarianism already present in today's America.

Just as Russia fears and "jams" radio broadcasts of *The Voice of America*, so, too, a fearful American government confiscates and destroys publications mailed from Iron Curtain countries unless addressees in the United States secure a special license to receive them.

CUREspondent Mary Hays Weik has viewed and described a half-dozen little-publicized concentration camps which the United States government keeps ready to imprison possibly "subversive" American citizens if and when a future conflict threatens.

Growing governmental secrecy imperils the public knowledge of public affairs, strangling the freedom of information which is vital to democracy.

The American founding fathers shunned a standing army as a standing threat to liberty. Today, for the first time, the United States has a powerful professional military class. CURE's consultants see dangers to American civil institutions in the military establishment of the Pentagon, in Selective Service, in chauvinistic veteran leaders, in the Federal Bureau of Investigation, in the civil prominence of former admirals and generals, and in the idolatry lavished upon a soldier President.

Civil factions in the United States, too, contain potentiali-

31

ties for democracy's destruction. CUREspondents detect such elements in reactionary business groups, corrupt labor unions and autocratic churches.

Educational institutions in America are the arena of a battle for the minds of the coming generation. Great universities can sometimes defy the bigots who seek to forbid them to hear all sides of a question; but lesser schools often suffer censorship of their books, their topics and their attitudes.

Many conferees see authoritarian trends in Southern racist demagogery. Yet the crude remedy of Federal intervention appears to others as an equally grave menace.

By reason of their very number such totalitarian potentialities are, as yet, relatively diffuse. If they should sometime coalesce around the figure of some false patriot, American liberty will be in bad trouble.

Already there have been hints of this. Many Americans saw an emerging dictator in Senator Joseph McCarthy of Wisconsin. The apparent contradictions in the brief if not brilliant career of this home-grown Hitler are worth our attention.

Early in the game, he won a primary election with the help of a Communist labor faction. As Senator, wooing a more respectable element in the community, McCarthy was one of a hundred or more sponsors of a joint Congressional resolution favoring steps toward world government. Later, almost by accident, he touched on the mainspring of American anti-Communist anxieties. He never uncovered a Communist (which was a wonder, for there were some around). But he did find a horde of American citizens ready to follow an American Führer in suppressing traditional freedoms of conscience.

Senator McCarthy's accusations of disloyalty in the State Department of the United States government were a "reactionary process", according to G. W. Greene, Salisbury, North Carolina, of the World Government Institute of Catawba College, "taking us back . . . to a time several centuries ago before we in the U.S.A. pointed out the way to real freedoms for citizens of a free country."

McCarthy's charges were fake. But there was nothing imaginary about the demoralization which he caused in the State Department, nor about the damage which his crusade

32

did to the foreign policy, to the military and educational systems, and to the scientific and intellectual life of the American nation.

And, ominously, public opinion polls reveal that a substantial minority of Americans still approve the purposes which "McCarthyism" represented to them.

Psychologists recognize a large element of illogic in anxieties. Ill-adjusted personalities may center their anxieties upon money worries, sex relations, health, or on getting along with other people. Often anxieties find expression in hostility toward another class of society, toward the opposite sex, toward a different race or religion, or toward foreign nations and foreign peoples. Scratch a McCarthyist and you will frequently find an isolationist, an anti-feminist, a racial bigot and a religious fanatic all wrapped up in the same warped human bundle.

A typical nationalist in the United States is activated "not by love of Americans and their culture," but by a sense of "hostility and anxiety in relation to other nations," according to Dr. Daniel J. Levinson, Assistant Professor of Psychology at Harvard University, writing in a paper presented before the American Psychological Association.

Isolationism is a group neurosis of a paranoid or fear-filled nature. It makes no rhyme or reason when the victims of an isolationist neurosis react to world disorganization by clamoring for more disorganization; yet that is the irrational nature of a neurotic fear. In this way national stresses mobilize the neurotic elements in a community.

These stresses can quickly inhibit intellectual progress. "There is very little branch or chapter activity in Florida at present," reports Dorothy S. Briggs, Adamsville, Rhode Island, former member of the Executive Council of United World Federalists. She says that advocates of world law in Florida "have more or less gone underground because of prejudice and misconception of UWF actively fostered the last four or five years" by veteran groups, patriotic organizations and reactionary political figures.

The protective conditions which produced Western democracy are vanishing. A climate of "pistol and claw" can result not only in the progressive suppression of rational thought, but in the gradual erosion of all personal freedoms.

Correspondent John Holt declares that the dread of an uncertain destiny is making inroads all the way down the line of the Bill of Rights contained in the Constitution of the United States.

"(1) Ex Post Facto: any number of men have been, and are being punished, for doing things that were legal when they did them.

"(2) Bill of Attainder: if the Smith Act is not a Bill of Attainder, as such was understood by framers of the Constitution, then the words have no meaning.

"(3) Double Jeopardy: the trick is to try a man for committing a crime. If he is acquitted, try him for committing perjury during his first trial . . .

"(4) Assumption of Innocence: this, the foundation of Anglo-Saxon law, has been abolished in security cases.

"(5) Jury of His Peers: General Yamashita convicted by a jury of his enemies.

"(6) Treason: Constitutional definition thrown out the window in the case of the Rosenbergs, who gave information (if they gave any) not to an enemy, but to a nation with whom we were at peace and with whom we had very recently been an ally.

"(7) Habeas Corpus: the Japanese internees during the war, arrested without a charge and imprisoned for years without a trial and without any opportunity to defend themselves. . ."

When panic strikes, suspicion rules. New politicians will arise to accuse their opponents of treason. Neighbors will spy on each other. Cloaked in respectable fronts such as veterans and patriotic organizations, financed by men with more money than brains, egged on by a few goosestepping newspapers, aided by a clandestine poison press, authoritarianism will gradually seep into the bones of America as it does into nations which fear America as an enemy.

"We could conceivably lose without a shot being fired," warns William A. Wheeler, Rochester, New York, former Chairman of Genesee Council of United World Federalists.

And John Holt adds, "if we can avoid war for another fifty years or so, only the difference in language will enable a man to tell whether he is in Russia or the United States."

If a dictatorship at some future time takes over the United

States of America, the betting among CUREspondents is six to one that it will come as a native American movement, rather than by the spread of Communist influence from Russia.

You Pay the Bill

Like any fear mechanism, tyranny inhibits the rational behavior of its victims. A dictatorship stifles the initiative and the individualism of its subjects, and for this reason fails to tap the best human resources available to it. Autocracy, no matter how well-meaning its leaders, no matter how hard-working its citizens, is fated to relative sterility, because it lacks the competition of ideas which stimulates new thought among leaders and citizens alike.

The competition of individuals is a constructive process when it occurs within a governed nation; but rivalry between nations is a destructive force when it exists in an ungoverned world community. It is from the disunity of nations that citizens have to fear totalitarianism. Today's world has changed so that it is internationalism, rather than nationalism, which offers the most lasting hope of leading peoples out of servitude. Tyranny reflects an inadequacy of government. Like a secretion of adrenalin into the human bloodstream at a moment of danger, totalitarianism is in today's world a preparation for battle.

Peace is not merely the absence of war. A state of potential war exists when there is an absence of the means to maintain peace. Since the advent of the United Nations the phrase "Cold War" has described world power conflicts which the present United Nations is inadequate to govern. War is implicit when peace is not positive.

The insufficiencies of the United Nations are different in degree, but not in kind, from the inadequacies of the League of Nations. In 1939 the outbreak of war presented to humanity the bill for the failure of the League of Nations to govern human conflicts.

The Second World War devoted to destruction a million times a million man-hours of labor. Such a quantity can be named, but hardly grasped by the mind. Its personal meaning, to many people, was several years of life preoccupied with the effort to destroy other people.

35

To a quarter of a million young American men, of an average age around twenty-two, its meaning was the end of life hardly begun.

The writer of this book knew some of them. Gunner's Mate Francis McKone was torpedoed at sea. Ensign James Maddox died after seventy-six days on a liferaft. Lieutenant Howell Murray was lost in the explosion of the destroyer Turner in lower New York Harbor. Marine Lieutenant Robert Nelson was killed on Saipan. Lieutenant Colonel Peter Dewey, son of a United States Congressman, was ambushed in Saigon.

Franz Friedrich Colloredo-Mannsfeld was born an Austrian count. He became a United States citizen and, in his thirties, joined the Royal Air Force. At Miami in 1940 young British pilots were training for the battle of Britain. Four out of five of them died before their job was done. Squadron Leader Colloredo-Mannsfeld was shot down in a Spitfire.

Carl Zeidler was the Mayor of Milwaukee and the brother of its present Mayor. He took a leave of absence from his office to join the Navy. He got sixty days' training and command of a four-inch gun on a merchant ship. Home on leave, he told Milwaukee reporters of sinking an enemy submarine at several miles' range. When headlines about this yarn reached Washington, annoyed Navy officials ordered him forthwith back to sea. A few days later Lieutenant Zeidler and his ship disappeared without a trace in the submarine-infested South Atlantic.

Each reader of this book, every citizen of Allied nations, can add tales of someone who vanished from his life.

The list of the soldier dead of the Russian nation was more than twenty times longer than America's own.

Make room in this tabulation for the dead Jews of Poland, the dead Chinese, the dead civilians of bombed cities all over the world. Add to these, if you have the stomach for it, the dead defenders of Japanism and Italianism and Germanism.

Three hundred billion dollars, as a direct cost to America of the Second World War, represents twice the sum of all previous American war costs plus the nation's peacetime expenses since its founding. The Second World War took a quarter of the oil reserves of Texas, a quarter of America's zinc and lead, and a fifth of American resources of copper.

The churches of Wren's London, the bridges of Florence, the Library at Louvain, the scientific museum at Munich all fell in rubble to pay for the failure of the League of Nations. Leipzig craftsmen labored for a century to engrave upon printing plates the music of Johann Sebastian Bach: Hitler needed the metal, and the plates went for scrap. According to a report of Harvard librarians, the destruction of books and libraries in World War II "probably exceeded by many times the destruction of all previous wars and catastrophes put together."

The costs of war are rising. American losses in the Korean War, a relatively minor conflict, equalled the nation's losses in World War II. Soon the costs of war may be total.

Power Never Balances

A failure to utilize the skills of free men in government loads the odds, not only against democracy, but against survival. Free men who engage in power politics against tyrannies accept, in effect, the enemy's choice of battleground. To accept battle where we are weakest courts defeat: we stand to lose our liberties and our lives.

A future struggle for supremacy by naked force will involve perhaps a brief war, perhaps a series of wars. Much of what now exists on earth will vanish. Even if everyone's goal should be a world government, much of mankind will not survive to be governed or to govern themselves.

Only 22% of correspondents polled by CURE think that a peace based on ungoverned balance of power can continue indefinitely.

"No balance of power can continue indefinitely because history shows that some nations decline in power while others increase," asserts John W. Schneider, Bay Shore, L. I., New York, Treasurer of New York State Branch of United World Federalists. "Eventually one side will either become strong enough to attempt to impose its will on the other side or will think it is strong enough. In either case, a world war is almost inevitable without a world government."

Dr. J. David Singer, Ann Arbor, Michigan, a member of the Department of Political Science at the University of Michigan, gives a typical case history of a balance of power.

37

"We pass through a momentary balance as one bloc overtakes and surpasses the other in an erratically upward spiral of actual power," writes Dr. Singer. "Balance is less stable as neutrals succumb to the centripetal force of one of the two power centers. Bi-polarity is the final phase before instability reaches the point of detonation."

"In theory a peace based on balance of power can continue indefinitely, particularly as the power in question is suicidal and therefore less likely to be used than the non-suicidal power of surviving wars," contributes Patrick J. Armstrong, London, England, Clerk to the British Parliamentary Group for World Government. "*But* there is a large 'area for accidents' and it is mathematically certain that 'accidents will happen'." •

If a band of aggressors assembles and detonates a nuclear bomb in some basement in New York or another of the world's great cities, against whom do we retaliate?

88% of CURE conferees agree that fear of retaliation will not prevent war. To base peace on the fear of retaliation is a counsel of folly; for it assumes that there are rational men on both sides. In actuality, there are many more than two sides, and men are not always rational.

Totalitarian leaders are especially not always rational. Totalitarian leaders sit atop irrational structures, and they usually earn their eminence. At the least, like all power-oriented individuals, they are neurotic menaces to society. At the worst, they may be psychotic heads of diseased mobs which behave as no individuals among them would act if they were in their right senses.

Flimsy hopes of co-existence which rely upon the threat of reprisals leave democratic men without real protection against any deluded zealot who starts a blitz. Some accident, a blip on a radar screen mistaken for an enemy, or a madman's push on a button will eventually put a period to any such wishful dreams. A moment's insanity will bring the end of a balance of power, for the innocent as well as for the guilty.

It is clear that in the present day world the existence of tyranny anywhere threatens the failure of all our civilization.

Chapter 3.

Can Freedom Survive?

The conflict between tyranny and democracy fills the human heart with dread. Too plainly it can spell disaster to all our lives.

Yet there is nothing we can do which will wipe out autocracy all at once. Democracy and tyranny have lived side by side for centuries, and both will continue to exist in the years immediately before us. The challenge is one of co-existence. Democracy's hope is to shift balances in its favor, to outthink, to outlast and to outbid tyranny in the struggle for the allegiances of men.

Hope cannot exist in an atmosphere of panic.

"Psychologists agree that people evade—often with ingenious mental twists—messages that create excessive fears, particularly if the communication does not provide realistic and feasible suggestions for dealing with the problem," say a group of motivation experts in a study, *Action for Peace,* prepared for the Institute for International Order under the direction of CURE conferee Earl A. Osborn.

"Fear appeals, while they are often successful in winning attention, may prove ineffective in producing the desired action on the part of the reader," the study goes on.

"In one experiment three techniques were used to promote dental care. One was a highly dramatic talk, with photographs, showing the gruesome results of lack of care. The other two were moderate, rational explanations. The dramatic version succeeded in getting more people to worry about their teeth, but surprisingly, these worriers adopted the recom-

39

mended remedies less often than those who heard the moderate warnings.

"The urgent need for international methods of preserving peace seems to be clearly recognized by most people; and apparent apathy and indifference may well be the result of fear and anxiety, which psychologists recognize as immobilizing forces."

The motivation experts who prepared this study included Frank G. Kelly, formerly with the International Press Institute; William N. McPhee of Columbia University, and William W. Wade, formerly pamphlet editor of the Foreign Policy Association.

From a labor union executive among CURE's conferees we have a corroboration of this theme.

"As one whose business is mainly based upon collective bargaining," observes Byrl A. Whitney, Kensington, Maryland, Education Director of the Brotherhood of Railway Trainmen, "I have observed that the real hopelessness in men's lives comes when men declare there is nothing to negotiate, not when they are willing to sit down around a conference table and negotiate the details that will bring them to the objective to which they have all dedicated their purpose."

A housewife puts it in a nutshell. "We have to start on a value basis," declares Anne P. Dennis, "not just on the 'atom bomb will blow us all up' basis."

Fear arguments, those based on atomic and missile perils, should not constitute a principal stress in peace persuasions, agree 74% of CURE's advisers. And 54% are of the opinion that the principal psychological block to progress toward world federalism is a widespread feeling that an individual is personally helpless to advance the cause of peace.

During the five years of the studies of the Conference Upon Research and Education in world government, man's hopes for peace have sunk to a new low. "What the world needs today even more than a giant leap into outer space is a giant step toward peace," the President of the United States said to his countrymen. But a speechwriter composed the phrase. Most citizens have given about as little serious thought to governing the affairs of mankind as they gave to perpetual motion. Man has made far more progress toward flight to other planets than toward peace on earth.

Humanity, writes Hollander Alfredo Rodrigues Brent, "is more bewildered, afraid and cynical than ever, and therefore less inclined to, or even capable of, consistent support for any rational effort for an orderly world."

Shall we believe that mankind is capable of taking a lucid look at its peril, and doing something about it? Or is it closer to the truth that the sense of doom, masquerading sometimes as indifference, has paralyzed men's will to act?

Is Planning Futile?

"All emotions and actions admit of excess and deficiency," Aristotle, the wisest and simplest of moral teachers, declared in his *Ethics.* "Prudence is a practical virtue," he said, and added: "the supreme form of prudence is statesmanship."

A deficiency of security in men's lives leads to terror and heartbreak and destructive conflict. An excess of personal security renders the individual dependent upon the state: its subject and not its master. In economic terms, a security of opportunity is something quite different from a security which encourages indolence.

As important as is the practice of prudence in determining policies of economic welfare, it is not directly the subject of our present study. The goal of CURE's debates, in the minds of 95% among Conference participants, lies not in the field of economic security, but in the area of political security. If we achieve a greater security from war, we will not necessarily deprive our future generations of their opportunity for struggle and adventure. Anyone knows this who has ever climbed a mountain, who has sought honors in scholastic work, who has run for political office or tried to make a living running his own business; anyone who has attempted to introduce a new idea anywhere, or perhaps endeavored to write a book. Guarantees of political security will, at most, help to protect our children from the loss of their homes and their lives by catastrophes beyond their responsibility or control.

But statesmanship, along with such virtues as foresight and prudence, has a way of going askew. "Don't worry. Things never turn out all right," says one of the wry aphorisms known as Murphy's Laws, while another asserts that "Nature works on the side of the hidden flaw." Wishful thinking can

41

endanger one's security, just as daydreaming can waste the imagination. No one may wisely allow his own security to depend upon someone else's plans and promises.

A good question for planners to ask themselves is whether planning is likely to do any good. Is there such a thing as prudent planning in politics? Can there be conscious foresight in statesmanship? Or, as some people fear, is all planning necessarily Utopian where it concerns international affairs, and hence unrealistic and futile?

Perhaps there is no hope at all. What about the Cold War? Are the great world antagonists, like dueling stags with antlers tangled together in the forest, locked in a mortal struggle that can end only with death?

And there are other perplexities. What about the unpredictable Russians themselves? They are likely to upset any plan.

What about America? History tells us that the creation of the United States of America as a democratic federal republic did not proceed according to any prearranged program. The United States, as a community, took form first in an army, second in a government, and only thirdly in a constitutional democracy with a Bill of Rights to guarantee its citizens against the monarchical abuses of power which had triggered the Revolution.

"I am continually amazed at the assumption that a good blueprint is *all*," exclaims Rachel Welch, Georgetown, District of Columbia, who speaks with the authority of a retired naval architect. And 85% of the Conference agree that formulas of their own logic will not end the Cold War.

"An armistice is unlikely to be produced by the positive attraction exerted by one alternative," predicts Hugh Nash, New York, N. Y., a staff member of *Architectural Forum*: "if it is to be achieved at all, it will come because the pressure of events may force the nations of the world into a corner where their freedom to be irrational will be circumscribed."

David Judson of Charlotte, North Carolina, Chairman of the Charlotte International Affairs Council, states that "logic won't bring an armistice, but pressure resulting from good formulas is a first step."

It seems apparent to many thoughtful observers that a large proportion of world public sentiment is emotionally prepared

42

to advance toward international government if anyone can show the way. The will exists. The way sometimes seems so appallingly difficult as to inhibit action.

"The peoples of the world will continue to be isolationist until we are able to define the internationalism which we ask them to accept," prophesies Neil Parsons, Dallas, Texas, former Executive Director of Iowa State Branch of United World Federalists.

Planning, in one sense, is a fictional analogy by which we visualize the future as we desire it. Concepts that do not relate to a person's previous experience, either by analogy or by a reasonable extension of already known facts, have real meaning only to the small minority of men whose imaginations are creative; for the average man, it is a lot easier to grasp new ideas by a circumstantial forecast of the future than by means of abstract reasoning or complicated theory.

Before anyone sets out to fictionalize the future he should first assemble all the available knowledge about it. Knowledge, in such a case, is that part of one's past experience which seems useful and applicable in predicting what will happen.

As an example, the formation of a federal union among the American colonies led to their subsequent freedom, peace and prosperity. Therefore, we may reason, a federal union among the world's nations, if it can be made possible, will permit all humanity to thrive in liberty and peace.

How can a world federal union become possible?

"I challenge most sharply the folks who suggest that anyone who works on such things is merely indulging a penchant for design like a youngster building blockhouses," argues Vernon Nash. "What is the Constitution of the United States or the Charter of the United Nations but a design? Whoever, said John Dewey, does not will the means does not will the end. Formal logic was still being taught in my college years. One thing at least stuck to me from it: 'An essential factor is seldom also a sufficient one . . .'"

An assembly or convention or conference which meets to study a constitution for an international federal government will need a background of preparation.

"Any assembly, official or unofficial, will be assisted enormously in its work (in my opinion) if there has been the widest possible consideration of the perplexities with which it will struggle—and the more explicit the suggestions discussed fully in advance the better," Dr. Nash continues. "The wide assumption that the task of unifying the world is so difficult or so nearly impossible that it is outright foolish to think of it . . . can be exorcised only as we are able to make and to publicize proposals for dealing with the worst of the perplexities, which seem to the average person to be plausible."

Good planning lends motivation. 71% of CURE's consultants think that drafting of formulas is a necessary step in mobilizing public opinion toward a solution.

"In the course of debate, the strong ideas will inevitably attract strong followings," prophesies Col. R. Frazier Potts. "One day, while the debate still rages, the 'right' approach will suddenly become an event."

Planners of history cannot afford mistakes. World federalists must know what they are talking about. There is likely to be no tolerance of error, no going back, no forgiveness of stupidity.

"The Federalist cause is an urgent one: it aims to avert a danger that is upon us now, where the stake at risk is millions of lives and whole civilizations," Col. Potts warns. "We cannot carry on with the detachment of a classroom debate. *We have to be right.*"

In war there is no second best. And in planning for peace none of us can count upon an opportunity for second guesses.

The Muddling Approach

Another good question is whether planning is necessary. Can we just muddle along somehow, experiment, improvise, play it by ear, while humanity prepares itselfs psychologically for eventual world union?

At the outbreak of the Korean conflict the body of diplomats who constitute the United Nations resorted to heroic expedients. The General Assembly of the United Nations sought to construct by inspired improvisation what the charter of the United Nations failed to provide in the way of good design.

On November 3, 1950 the General Assembly adopted a resolution titled "Uniting for Peace" which claimed for the General Assembly a right to act in the event the Security Council fails to exercise its responsibility under the Charter for preventing aggression. The General Assembly's assumption of peace enforcement powers was in direct violation of Articles 12 and 27 of the United Nations Charter, which limit the General Assembly to an advisory role. Nonetheless, the United Nations proceeded to fight the Korean War on the basis of the "Uniting for Peace" Resolution of the General Assembly. On the later occasion of the Suez incident, even the Russians endorsed the doctrine of "Uniting for Peace", and it has now become, for all practical purposes, an effective amendment of the Charter.

Inspired by this example, some people contemplate that the United Nations may continue to grow in strength by "re-interpretation" of the "implied powers" of the Charter, in a process resembling the gradual growth of the British constitution from precedent to precedent.

A 57% majority of conferees agree that the British type of flexible, "unwritten" constitution is a *possible* way to create the institutions of a world government. But 92% of those voting doubt that the process of "re-interpretation" is a *desirable* pattern of growth for a world constitution.

An "unwritten" constitution would be "too dangerous for an international government," thinks Henry C. McIlvaine, Jr., Captain, USNR (Ret.), San Diego, California, a member of the Board of Directors of the San Diego Chapter of the American Association for the United Nations.

The British type of "unwritten" constitution might serve the world community "provided an adequate period of time were involved," suggests Col. C. A. Edson, Syracuse, New York, President of the Onondaga Chapter of the Atlantic Union Committee. But John W. Schneider observes that "the British people enjoy a homogeneity and a long period of common customs and tradition to curb any possible usurper of power, which is, and will be for some time to come, lacking in the world community."

"No one of the independent dominions in the British Commonwealth followed the precedent of the United Kingdom; all framed and adopted written constitutions," notes Vernon Nash.

Mrs. Paul Hanson, Lexington, Massachusetts, Foreign Affairs Chairman of the Lexington League of Women Voters, declares that "I strongly believe a written constitution is

45

necessary because of the diversity of member governments and the shortage of time to establish precedents."

"The more divergent the uniting states, the greater the need for a highly specific written constitution," concurs Edith Wynner, New York, N. Y., lecturer and co-author of *Searchlight on Peace Plans*. "Since August, 1945, the 'inhuman' race no longer has so much time for slow evolution."

"An unwritten world constitution would evolve very slowly as the balance of power system has evolved from 1648 to 1920," believes Professor Quincy Wright. "There has been a more rapid evolution through such written instruments as the League of Nations Covenant and the United Nations Charter since. Thus I think the use of written instruments is desirable in developing the world's constitution, but practice and precedent are also important in developing the basic framework established by the written documents."

"It is not proper that the representative body of any organization should take unto itself new powers without going back for authority to those nations or people who created it," cautions Stanley K. Platt, Minneapolis, Minnesota, Vice-Chairman of the World Affairs Center of the University of Minnesota. "It is true that by default of adherence to the wording of the Charter, the United Nations could become a world government, but it is desirable that such a development should be with the consent of the governed and that limitations, safeguards, a bill of rights and an adequate system of courts of justice and equity be included at the same time. When we make a move like that, we should know what we are doing."

Nevertheless it is desirable that the written language of a charter or constitution should not become a straitjacket to strangle progress.

"The strength and durability" of the United States Constitution "have depended upon the flexibility of its language, an indication that power lies in escaping the written word," points out Jean S. Barnard, Mill Valley, California, Chairman of the Mill Valley Chapter of United World Federalists.

The attitude of Americans in the matter of constitutionality deserves a full measure of everyone's respect. Citizens of the United States have had nearly two centuries of experience in distinguishing the desirable flexibility of a constitution from undesirable changes which would amount to its violation. American feelings toward questions of constitutionality offer a useful guide for planners of a stronger United Nations.

Re-interpretation of the United Nations Charter by other than constitutional means is, in the view of 73% of CURE conferees, a dangerous process. The constitution or charter for a world government should be subject to ratification "by both peoples and governments," declares Edith Wynner, an opinion shared by a 78% majority of CURE's debaters.

Revolution or Evolution

As we explore gingerly into that jungle of human emotions which is world politics, it is well to be in earnest about our task, but not to take ourselves too seriously. Realities stare us in the face. Recognizing the facts of political life, 80% of CURE debaters doubt that it is practical to achieve a true world government in a single step by revision of the United Nations Charter.

Would it be possible, then, to improve the United Nations in several successive steps so that it eventually becomes an international government? Could humanity make so laborious and repeated an effort?

Some CUREspondents think not. "There is no such thing as half-a-government," insists Neil Parsons. "The first step toward government *is* government."

An eloquent spokesman for this point of view is Vernon Nash. "No grouping of sovereign political units in the past was ever able to patch its way piecemeal out of anarchy into order," he says flatly.

"In the task of creating a workable world union, we face at least two differences from previous conditions when federal systems came into being which are so great in degree as to be almost differences in kind," Dr. Nash continues. "The first is extreme variation in size and power of national units. The second is a similar contrast in standards of living. Both situations increase incalculably the difficulty of uniting the nations.

"In all our considerations," he advises, "emphasis should be placed on workability rather than presumed acceptability. We should bear in mind that unions by consent were rare indeed prior to 1789, and that our own nation and the similar federal

47

systems which have been formed since were produced mainly by the pressure of circumstances. 'Our union,' wrote John Quincy Adams, 'was extorted by grinding necessity out of an unwilling people.' Granted that the difficulties before us are staggering; it is also just as true that the pressures upon us to end anarchy are far greater than ever before.

"We shall get a united world when enough peoples see that it is preferable to any conceivable alternative; we can facilitate that recognition by making our proposals as palatable as possible. We must not, however, dilute an essentially revolutionary suggestion down to the place where it would prove unworkable even if attainable."

From Peter Birk, Princeton, New Jersey, we hear a grim reminder that this discussion is not taking place in a vacuum.

"A step such as the creation of a world government cannot be sneaked by the nations gradually. It will only become a reality when all the nations realize the need for it, and consciously create it," Mr. Birk says. "Unfortunately, I suspect it might very well take a full-fledged atomic war to make them realize this need."

Despite these reservations, a 72% majority of CURE consultants expect that the evolution of the United Nations toward world government is more likely to take place in several steps over the course of years, than in one sudden transformation.

"As we have discovered constantly with the development of the British House of Commons—and every country has its own case-history of this constitutional growth—collective institutions of value to millions of citizens, whatever their specific origins or legal authority, throw up their own rules and procedures, and, more important, their own special mental habits and emotional loyalties," writes James Avery Joyce, London, England, Professor of International Law and author of *Revolution on East River* and other books.

Among various historical examples of constitutional evolution is the Continental Congress which attempted to govern the United States during the first fourteen years of its independence.

"If history points the way for us here, then we must conclude that the United Nations is more likely to lead us to federation by its faults and failures, than by its successes and radical evolution," asserts Frazier Potts. "In 1787, how was it that our United States Constitution—one of mankind's greatest achievements—came about? Certainly it was not because the Articles of Confederation were so successful that we decided we needed a stiffer dose of the same medicine for our own good. No; on the contrary, the thirteen states were near chaos and despair; and the Philadelphia Convention, with a sharp sense of the inadequacy of the Articles of Confederation, junked the Articles bodily and invented something new—our federal union."

Those who are opposed to the evolutionary concept rightly point out that the history of American constitutional development was not a *gradual* change.

"Many radical changes have come suddenly in history," Vernon Nash reflects. "They have been like mutations or saltations in nature, or like jumps from one plateau of learning to another in education. Such changes have been a dumbfounding surprise to most persons alive at the time; to the most competent judges of human behavior, as well as to those of lesser intelligence. Apparent miracles happen because the needed change becomes the one alternative to imminent disaster."

The acceptance of change may occur as a result of underlying psychological preparation which, for other reasons, finds little superficial expression.

"Who is ever ready for crisis?" asks Frances Fenner, Afton, New York, Secretary of the New York Citizens' Committee for a Peoples' World Convention.

Anyone who has engaged in politics has observed instances when the opposition to a desirable measure collapses even as it blusters loudest.

At the time when the United States took its major step toward government, the act of creating a Constitution, its greatest leader of men, George Washington, admitted his own astonishment. On May 28, 1788, he wrote to General Lafayette: "I will confess to you sincerely, my dear Marquis ... (our new union) will be so much beyond any thing we had a right to imagine or expect eighteen months ago, that it will demonstrate the finger of providence as visibly, as any possible event in the course of human affairs can ever designate it."

Conferees cite several other examples of stepwise develop-

49

ment in government, both past and present.

"We have had examples of unofficial bodies (rather than necessarily popularly elected ones) such as the Indian Congress party and in 1918 the so-called Hungarian National Council under Count Michael Karolyi becoming the actual republican governing power," Edith Wynner reminds us. "Moreover, this practice of starting first with an advisory elected body seems to be rather general in British colonial efforts at ultimate self-government."

When the Continental Congress met in 1787 to consider some limited improvements in the Articles of Confederation of the American states, there was little hint of great events impending. The delegates had no mandate to form a federal union or to write a new Constitution for the United States. In the course of the sessions, the delegates wrote a new Constitution because they found it necessary; many of them were influential merchants who felt there was sufficient reason in the need to protect their property and prosperity.

Similarly, many Federalists feel today that plans to strengthen the United Nations in limited ways will not necessarily end in ineffectual compromise. Once again, as in 1787, plenty of people have selfish reasons to achieve a great human good.

Once a limited breakthrough begins, a United Nations Charter review conference may go well beyond the goals assigned to it. Such a conference may build a structure adequate for decades or centuries of future development. If amendments to the Charter become blocked by vetoes or other entanglements, popular pressures may well demand the inauguration of a fresh start toward the government of mankind, perhaps in other forms than the United Nations. When change is imminent, the possibilities for achievement are limitless.

This is the mutation, the sudden blaze of development, which Federalism foments.

Where There Is a Way, There Is a Will

A Federalist solution must build on motivations of hope, not fear. It must follow constitutional principles. It must provide a plan permitting further flexibility and growth; it need not seek to be a panacea, a cure-all, but should be a method by which the solution of other problems becomes possible. And it must be politically practicable at each step.

In screening our proposals we must consider the objections of those persons who hold extreme views, as we must also consult the indecision of those persons occupying a middle ground.

At one extreme there are those who are so fearful of foreigners that they hesitate to improve the United Nations because it might limit the independence of their own nation.

At the other extreme are those who fear war so much that they want world government immediately, without stipulating the democratic nature of its institutions.

In the middle stand a large body of people who have only a vague notion what a world government will be. The uncommitted person, and that is most of us, seeks to avoid the costly consequences of war. Some of us fear that a greater scope of government must necessarily mean lesser liberties for the individual. Almost everyone feels in greater or lesser measure the qualms of facing an unfamiliar future. In helping many of these persons to make up their minds, the task isn't to argue *why* the world needs government; it is to explain *how* mankind can acceptably govern itself.

Among so many conflicting demands, is there any area for common agreement?

Can any proposals win widespread support?

Is there any real alternative to the suicidal insanity of an arms race?

The first thing we realize as we enter into a study of these problems is that very little of the ground is as yet explored.

There have been eloquent books to demonstrate the need for mankind to gain control over its destinies by means of a government of international affairs. Members of the Conference have written more than a score of books on various aspects of this subject. Among familiar titles in this field by other authors are *How to Think about War and Peace,* by Mortimer Adler; *Peace or Anarchy,* by Cord Meyer; *The Anatomy of Peace,* by Emery Reves; *The Commonwealth of Man,* by Frederick L. Schuman, and *Who Speaks for Man?,* by Norman Cousins.

These and other able books have established a convincing

51

case *why* world law must grow. The purpose of this study is to examine in increasingly practical terms *how* free men can progress toward international government. An overall examination into the practicability of a government of international affairs has psychological, sociological, economic and political aspects. A whole library of books could usefully examine the complexities of the subject which we can only touch upon here.

"We have a terrific amount of education to do, even among our own supporters," comments Byrl Whitney. And he harks back once again to the founding of the American republic. "Having determined to bring law and order, through government, in the affairs of nations as within nations, we will find a way to implement that idea, even as in the darkest days it was given to Ben Franklin to come up with the bicameral legislature as the final means by which agreement was reached."

If there can be substantial hope of forming some sort of world government which will offer mankind a measure of peace and freedom, CURE's advisers expect that vigorous public support will develop to impel such steps.

"Resistance to the creation of an organic world government is prodigious," comments Vernon Nash, "but so also is the pressure toward it.

"Could Switzerland be said to have been ready for full organic union in 1847 when almost a third of the Cantons voted against it? Or we, with the desperately close vote in most of the large crucial states?"

"I introduced in the Senate the first resolution proposing a United Nations," Claude E. Pepper, Tallahassee, Florida, former United States Senator from Florida, tells CURE. "An effective world organization is bound to come. The only question is when! World events, conditions, and opinions are vastly accelerating the evolution of such an institution. Yet, when we look back to the Amphyctian League and the Italian city states and follow the concept of such an organization through the centuries we must marvel at what we have done not only in our time but in a decade. The important thing is to keep the organization we have functioning and not wreck it, for time and circumstances, some unhappy, are moving the world to order its affairs so that we will have law and order among nations and the means of promoting the general world welfare."

To believe in the possibility of human survival requires faith in man's capacities.

"Never overestimate the people's information," said reporter Raymond Clapper, "but never underestimate the people's intelligence."

If we hold fast to a faith in man's best capabilities, nothing is impossible.

Life is full of problems, as it is of joys and sorrows. But we may be sure that unless mankind solves the primary problem of global self-government, the lesser worries of living cannot long concern us. Without a solution of this problem, our other problems soon may not even exist.

Chapter 4.

A Parliament of Man

A principal goal of the United Nations is to serve as a parliament of man: and to a considerable degree the United Nations, from its inception, already serves as a forum of world opinion.

Laird Bell, Winnetka, Illinois, lawyer and a former Alternate Delegate of the United States to the General Assembly of the United Nations, tells CURE "I do not see how 'peoples' are going to elect representatives except through their political institutions; and the political institutions of 76 nations now send representatives to the United Nations, so that I should suppose most nations would say that their peoples have already a United Nations voice."

Mr. Bell contributed his comment to the Conference Upon Research and Education in world government shortly after he spoke for the United States in the General Assembly of the United Nations in favor of a conference to review its Charter. But it is obvious that citizens do not participate as directly in the United Nations as they do in democratic governments. Mr. Bell, speaking before the General Assembly, did not express his personal views. He did not speak for constituents who had elected him to be their representative. He was appointed to his post by the President of the United States, and the speech which he delivered was written for him by staff members of the United States Department of State.

Nor, when the delegation representing 170,000,000 Americans cast a vote for review of the United Nations Charter, did their ballot carry any greater weight than that of a small nation one one-hundredth the size of the United States. Because they were voting in a diplomatic assemblage of sovereign nations, the ballot of the United States delegation was exactly equal to that of representatives from the smallest or the largest nation. Each member government cast one vote, no more, no less.

The United States Ambassador to the Security Council of the United Nations, who during the several years of these studies was Henry Cabot Lodge, is in a similar position. His title and rank is that of a diplomat. The American Ambassador's ties to the voters, observes Rachel Welch, are "too indirect to influence him."

Citizens of democracies are accustomed to elect their legislators. Most people expect a democratic legislature to include at least one house in which representatives are seated in proportion to populations.

"Not one of the delegates of the United Nations' member countries today, worthy though he may be, actually represents or speaks for his country's people, for the people themselves had no hand in his choosing," comments Mary Hays Weik, Cincinnati, Ohio, Director of the American Registry of World Citizens. "This is the first and most obvious lack, the greatest injustice which we must correct in any honest plan for a revised Charter. How? by replacing today's appointed delegates with a representative body—a balanced Assembly of two Chambers. Let us be clear on one point: either all the world's people are to be given a voice in its government from the start, or no one's liberties anywhere will be safe for long."

"In any political community the individual can be either a citizen or a subject. If a man isn't the one he must inevitably be the other. And, indeed, subjects is what we all are in the political structure of the United Nations, the NATO, the South Pacific set-up," declares Alfredo Rodrigues Brent.

This role "is somewhat humiliating to Americans whose forebears rejected their subject status on July 4, 1776, replacing it by a citizenship," continues Mynheer Brent. "It is no less humiliating to the English whose forebears were factually raised from the status of subjects to citizenship by the Bill of Rights enacted by their King William III on January 22, 1689; nor to the French who adopted equality before the law of all citizens whose citizenship was described in their 'Declaration of Human Rights and Citizens' Rights,' which

55

new status commenced on August 4, 1789; nor to the Dutch whose forebears rejected their status as subjects of King Philip of Spain in order to adopt the citizenship of the Republic of the United Netherlands in 1579.

"Citizenship, that is miserably missing in the present-day 'Declaration of Human Rights,' was emphasized in the French 1789 issue entitled specially, 'Déclaration des Droits de l'Homme *et du Citoyen*.'" Mr. Brent emphasizes the significant phrase.

Participants in CURE's forum have a strong feeling that, even without increases in the powers of the United Nations, the peoples should be more directly represented in it. Three of the Conference's prominent educators express this view:

"A popularly elected chamber without power, but with capacity to voice world public opinion," writes political scientist Quincy Wright, "might assist in the emergence of a world public opinion and a world legislative body."

Edward J. Sparling, Chicago, Illinois, President of Roosevelt College, holds that "if salaries could be greatly increased and national elections held for delegates, the educational value of such a campaign would bring peace and security to the world far faster than under our present system."

"It is practical to choose by popular election delegates to the United Nations' Assembly, if we want to see 'diplomacy' replaced by 'law'," concurs Claude L. Bourcier, Middlebury, Vermont, Dean of the Department of French of Middlebury College; and he adds, "the Machiavellians are no longer the true 'realists'—we are."

One of the characteristics of a federal system is that not only the government of the states, but also the federal government "must rest directly on the rights of each individual citizen," stresses Hollis E. Suits, St. Louis, Missouri.

Mildred Riorden Blake, Dobbs Ferry, New York, former member of the National Executive Council of United World Federalists, defines the federal principle as one in which there is a "direct relation of the individual to several levels of government."

A dual and direct relationship of citizens with state and federal levels of democratic government rests upon the popular election of a least one chamber in each legislature. If a federal government is to be other than paternal, a direct representation of the people in its parliament is essential. Unless the people win the right to elect their representatives to the United Nations, that international organization is fated either to remain ineffectual or non-responsible, or most likely both.

"The primary purpose of such elections," argues John W. Schneider, "is to bring about direct contact beween the United Nations and the people. Many whose approach to problems confronting the United Nations has been 'what can I do about it?' or 'leave that to the diplomats' will realize that the responsibility is theirs."

That which the people make their own will, in time, become an instrument of popular sovereignty. A popular chamber, two-thirds of the Conference think, even if initially limited to advisory functions, will continually grow in its actual powers as part of a government.

An obvious example is the House of Commons, which during the course of centuries has gradually reduced the House of Lords to a vestigial function in the British Parliament.

A Compromise in Representation

"So long as we keep a straight one-nation-one-vote system in the present United Nations Assembly," maintains Vernon Nash, "it seems to me virtually certain that no real powers of any consequence will be entrusted to it."

There are a good many observers who feel that a popular chamber in the United Nations should allot seats in direct proportion to populations.

"There are no democratic alternatives to straight population representation," declares Alvin M. Kaye, Philadelphia, Pennsylvania, member of the Department of Zoölogy of the University of Pennsylvania.

Frances Fenner believes that the "dignity of the individual" is best served by representation in direct proportion to populations.

"Any other method will be too complicated and difficult for the general public to understand or maybe to enforce," agrees John W. Apperson, Memphis, Tennessee.

"I—and I hope many of my fellow world citizens—would refuse to be ruled by an undemocratic authority, at the world level as well as at the national or local level," states Jacques Savary, Paris, France, Secretary General of the World Council for a Peoples' World Convention. "The fundamental principle of democracy is the right of all men and women—their equal right—to participate in the conduct and control of public affairs through the intermediary of representatives elected by them. In conformity with the principle of equal rights and duties—a principle which is the very essence of democracy—all the citizens of the world should have equal representation in any world assembly."

Other conferees put the principle of equal representation in a less immediate perspective.

"The lower assembly must inevitably be on a straight population basis, though initially it will not be," predicts David Judson.

Col. R. Frazier Potts states "it is an axiom that 'a representative government is only as good as the electorate which it represents'. If and when India or China should have a well-informed, educated electorate, I would have no fear of the consequences of straight population representation," and he adds that it is "the ideal goal."

Whatever the reason for the reservations of most conferees, only a minority of 12% in CURE's debates vote for unmodified population representation in a world Assembly of Peoples. An additional 12% approve a method of seating based on population, subject only to an upper limit on the delegations of big countries.

Including this latter group, an overwhelming majority of participants in CURE's forum (88%) recommend some modification of straight population ratios.

Economic and Educational Weighting

"A world union must give nations voting strength in some proportion to their stake in the maintenance of world order," Vernon Nash offers as a rule-of-thumb for judging various types of representation formulas.

Inventor John Rust, whose cotton-picking machine has emancipated hand-laborers in the fields of the southern United

States (as a century earlier the McCormick reaper had freed the agricultural laborers in the North) possessed an inquisitive mind able to ponder on political concepts as well as upon machines. One of inventor Rust's ideas was the suggestion that a system of representation in a world parliament might be arranged "in direct relation to the relative amount of 'prime movers' or technological power used" in any given country.

There are, at least in theory, several ways to set up a system of representation based on other factors than population. Such suggestions include not only Mr. Rust's proposed factor of technological productivity, but other possible factors like education, or perhaps a country's financial contribution to the United Nations budget.

Dr. J. David Singer thinks that a compromise of population with other factors is "best, if possible to determine."

"Utilization of the square root or the cube root of populations and of contribution to the United Nations budget would provide two scales which might be used separately or in combination, for counting votes on different types of resolutions," suggests Professor Quincy Wright. "The present vote system could be used on some resolutions."

A stumbling block in the path of these propositions might be one of psychological nature. People might not like to have their votes weighted in proportion to their machines, or their wealth, or their mastery of an educational curriculum. A system of representation weighted by such factors might be embarrassing to explain to the poor people of the earth, to people who have no cotton picking machines, who earn scarcely any money or are just learning to read and write.

But it would work. If public opinion found it acceptable, a weighted apportionment of voting would bring an improvement in representation for the populous nations of the earth in comparison with the present single vote for each sovereign government. In the course of time, a system of this nature would reward the increased standards of living and improved levels of education in progressive nations with a growing voice in world politics. Some form of weighted representation offers one type of solution for the seating of a world Assembly of Peoples.

Weighting On a Graduated Scale

Other possible ways to achieve a workable voting allocation in a world chamber of peoples might rely simply upon a graduated mathematical scale to modify a straight population ratio.

There is a good deal of room for mathematical compromise between the one-nation-one-vote system and a straight population ratio of representation. In the General Assembly of the United Nations, if representation were based on populations, the largest nations would have over a hundred times more votes than the smallest nations. If a future Assembly of Peoples in the United Nations is based on an adjusted mathematical scale giving the largest nations, for example, ten times more votes than the smallest nations, the smallest nations will still keep ten times more representation *per capita* than the biggest. In such a compromise solution, the little nations will retain a greater proportion of votes than their populations alone would justify, but large nations will acquire a more nearly representative proportion of votes than they have at present. Such a compromise would maintain the influence of national sovereignties, but in a modified form.

In the United Nations of today, small nations by virtue of the one-nation-one-vote system serve as the arbiters of great power disputes. A mathematical type of compromise in the United Nations voting system would preserve some of this balance of power now vested in smaller nations. The role of smaller nations as arbiters between great powers would remain clear (even though the world's two great antagonists, Russia and the United States, are not actually the largest in population, but rank behind the world's two most populous nations, China and India).

A formula of representation based on a graduated scale of populations has another advantage: it can be framed in ordinary legislative phraseology, rather than in sociological or technological terms. In a statute based on a graduated scale of populations, no one need refer to such criteria as the production of kilowatt-hours of electrical energy, nor need the United Nations set up a worldwide system of educational testing in order to allocate the number of representatives for each country. A graduated scale of representation requires only a simple table as its explanation.

A typical formula using a graduated scale might, as an example, assign to each nation a number of seats equal to the square root of the number of millions of persons in its population. Table I shows how this particular formula works out in practice. For the sake of illustration, the table is based upon the nations of the world as listed in *World Peace through World Law,* by Grenville Clark and Louis B. Sohn, without regard to their present status of membership in the United Nations.

TABLE I

Seating in the United Nations Assembly of Peoples based upon the square root of the number of millions population of each member nation.

POPULATION	SEATS		NATIONS		TOTAL
up to 1 million	1	x	3	=	3
1 to 4 millions	2	x	25	=	50
4 to 9 millions	3	x	20	=	60
9 to 16 millions	4	x	16	=	64
16 to 25 millions	5	x	12	=	60
25 to 36 millions	6	x	5	=	30
36 to 49 millions	7	x	—	=	—
49 to 64 millions	8	x	5	=	40
64 to 81 millions	9	x	—	=	—
81 to 100 millions	10	x	3	=	30
100 to 121 millions	11	x	—	=	—
121 to 144 millions	12	x	—	=	—
144 to 169 millions	13	x	—	=	—
169 to 196 millions	14	x	1	=	14
196 to 225 millions	15	x	1	=	15
225 to 256 millions	16	x	—	=	—
256 to 289 millions	17	x	—	=	—
289 to 324 millions	18	x	—	=	—
324 to 361 millions	19	x	—	=	—
361 to 400 millions	20	x	1	=	20
400 to 441 millions	21	x	—	=	—
441 to 484 millions	22	x	—	=	—
484 to 529 millions	23	x	—	=	—
529 to 576 millions	24	x	—	=	—
576 to 625 millions	25	x	1	=	25
TOTAL IN ASSEMBLY OF PEOPLES			93		411

The United States, by the working of this particular formula, will receive fourteen seats out of 411, or roughly 1/30 of the total of votes: more than the 1/82 of total votes Americans now possess in the General Assembly of the United Nations, but less than the 1/14 proportion of all votes which the United States would receive in an allocation in direct proportion to populations.

To examine another aspect of this formula, the votes of a smaller nation such as Belgium, Peru or Portugal, each with approximately 9,000,000 inhabitants, will be in a ratio of 3:14 to United States votes, rather than the 1:1 ratio of equal nations or a lopsided 1:20 inferiority which would result from apportionment on a straight population basis.

A possible objection to a mathematical scale or table such as this is that it lacks the elasticity of formulas based on education or productivity. With a graduated scale, the bias in favor of small nations is built-in. The curve is skewed to stay. Periodic reapportionment under such a scheme would take cognizance of changes in populations of the various nations by moving them from one bracket to another. Its framers would not intend to change the formula, but merely its application in the wake of each census.

Later on, when we come to the problem of the veto, we will consider one way in which great continental federations might retain special rights as a compensation for their less than proportionate representation in an Assembly of Peoples constituted under a graduated scale formula of this nature.

Logic of a Bicameral Assembly

In November, 1951, an international group of some 400 citizens of various countries, without success, petitioned United Nations Secretary General Trygve Lie to bring before the General Assembly, or before a commission of the United Nations, a proposal for the addition of a chamber of elected representatives which would serve initially in an advisory capacity to the existing bodies of the world organization.

Some advocates have suggested that the creation of such a peoples' assembly might make it possible to eliminate all representatives of the national governments from the United Nations. Conferees Grenville Clark, Dublin, New Hampshire, international lawyer, and Louis B. Sohn, Cambridge, Massachusetts, Professor of Law at Harvard University, joint authors of *World Peace through World Law,* recommend that a reconstituted United Nations parliament comprise only a single elected chamber.

Legislatures consisting of a single chamber are common at the lower levels of government. Municipal councils, for instance, usually consist of a single body.

At the intermediate level of state government in the United States only Nebraska, with 0.8% of the nation's population, has a unicameral legislature.

Among members of the United Nations, Costa Rica, New Zealand, Pakistan, Turkey and Denmark, comprising about 6.5% of the populations outside the Russian empire, base their governmental structure upon a single legislative chamber. 93.5% of non-Soviet ruled United Nations populations provide legislative structures consisting of two chambers.

Other theorists, at the opposite extreme from conferees Clark and Sohn, have proposed that a world legislature might have as many as three chambers. The Committee to Frame a World Constitution which met at the University of Chicago shortly after World War II suggested a world parliament of three houses, together with equally elaborate executive and judicial arrangements which they thought would befit the dignity of government at an international level.

In visualizing the United Nations as a world parliament, most Federalists recognize in it a classic example of the necessity for a least a bicameral legislature. A majority of Federalist opinion supports the Declarations framed in 1953 at Copenhagen, Denmark, jointly by the World Association of Parliamentarians for World Government and the World Association of World Federalists, proposing that the United Nations shall have a legislature of two houses, one with equal votes for each government, and another with representation based upon factors including population. It may be that one of the solutions which will make it possible for a world legislature to come into being is this device, which represents governments and peoples in two separate chambers, and requires the assent of both chambers for the passage of legislation.

"I'll bet heavily that we'll end up with two houses," prophesies Dr. Vernon Nash, "since all federal systems have adopted that compromise after long struggle in constitutional convention."

The device of the bicameral Congress, for instance, made possible the creation of the United States of America. John Boardman, Syracuse, New York, graduate student in theoretical physics at Syracuse University, reminds us that "for most of this country's history the United States Senate represented state governments and not the people of those states." It was more than a century after the founding of the United States until the people, by means of the 17th Amendment to the Constitution, acquired the right to elect Senators representing their states in the upper house of the American federal Congress.

The proposal to endow a United Nations parliament with lawmaking powers in international affairs will confront a conference for the review of the United Nations Charter with a dilemma comparable to that which faced the Constitutional Convention of 1787 in Philadelphia.

"The United Nations is already with us: too early to be a true Parliament of Man, but too late to be just a conference of foreign ministers," writes CUREspondent James Avery Joyce.

Although the United Nations is already more, it still remains in large part a conference of foreign ministers, other conferees point out.

"Representatives to international bodies have traditionally been appointed, to enable the government represented to have full control over its representatives," remarks Niels T. Anderson, Kearny, New Jersey, past President of New Jersey State Branch of United World Federalists.

For these reasons, 85% of CURE's debaters doubt that the addition of an Assembly of Peoples would make possible the elimination of a chamber of governments to serve the functions of the present General Assembly of the United Nations.

Because a federal system formed among the nations of the world would combine greater extremes than in any existing federation, not only with regard to size of populations but many other features, it may be necessary to employ several different forms of compromise in the construction of its legislature.

It seems possible to accomplish the various purposes of compromise without entering into so elaborate an arrangement as a third chamber in the world parliament. For instance, in the chamber of governments of a bicameral world legislature we may question whether the theory of national sovereignties need be so rigid as to prescribe that each government must possess an exactly equal voice. Russia has already set a precedent by bargaining for and winning three seats for herself and her Soviet provinces in the present General Assembly of the United Nations. Major continental federations such as the United States may approach a conference for the review of the Charter with other comparable demands, if only to prepare themselves in a favorable position for bargaining. It is inconceivable that a United States of Europe, for another example, if it becomes a sovereign federal nation at some future time, should accept a status in a world senate which places even the smallest independent nation of the world in sovereign equality to it.

Some sort of a graduated scale based partly on populations may possibly emerge as a basis for voting in a chamber of governments as well as in the Assembly of Peoples of a bicameral world legislature. However, a chamber of governments may logically lay more weight on the principle of national sovereignties than would be the case in the chamber of peoples which we have previously discussed. In the chamber of governments a graduated scale, rather than using a square-root formula, might allot a number of seats to each nation equal to the *cube* root of the number of millions of persons in its population. The distribution resulting from this cube-root formula, shown in Table II, gives each nation from one to nine "senators".

In offering any of the foregoing proposals as an agenda in a conference for the review of the United Nations Charter, it may appear desirable to minimize their novelty, and to maintain as much continuity as possible with existing institutions. One possible way to make the United Nations into a workable government would be to divide the present General Assembly into two chambers, an Assembly of Nations and an Assembly of Peoples, and to transform the present Security Council into an executive branch responsible to the legislature.

Alternatively, a Charter Review Conference might find it

expedient simply to enlarge the Security Council so that it includes all member nations, and so make of it a senate or chamber of governments. The review conference may then make the General Assembly into an elective chamber with a system of

TABLE II

Seating in the United Nations Assembly of Nations
based upon the cube root of the number of millions
population of each member nation

POPULATION	SEATS		NATIONS		TOTAL
up to 1 million	1	x	3	=	3
1 to 8 millions	2	x	42	=	84
8 to 27 millions	3	x	32	=	96
27 to 64 millions	4	x	9	=	36
64 to 125 millions	5	x	3	=	15
125 to 216 millions	6	x	2	=	12
216 to 343 millions	7	x	—	=	—
343 to 512 millions	8	x	1	=	8
512 to 729 millions	9	x	1	=	9

TOTAL IN ASSEMBLY OF NATIONS 93   263

representation more realistic than at present. Using this approach, the Charter Review Conference could then proceed to enlarge the duties of the Secretary General and his staff in order to constitute them an answerable executive.

Certainly it will be a good idea for one or more of the participating nations to place such proposals, as part of an agenda, before a conference for the review of the United Nations Charter.

Democracy Bores from Within

The proposal for a bicameral United Nations parliament will first receive a serious opportunity for consideration in a review conference under the terms of Article 109 of the United Nations Charter. In the pattern of CURE's studies we see a better system of representation in the United Nations as a key step which makes other steps possible. A Charter Review Conference, given adequate public support, can reasonably hope to achieve at least this first step.

66

To "put the people in the United Nations" seems a simple idea. But this accomplishment will be one of the most momentous events in human history.

"Extending democratic law into the arena of international affairs is a great revolutionary proposal," declares Ralph Templin, Cedarville, Ohio, Professor of Sociology at Central State College.

A world Assembly of Peoples will stir new desires for self-government in nations whose institutions now lack popular representation. No one, not even the so-called free peoples, will be indifferent to the effects of a world popular chamber. Even for citizens of "free" countries, it will be a new experience to elect delegates who sit in a legislature alongside representatives of other races, other countries and other continents.

The citizens of totalitarian countries, accustomed to rigged "elections", will undoubtedly vote, at first, to elect a stacked slate of candidates to the world parliament. Other peoples who are wiser in their experience of democracy can afford to be patient with politically backward nations. Democracy takes time to sink in. Democratic countries themselves are only comparatively more advanced; all of them have had less democratic epochs in their pasts, and most of them are not entirely proud of certain aspects of their present institutions.

Just as one example, the United States at its inception was far from a democracy. The word democracy does not appear in the American Constitution. And democratic methods had only a dim role in its drafting at the Constitutional Convention of 1787.

"I hope you will also remember the highly aristocratic character of American politics at that time, the limited democracy in the election of delegates, the fact that they violated such instructions as 'the people' gave them, the extraordinary secrecy in which they worked, not only locking the doors but agreeing they would *never* reveal what had gone on, even after it was all over, a promise that Madison broke long after, and the facts that the resultant Constitution barely squeaked through, that it was never submitted to popular ratification, and that if it had been it would doubtless have been rejected, either by more than a quarter of the states, or by one of the needed big three, New York, Pennsylvania and Virginia, and that where it would have been ratified by 'popular' vote, the voters were only, on the average, 1/11th of the adult population of males," writes Dr. S. Colum Gilfillan, Chicago, Illinois, author of the UNESCO book *Social Implications of Technical Advance.*

"In short, the American Constitution and union was a highly aristocratic achievement, and was largely intended to protect the property and position of the aristocracy," he adds. "And we're all highly grateful for it."

The founding fathers of the American nation left it to each state to select its minority of "the wise, the good and the rich", as Fisher Ames bluntly called them, who were to vote in elections of representatives to the federal Congress. The United States Constitution gives individual American states the responsibility for the conduct of federal elections within their borders. It is noteworthy that in matters of representation the United States and other existing democracies have allowed a good deal of leeway, and even abuse, and yet they have still managed to function fairly well.

By similar reasoning, a world federal union need not demand a Utopian perfection of electoral practices within its member nations. Neither Russia nor America, nor perhaps many other nations, would welcome United Nations supervision of their citizens' balloting for delegates to an Assembly of Peoples in the United Nations. 61% of Conference participants agree that United Nations agencies should not attempt to supervise United Nations delegate elections in member nations.

But, say 66% of respondents, the United Nations can adopt a Bill of Rights establishing standards for democratic elections of United Nations delegates within member countries.

"The main trick in federation is to combine a maximum of voluntarism (no coercion of states as such, for instance) with a maximum of conflict-solving procedures and institutions," says William Bross Lloyd, Winnetka, Illinois, author of *Waging Peace: The Swiss Experience* and Editor of *Toward Freedom.* "It seems to me that the first step is for the United Nations to draw up model election laws and procedures, approve them, and recommend them to member nations for use in the election of United Nations delegates, much as the United States federal government draws up standards for state practice in social legislation."

The debut of world democracy in the forum of the United Nations is not an occasion for coercion, but for persuasive pressures.

How Democracy Defends Itself

No self-respecting person is likely to give anyone else a share in making his decisions unless there is a pretty good reason for doing so. Only the most compelling circumstances can persuade democratic citizens to share their decision-making with totalitarian co-voters. And totalitarians are sure to be even more reluctant to entrust any decisions to a parliament whose majorities are hostile. Apprehension colors attitudes on both sides.

The discipline by which totalitarians infiltrate faction-ridden democracies could become a menace in a world legislature. "No 'Peoples' Representative' from a 'Peoples' Democracy' would vote against his government's point of view without asking for asylum, whereas free-world representatives will be voting their own respective consciences (or party platforms)," objects Frank E. G. Weil, New York, N. Y., lawyer and member of the Special United Nations Subcommittee of the American Veterans Committee. The result, he fears, might be a "lopsided" rout of democratic forces.

But other conferees point out that a minority seizure of power is a danger principally where government is absent or ineffectual. In broad terms, as we have seen, a world legislature, as it establishes world security and world law, will nourish democracy and undermine dictatorship everywhere.

And John Holt reminds us that the Communist "hard core" is far from solid at the world level.

"There is plenty of disagreement between Russia and China, or Russia and Poland," he remarks.

The power of minorities in a representative legislature is defensive rather than aggressive. Democratic legislation must thread a maze of resistance by minorities. According to the interpretation of David Riesman and other sociologists, the real control of events in a democracy rests not in the hands of any mysterious "they" who run everything, but resides in a nega-

69

tive way with an array of "veto groups" which strongly oppose any invasion of their vested "rights": farmers, labor unions, investors, war veterans, civil servants, racial, religious and regional blocs, to name a few. In a democratic society each of these groups is a minority not only in numbers but also in influence. Although none of them has enough power to act much outside its own area, each "veto group" has a deeply felt commitment to defend its own territory. Possession is nine points of a sociological attitude, as it is of the law.

"The Communist party will not be the only ideological bloc in a world legislature," forecasts John Boardman. "Socialists, Clericalists, anti-clericalists, Centrists and Conservatives would also crystallize out into party organizations transcending national boundaries. The situation would resemble a European parliament, where a Communist bloc vote exists, but is maneuvered around by the parliamentarians of other parties. The presence of large and vocal Communist parties in the parliaments of France, Italy and Finland does not give the result predicted by Mr. Weil for a world parliament."

This reasoning guides an overwhelming 83% of CURE's participants to believe that a totalitarian minority could not force through a world legislature measures which a free world "veto group" strongly opposes.

If anything, the real problem is the other way around. 61% of Conference voters express a doubt that the Communist world as a "veto group" could prevent encroachments upon its vital interests by a democratic majority. For this purpose, if for no other, we will consider later in this report the desirability of protecting the vested interests of minorities by means of a modified constitutional veto in a revised United Nations Charter.

Subject to such conditions as may be necessary to protect the vital domestic interests of great powers in this manner, it seems clear that it will be possible to interpose the democratic process of decision between the conflicting interests of nations at the world level. An international legislature is, today, the spot where humanity most needs the influence of a representative system.

It will not be perfect. What ever is? But it will develop in its support the enormous force of individual self-respect. The creation of an Assembly of Peoples within the United Nations will establish an entirely new fount of sovereignty. Even if some nations do not permit their peoples to choose representatives in honest elections, those which do so will establish satisfactorily the representative nature of the popular house.

A majority of nations will comply willingly with the spirit of the new world statute. From the start, representatives of democratic nations will be in a numerical majority. But more important than static numbers will be the dynamic advantage which democracy enjoys in a climate of opportunity. Men learn about democracy by practising it.

Chapter 5.

Life, Law and Liberty

The establishment of an Assembly of Peoples will enable the world to entrust more responsibilities to the United Nations.

A 91% vote affirms this belief among participants in the Conference Upon Research and Education in world government. In an inquiry among leaders of 135 organizations affiliated with the World Veterans Federation, totalling some 20,-000,000 former soldiers, sailors and airmen of the earth's wars, two-thirds of organization spokesmen who reply share this opinion. And eight out of ten Americans polled in neighborhood discussion meetings express the same view.

We have seen that the United Nations, as a representative body, already has some of the qualities of a world forum. And in the same way there already exist precedents of world law which, in a primitive and tentative form, foreshadow the legislative responsibilities of a true world legislature.

"The United Nations constitution is, in its day to day operation, as distinct from its legal text, nothing less than an outline structure of government of world-wide dimensions," writes analyst James Avery Joyce.

Justice Robert Jackson, American member of the international tribunal for post-World War II trials of war criminals at Nuremberg, Germany, maintained that both the common law and international law may, on particular issues, have "a twilight existence during which it is hardly distinguishable from morality or justice, till at length the imprimatur of a court attests its jural quality."

And Professor Quincy Wright comments that "the Nuremberg tribunal gave the court's imprimatur to notions of the criminality of war which, it said, had been gradually developing through pronouncements in the League of Nations and such instruments as the Kellogg-Briand pact."

The evolution of morality into law is characteristic of man's efforts to attain the institutions of government.

"From a study of comparative constitutional history of all polities which have been formed out of many smaller polities we can detect the sequence of developing forms in institutions of government. From this study we find that pre-state polities gain their identity in a mesh of legal rights and duties," writes Waldo Mead, Buffalo, New York, minister and former Managing Editor of the student Federalist publication *World Frontiers*.

"An example of it is to be found in the Hanseatic League. This was a legal structure limited to trading activities only of the Hanseatic cities," Mr. Mead continues. "This league was governmental, but it was based upon functions rather than territory with its territorial jurisdictions incidental to its functions.

"The essential quality of government in such an order is the provisions for prescribing procedures through institutional action, avoiding the traditional problem of 'giving up sovereignty'."

It is instructive to note how wide a scope of duties a pre-state polity or functional "government" can take upon itself.

"The Hanseatic League was formed in 1241 in order to protect its members' ships against the pirates of the Baltic Sea and to protect its members' true or alleged privileges against German princes," Alfredo Rodrigues Brent comments. "Its principal centres were at first Hamburg, Bremen, Lübeck and Cologne. Its structure was definitely a political confederation.

"By the end of the 15th century it comprised 64 cities, some of them Dutch. It enjoyed and jealously preserved a monopoly of all trade in the Baltic Sea. Its government had its own consular service, extending from England to Novgorod in Russia. It had also its governmental treasury, a navy and an army."

And Mr. Brent goes on to relate that the Hanseatic League "went into decline in the 16th century, when the Baltic trade became secondary to the newly developing colonial interests in the East and West Indies."

73

The development of pan-European institutions today, as another example, is proceeding along lines of functional government similar to those of the Hanseatic League. 86% of CURE's correspondents interpret the European Coal and Steel Community as a pre-state polity. These omens, most conferees think, presage the birth of a true United States of Europe.

There are dangers in functional government, however. Rachel Welch sees in Europe's development "a cartel with political overtones." Mr. Brent warns us:

"The Coal and Steel Community is the old (pre-war) steel trust, remodeled and with a few new features. In its political aspects it is the nearest approach to the fascist and national-socialist ideal of the 'corporate state' ever realized. Because of governmental participation and labor influence it is definitely mercantilist in character.

"World federalists wishing to advocate a pre-state concept should make sure that this concept is democratic in character and avoid technocratic concepts as carefully as they would theocratic concepts and also corporate concepts of national-socialism or fascism."

The emphasis here is upon the *nature* of the government, and not upon its jurisdictions. The European Coal and Steel Community lacks a popular parliament to give it democratic sanction. A functional government, no less than one with territorial jurisdictions, should be responsible to those whom it governs.

The United Nations already has some degree of functional sovereignty in the sense that sovereignty is simply a power or a competence to do certain things. Some illustrations of this are familiar to everyone. The United Nations has its own uniformed headquarters police. It can muster sizeable armies under its military command. It employs a numerous staff who take pride in their status as members of a world civil service. The various specialized agencies of the United Nations act with what may be called sovereignty in their fields simply because there is no one to stop them and there is a general desire that they should do so.

But the powers of the United Nations are not adequate to discharge the minimum tasks of an international government. Each specialized agency, instead of acting as an executive arm

74

of a world parliament, forms in itself an independent petty parliament of participating nations. The General Assembly of the United Nations, like the European Consultative Assembly, lacks the popular sanction that would fit it to direct the agencies as departments of government. Coupled with the handicaps of an unrealistic system of representation, this legislative structure does not inspire the confidence necessary to any truly decisive powers.

A World Development Authority

Among the specialized agencies are several which have sprung up, loosely grouped within the United Nations, aiming to deal with the most pressing economic needs of humanity.

The Economic and Social Council (ECOSOC) has a general responsibility for the co-ordination of other agencies in the field of international economic co-operation. The World Bank, whose origins stem from the Conference at Bretton Woods in 1944, has as its field the making of loans which can offer good security for the repayment of principal. The International Monetary Fund exists to help stabilize national currencies. The Technical Assistance Program covers a wide range of services to aid backward countries. The Food and Agriculture Organization acts as the world's farm management bureau in developing better crops.

These existing international economic agencies fill useful and necessary roles, but they are hardly a complete answer to the world's economic problems. No present agency has funds available for relief and rehabilitation in circumstances where repayment is unlikely. Emergency aid programs must therefore rely upon the bounty of individual wealthy nations. The granting of contingency aid falls largely in the realm of selfish political strife between donor nations, and usually fails to employ co-operative procedures which would gear aid to need and strengthen the arbiter role of a world organization.

A near-unanimous 96% majority of conferees believe that there is a need to improve the United Nations as an agency for economic co-operation throughout the world.

The proposed Special United Nations Fund for Economic Development (SUNFED) is one way in which nations can work together to raise worldwide standards of living.

Another desirable step is to simplify the existing and often overlapping agencies and to link them in a more responsible relationship to a world parliament.

A revision of organizational relationships within the United Nations, therefore, might logically set up a World Development Authority as an executive branch with general responsibility in economic fields under the direction of the United Nations legislature. Such an authority will supervise a good many of the functions of the present quasi-independent specialized agencies. It will acquire other and broader duties in order that world economic co-operation may replace economic feuding for spheres of influence by powerful nations.

A 97% consensus of CURE respondents believe that the United Nations has need of such a World Development Authority; and 67% are of the opinion that this authority in its functioning will not infringe upon the sovereignties of individual nations.

A World Development Authority, as an executive branch responsible to the world parliament, can extend the sovereignty of the world's peoples in international fields most vital to their daily welfare.

Atoms for Peacekeeping

Another area of international responsibility already established by United Nations statute is the International Atomic Energy Agency.

Here, again, is a self-contained specialized agency, not responsible to the deliberative processes of the United Nations, but constituting an independent pocket parliament. The United Nations statute which created the International Atomic Energy Agency eliminated the veto from its governing procedures. Its powers, however, are limited to the peaceful uses of atomic energy. It falls far short of the regulation of atomic armaments which the world, for its peace, must entrust to the hands of an international governmental agency.

In today's world the creation of international regulatory powers over national armaments would be a drastic encroachment upon the sovereignties of individual nations, particularly in the case of those nations which, being most powerful, are stuck with the most sovereignty.

76

Perhaps the most we can hope from present revision of the Charter of the United Nations is to enlarge the competence of the International Atomic Energy Agency so that it can eventually accept responsibility for control of nuclear arms when the opportunity comes as a consequence of later pacts and treaties among the nations. As in the case of other administrative jurisdictions, an essential step will be to subordinate the International Atomic Energy Agency under the general authority of the world legislature. Before it can have real power, it must be answerable to the people whom it serves.

Three out of four CUREspondents think that improvements in the United Nations as a parliament will hasten the growth of world authority in nuclear control. Whether or not it is possible to take such a step initially, CURE conferees agree by a 97% vote that mankind should seek as soon as possible to give the world atom authority an effectual control over all national armaments.

"Without preventing the use of atomic energy for war weapons," warns Philip Isely, "the peaceful use of atomic energy is a mockery."

"An authority without authority is useful as an educational step but little else," seconds Donald Hensel, Boulder, Colorado, past President of Morgan County Chapter of United World Federalists.

An atom agency for peaceful uses, John Boardman argues, is "useful for scientific reasons," but has "absolutely no relation to the cause or to the prevention of the armaments race."

Despite its initial lack of supervisory powers over national armaments, CURE participants by a preponderance of 71% agree that the International Atomic Energy Agency has substantial value in its educational and preparatory functions. A world atom agency will command much of the world's best scientific brains. To it will gravitate new resources and techniques, many of them developed at great cost elsewhere as byproducts of arms programs.

"The plan for 'have' nations to contribute fissionable materials to a common stockpile, to enable the 'have not' nations to develop their economics and resources, offers an immediate and practical plan for relieving some of the international tension," feels Evadne M. Laptad, Lawrence, Kansas, President of the Douglas County Health Council.

W. B. H. Corkey, Goldsboro, North Carolina, hails the program as one which promises "demonstrations of good will through actual projects."

Professor Quincy Wright adds that a program of atoms for peace will "build a spirit of co-operation in this field among scientists and technicians of the United States, the USSR and other countries."

A substantial 85% of conferees foresee that the growth of a non-regulatory atom agency under the United Nations will make hostile action by an outlaw nation increasingly difficult.

"Yes, but not difficult enough," Dr. David Singer qualifies his vote: "this is one case where half a loaf could be suicidal."

And the majority of conferees agree that an atomic authority for peaceful uses is no more than a preliminary step toward disarmament. In combination with other executive functions under the general responsibility of a world legislature, the jurisdiction of an initial world nuclear authority is an asset to world peace only if it accelerates our progress toward world law. The International Atomic Energy Agency should be organized within the United Nations so that it is fully capable not only of this preliminary duty but of the awesome responsibility for the custody of ultimate force which it must accept in the future.

Making Use of the Trusteeship Council

Another type of international responsibility still in its early stages of development is the United Nations' trusteeship of non-self-governing territories.

The present Trusteeship Council does not itself administer the non-self-governing territories under its jurisdiction. Although under the terms of the United Nations Charter the Trusteeship Council may administer directly such territories, in practice it assigns each Trust Territory to an individual nation as administrator. The Trustee nation is almost inevitably a colonial power more interested in the exploitation of its wards than in their progress toward independence.

The General Assembly appoints the members of the Trusteeship Council. But the members represent their nations, and are not responsible to the General Assembly. The General Assembly cannot remove its appointees from office during their three-year terms. While the Charter directs that the Trusteeship Council shall function under the direction of the General Assembly, in actual operation, like other administrative agencies of the United Nations, the Trusteeship Council is largely independent of its parent body. It is not an executive branch answerable to a United Nations legislature.

92% of CURE's consultants feel that the Trusteeship Council should be reconstituted as an executive branch under a democratic world parliament. 93% believe that all colonial peoples should have the rights to petition, to report and to consult, which are now extended by the United Nations to Trust Territories only. In the opinion of 94% of conferees, the Trusteeship Council should exercise its authority under the Charter to offer direct trust administration as an aid in the progress of colonial peoples toward independence.

There is good historical precedent for a wider responsibility of trusteeship under a world organization. Quincy Wright cites the fact that "the League of Nations successfully administered the Saar for fifteen years through a commission."

William Bross Lloyd refers to post-World War II commissions under the United Nations which supervised Libya, Eritrea, Italian Somaliland and Indonesia. "In the latter case United Nations powers covered important political, economic and social fields, amounting for a time almost to United Nations administration," he notes.

Improvement in the legislative and executive structure of the United Nations will put the Trusteeship Council in a better position to undertake the direct administration of Trust Territories. "In dealing with the power of direct trusteeship," affirms Waldo Mead, "the United Nations would be competent for such a power once it becomes truly representative of the people."

Direct administration of trusteeships by the United Nations will provide a transitional stage between the former sovereignty of the colonial power and the future sovereignty of the population itself.

Plans for eventual revision of the United Nations Charter, in the opinion of conferees, should seek to ensure that direct

United Nations trusteeships shall not invade the rights of any people or of any nation. Conferees by a 92% margin would permit the Trusteeship Council to assume a trust only with the assent of the previous colonial power. Moreover, says William Lloyd, the United Nations should undertake trusteeship only "where specifically requested by a majority of inhabitants" in a plebescite held in the territory.

"The crux of the problem" is "all parties willing," declares Arnold Goodman, Racine, Wisconsin, President of the Midwest Branch of United World Federalists.

"Giving colonial peoples their choice between two temporary rulers—the administering power and the Trusteeship Council—would be a spur to both, and a needed safeguard for government by consent of the governed in the future," Mr. Lloyd suggests. "This could be spelled out by requiring the establishment of minimal time-tables for complete independence in the cases of all colonial peoples electing to come under direct United Nations administration.

"On the other hand there is a danger in world authority which should be faced frankly. Will a world organization which is strengthened in its power over colonial areas become dictatorial and itself a danger to freedom? Who can say that a world bureaucracy administering colonial areas will be much more enlightened in the long run than the old-line colonial nations have now become? Nationalist movements are leary of endorsing United Nations administration. First give us independence, they say, and then you will see that we will be glad to join the United Nations like any other country."

The hitherto unused powers of the United Nations to accept direct trusteeships, once dusted off and brought into action, can help to direct native yearnings for independence into constructive channels. As an addition to these powers, Mr. Lloyd advocates the establishment of more direct communications between the Trusteeship Council and those trust areas which continue under an administration by individual trustee nations.

"A permanent United Nations privilege in all colonial areas should be a United Nations radio network—to which television might in time be added (Brazil is already planning use of this medium in the education of jungle tribes)," he proposes. "One

United Nations radio station in each territory would supplement—not replace—stations operated by the administering authority, and could ensure a clear popular understanding of United Nations activities leading toward self-government."

An 82% majority of CURE's forum back Mr. Lloyd in his recommendation that the Trusteeship Council should have a right to operate radio stations in any Trust Territory under its cognizance.

Even a cautious plan for change in colonial relationships may have explosive potentialities.

"Colonies are a major part of the power struggle," states William A. Wheeler.

"We are in favour of extending the powers of the Trusteeship Council," comments Gilbert McAllister, London, England, Secretary General of the World Association of Parliamentarians for World Government and a former Labour Member of Parliament. But his parliamentarians might not endorse the proposal of direct trusteeship: "one has only to think of France's 'walk out' to see what political dynamite that is," Mr. McAllister cautions.

In many cases, consent of the colonial power to a transitional United Nations trusteeship would come "only by continuous concentrated pressure of world opinion," in the belief of Mr. Lloyd.

Present unrest and pressures for independence in colonies suggest, however, that United Nations interim administrations may come to be regarded by colonial powers themselves as a safeguard for their continuing economic interests in territories where they have investments.

Another type of international administrative responsibility may develop for certain of the earth's areas which lack permanent populations.

"I believe that we ought to concentrate first on Antarctica," suggests Isaac James Pitman, London, England, Conservative Member of Parliament and Chairman of Sir Isaac Pitman and Sons, publishers. "The introduction of the rule of law there will tread on no one's toes—indeed it will let out many nations from liabilities which they would gladly shed providing the shedding may be satisfactorily done. Nations attach, I believe, small importance to their territorial claims in Antarctica and would

81

regard their claims as 'an insignificant but real amount' of sovereignty."

Several nations assert claims to parts of Antarctica, some of them conflicting. A necessary first step toward United Nations responsibility for the Polar continent might be an international treaty among the nations which claim portions of the snowy wasteland. Underneath the snow and glaciers, patrolled by penguins, there may lie vast Antarctic natural resources which will provide revenue for the United Nations, and which will help to untie world budgets from the purse-strings of individual member nations.

A four-fifths majority of the participants in CURE's discussions concur with the suggestion that Antarctica should be placed under United Nations trusteeship.

"Antarctica differs in that permanent United Nations ownership and control should be envisaged," declares William Lloyd; a principle, he adds, "not so with colonies," where "a time table for complete self-government and full United Nations membership should by all means be specified."

Strategic Areas

Still another large share of the world's turmoil springs from disputes over the control and use of various strategic waterways and harbors.

In many cases the access to a vital canal or port, or the control of a strategic strait, affects the economy and safety of many nations. The interest of an actual possessor may be only to prevent adverse possession by others. Such cases occur, as instances, at Gibraltar, Panama and Singapore. In other instances, such as Suez and the Bosporus, an owner nation inhabits the land around the waterway. But regardless of this distinction, it is in the interests of world peace that international shipping traffic through any key maritime passage should not be subject to the whim of a particular nation.

Where international waterways are concerned, "there is good reason to believe that the still powerful ethical appeal of the United Nations as the representative of humanity would lead to popular acceptance of United Nations administration," in the opinion of William Lloyd. "Such direct administration would be an important milestone on the way toward world federation."

The trusteeship powers of the United Nations are broad enough to accept the civil administration of populations in zones controlling strategic waterways, wherever such a procedure seems advisable; in most strategic zones, however, the populations have natural allegiances to governments which can well accept the civil responsibility for such areas. The world's need in such zones is primarily for technical administration of the facilities for international navigation. International waterways will be an important source of revenues for a future United Nations. Their administration will embrace many aspects of engineering and of financial planning as well as the duty of efficient and impartial service to the commerce of the world.

An administration adapted to such purposes might evolve from a broader interpretation of the present trusteeship provisions of the United Nations Charter. In principle, however, a better procedure will be to create as a part of a revision of the Charter something in the nature of an International Waterways Administration, intended, like other executive divisions of a future United Nations, to function in accordance with legislation provided by the world parliament.

A time of crisis such as the Suez difficulties may bring an invitation for the United Nations to accept responsibility for an international waterway. The status of international passages may develop by common consent, by horse-trading among various governments seeking concessions in other fields, or by request of local governments desiring funds for development. The more trouble a particular spot causes, the more logical is United Nations administration there. The eventual result we may foresee as a series of international buffer zones at vital points of the earth's geography.

Administration of prominent trouble spots "as a first step to give the United Nations actual temporal powers and allow its feet to touch the ground, however tenuously, is a very good idea," comments Yehudi Menuhin, Los Gatos, California, concert violinist. Establishment of United Nations responsibility for danger points such as strategic waterways will hasten its growth toward true government, 59% of participants in CURE's conference agree.

Differing types of trusteeships under the United Nations can assert the sovereignty of mankind in various jurisdictions where national sovereignties are least precise and most troublesome. "Give me where to stand," said Archimedes, "and I will move the world." The administration of friction areas, establishing the United Nations as a world-wide buffer state, will create an Archimedean leverage for world peace.

NeptUNO Rules the Seas

National governments lay claim to most of the world's lands. Nations assert ownership of waters near their territories. Yet the claims of all governments to territorial sovereignty cover only a fraction of the earth: the rest is ocean.

"Proper government of the high seas," writes Patrick Armstrong, spokesman of the British Parliamentary Group for World Government, "is no mere academic problem."

Mr. Armstrong enumerates increasing threats to these traditional freedoms of the seas which the English-speaking navies have long defended.

First, "by the encroachment of nation-states with claims to ever larger territorial waters from the customary three miles to four (Norway), twelve (USSR) and even 200 (Peru, Ecuador, Chile).

"Secondly, by further encroachment by oil-drillings outside territorial waters, through the theory of a 100-meter continental shelf extending sovereignty over the sea-bed often for hundreds of miles, according to the accidents of geography.

"Thirdly by the insufficiency of international conventions, even that of 1954, for the prevention of oil pollution by tankers.

"Fourthly, by the problem of testing atomic weapons in the oceans and the uncertainty about the siting or the extent of testing areas, and the lack of international regulation for the disposal of atomic waste.

"Fifthly, by the lack of sanction for the numerous fishing conventions which groups of nations have adopted."

The United Nations tries to cope with these problems through its International Law Commission, set up by the General Assembly to assist in the codification and "progressive development" of international law.

Representatives of 86 nations met at Geneva, Switzerland for two months in 1958 in an ILC session on the law of the sea. Four "conventions" proposed by most of the participating maritime states made some progress toward agreement on this "law" which is, in reality, only a structure of treaties.

The conventions of 1958 included (1) a reaffirmation of the principle of freedom of the high seas and of the air space above them; (2) provisions for arbitration in disputes about fishing and conservation of living resources in the seas; (3) a new code for the exploitation of submarine resources on the "continental shelf" of coastal nations, and (4) a restatement of national sovereignty over marginal seas adjacent to coastlines, with an attempt to define "innocent passage" through such territorial waters by the ships of other nations.

The Geneva Conference was unable, however, (1) to establish any rule of "law" with respect to the conflicting claims of nations to "sovereignty" at varying distances from their coasts; (2) to put any teeth into agreements against oil pollution by tankers, or (3) to restrain the United States from dumping its atomic wastes in the open ocean.

Clashing claims of sovereignty on the high seas are a historic source of international frictions. Like conflicting claims on land, to assert a nation's rights wherever its flag sails is asking for trouble. As we pass out of an era when war was an accepted instrument of national policy, the need for mankind to establish a rule of the oceans increases correspondingly. The reasons for formalizing the international character of the high seas are not only political, but also technical.

"The regime of the high seas has functioned reasonably well up till recent times because nations had no way of developing their rights beyond the limits of their land boundaries," Mr. Armstrong continues. "The advance of science in promoting fisheries, the vastly increased range of fishing craft, the coming of nuclear energy and the disposal of its waste, the raw materials which now can be derived from the sea have made some kind of new regime highly necessary."

Mr. Armstrong reviews the votes of CURE's Conference which propose that United Nations jurisdictions shall include an Economic Development Authority, the International Atomic Energy Agency, and powers of direct trusteeship as executive departments under a world parliament.

"The all-party British Parliamentary Group for World Government, which was founded in 1947 and has a membership of

85

131 in Lords and Commons," he writes, proposes "what would be a fourth direct grant of powers to the United Nations: that the high seas, sub-soil and seabed outside whatever the United Nations Law Commission should decide to be territorial waters, should be declared 'world territory' under United Nations ownership."

This, together with the British proposal of an internationalized Antarctica, "would put the United Nations into the real estate business to the extent of five-sevenths of the planet's surface, without (except in parts of Antarctica) infringing anyone's sovereignty," he adds.

"The advantages of giving the United Nations jurisdiction and control over the high seas and Antarctica are manifold," Mr. Armstrong points out. "For the first time the United Nations would have some real estate to administer and would require 'sea-traffic police' to do so. Acts of piracy or oil-pollution by nation-states could be dealt with so that 'the freedom of the seize' was an act of impartial justice rather than, as now, the unilateral action of an interested nation. The United Nations would, as befits its function, have the task of keeping open for all mankind the world's vital water highways. By settling the status of the high seas outside territorial waters the nation-states might well be less exorbitant in their claims and thereby make easier an agreement on the reasonable extension of territorial waters and continental shelf.

"The United Nations could derive an independent income from leasing out to member states or private concerns development rights of the sea bottom and Antarctica. The coastal state would presumably be given the right of first refusal by the United Nations for the development rights. But there is no reason why United Nations ownership should upset the exploitation of the sea and of the sea-bed which has taken place up to now."

An 84% consensus of CURE correspondents share the British Parliamentary Group's opinion that a high seas administration should be a sovereign jurisdiction of the United Nations.

If these British "NeptUNO" proposals become a part of a world law, the oceans, which gave us being, will once again provide an element favorable to our survival.

Man in the Realm of Space

For thousands of years men have travelled the familiar seas; within living memory man first took to the air. In the early part of the twentieth century aviation made use of an atmospheric layer of air only a few miles thick above the earth which, like the waters adjacent to a coastline, is subject to the effective control of a neighboring nation. The second half of the twentieth century is witnessing the breakthrough of man's realm into space above the atmosphere. Science is translating the concepts of manmade satellites and space ships from the comic strips to the commonplace.

Manmade moons and missiles presage new modes of destruction. A gleaming pinpoint drifting across the evening sky may be an innocent and interesting visitor; but its successor may carry a warhead aimed and armed to blast a teeming city out of existence.

If it is desirable that freedom of the seas shall become the United Nations' sovereign responsibility, it is equally logical that the United Nations should undertake to supervise man's exploration of space beyond the gaseous envelope of the earth's atmosphere.

80% of Conference debaters think that United Nations jurisdictions should include authority over space navigation. Like an Atomic Energy Agency, a "Bureau for Extra-Atmospheric Space Travel" may begin with nominal powers, ready to take over war weapons with the growth of peace.

Far beyond the paths of military missiles and the narrow orbits of artificial satellites lie wider realms awaiting exploration. If man survives his own earthbound follies long enough, his investigation of the sun's other planets may well occupy him for a century to come. Such adventures fill even the bored and anxious soul of modern man with wonder. Compared to the unfamiliar difficulties of spanning space, even the task of creating a world government seems easy.

Sometimes we hear or read allusions to the "control" of outer space. Such talk is presumptuous. The distance of one day's travel at the speed of light bounds a volume of space in which the earth would appear as minute as does one grain of sand in relation to the globe on which we live. The nearest star is more than one thousand times more distant again. Multiply its distance by another thousand, and you could "explore" our universe. Multiply it by a thousand once more, and a "traveler" could reach other universes! It is entirely probable that life exists elsewhere than on our miniscule planet; but it is also quite possible that we may never bridge the enormous gaps of time and space which separate us from other intelligent existences.

The perspectives of space perhaps more powerfully than any other knowledge help to focus our understanding upon the frailty of man. An exploration of voids beyond our terrestrial homeland asks of us the humility and the boldness which befit an undertaking in the name of all the earth's inhabitants.

Powers We Do Not Need

Areas where sovereignty is uncertain are a fertile cause of wars. The proper function of a strengthened United Nations is to stabilize those fields of friction where nations come into collision. We may describe its powers in these jurisdictions as arising out of necessity, rather than convenience or idealism.

"Affairs of world concern should be regulated by ultra-national authority," writes J. W. Walker, Johnson City, New York, past Chairman of the New York Citizens' Committee for a Peoples' World Convention. "However, it is all-important that the powers of such an authority be strictly specified and limited. No one can say now just where the line should be drawn. The important thing is that it be drawn, definitely, after proper consideration."

Since necessity is to be the mother of the new United Nations, we need not invent any powers for it which are not directly connected with the keeping of peace. Many functions familiar to us at the level of national governments are not actually necessary to an international federal government, votes of CURE indicate.

A common coinage is not necessary to a federation of nations, the Conference believes (87%).

Free immigration is not necessary to a world federal government (80%).

And, though less decisively, free trade is not necessary to the establishment of a world federation (63%).

With regard to world authority in such spheres, "I happen

to think that all three objectives are good, and that the world (even including Americans) may some day realize it," is the typical view of Henry C. McIlvaine, Jr. But, he says, it is going to be difficult to secure the basic necessities of world order; "why make it more difficult, if not impossible within any foreseeable future, by advocating all these additional powers?"

It seems preferable, at least in the immediate future, to leave matters not directly affecting peace as a continuing area for diplomatic negotiations among members of the United Nations, subject to agreements rather than to enforceable legislation.

Selection of an Executive

Within these carefully delineated areas of jurisdiction, the improved United Nations must have a clear competence to function. The organization of its executive departments must provide the channels of leadership and responsibility which are necessary for effective administration.

It is the view of CURE's two-thirds majority that at the level of international government a cabinet or collective type of executive is preferable to a strong individual executive on the American style.

"A single executive is primarily useful where the military concerns are predominant. These should be less important in a world community," states Dr. Martin T. Hutchinson, New Brunswick, New Jersey, Rutgers University entomologist and past President of New Jersey State Branch of United World Federalists.

Debates among CUREspondents reveal a trend in favor of a "neutralist" type of executive administration at the world level, such as might evolve out of the present administrative staff of the Secretary General of the United Nations. 70% of conferees feel that a future United Nations cabinet slate might include candidates who are not members of either branch in the proposed bicameral General Assembly, for instance, career members of the world civil service.

The strengthened United Nations can de-emphasize politics in its executive branch by the manner of electing its cabinets. A possible procedure is to hold a series of preferential ballots, in which the members of both houses of the legislature vote by

89

numbering the order of their preferences among the various cabinet slates. Each ballot, by this system, will eliminate one slate receiving the fewest favorable votes. A progressive elimination of lowest slates will result in the election of a conciliatory or "least objectionable" executive. 61% of CURE conferees believe that a system of preferential elimination would provide a practical way to choose the executive branch of the international government.

A requirement of a two-thirds vote to cause the interim dismissal of a cabinet seems desirable to 73% of CURE's consultants. Such possibilities suggest that it will be feasible for an amended Charter to provide adequate stability together with democratic responsibility in the executive structure of a revised United Nations.

Sources of Finance

In addition to a power to act, an international government must have the ability to pay its bills.

Delegates in the Assembly of Peoples of a world legislature should draw their salaries from an international treasury rather than from the nation of their origin.

A world treasury, in turn, should not depend upon the voluntary financial contributions of individual nations, which might be withheld as a pawn of politics or by reason of parsimony. An international government must stand on its own financial feet.

Theorists of government including Dr. Mortimer Adler have asserted that a sovereign government must be able to tax individual citizens. And so it must, in the case of any individual nation larger than a postage-stamp principality. But it is less clear that an international government will need the power to tax all of its billions of citizens.

"An international government must have the power to levy taxes rather than depend on voluntary contributions, but it need not be directly on the individual," suggests John W. Schneider. "In the State of New York, for instance, the county governments depend for their revenues on a tax levied on the cities, towns and villages in their jurisdiction. No city, town or village budget omitting the county tax is valid."

Without venturing to forecast exactly how a revision of the

United Nations Charter may eventually establish the financial basis for a world federal government, we may predict that the fiscal aspects of an effective international regime will offer no insuperable difficulty. The fiscal program of a revised and strengthened United Nations will rest upon a base of taxable wealth so enormous as to stagger appraisal. Its income will draw on many sources. It will be in business as a world bank. It will gain revenues from international shipping. It may quite conceivably become heir to all customs receipts of the individual nations. The United Nations of the future will license fishing rights in international waters, lease oil rights on the bottom of the sea and mineral rights in the Antarctic. It will control vast outputs of atomic power and of fissionable materials. The armaments expenses of a future United Nations, as we shall see, will be relatively modest. The actual costs of government (as distinct from welfare programs) will be a burden easily borne, whether they fall upon nations or upon individual citizens.

Whatever mode of levy comes into use will represent not an expense, but an economy to the individual citizens of the world's nations. Let us suppose, for illustration, that a United Nations of the future might cost so much that its budget would increase twentyfold. The resulting international stability will enable the United States to eliminate, let us say, three-fourths of its present arms budget. In terms of the average American's pocketbook, the net saving would cut in half his total burden of taxation for national and international governments!

World Law in Everyday Life

Since its creation the United Nations has had certain powers, certain competences and sovereignties, however limited they may seem in the scale of its giant task. The powers of today's international organization already far exceed those possessed by any previous league or treaty authority which has linked the world's nations. Yet, from the start, the United Nations has been inadequate to conduct a peaceful government of international affairs: its powers are uncertain and its sovereignties suspect.

"The United Nations is already loaded with words like 'trusteeship', 'law', 'court'," Vernon Nash remarks, "which mean

91

very different things internationally to what they designate locally."

Such government is, at best, ambiguous. "I doubt that any body may properly be called an 'authority' unless it either has power to compel in its own right, or is a subordinate agency of a government," Dr. Nash adds.

The decisions of an effective international tribunal must be enforceable within its carefully chosen areas of jurisdiction. Because the jurisdictions which this chapter describes are international in nature, enforcement in these domains need not invade the domestic sovereignty of any individual nation. In these international areas a growing reliance upon peaceful means of decision will minimize the use of force. Planes or Jeeps or ships which fly the ensign of the United Nations will have little need for weapons, for the blue banner which they bear will proclaim the authority not of a single nation but of nearly one hundred nations.

As the international jurisdictions of the United Nations become consolidated in everyday practice, it will become manifest to everyone that its powers of enforcement are, in fact, ordinary police functions. A government which is widely recognized as useful does not need to resort to military force to impose its wishes upon the citizens whom it governs.

"For a first period of, say, four to eight years, an executive cabinet can, and should, pick and choose the uncontroversial items out of its enormous range of loose ends left about by United Nations and international negotiations. This will enable one or two cabinets in this first period to produce excellent 'results', visible to the man in the street, with astonishing rapidity," prophesies Alfredo Rodrigues Brent. "Though we are idealists, we should nonetheless be practical, recognize that nothing succeeds like success and by this token establish the new world federation firmly 'in the minds of mankind'."

CURE's majorities have made recommendations for United Nations sovereignty in specific jurisdictions of economics, atomic energy, trusteeships and navigation. These jurisdictions are international by nature. No single nation can effectively "govern" the matters which they concern. If a Conference for the Review of the United Nations Charter can make the General Assembly of the United Nations more adequately representative of the world's peoples as well as of their national governments, it is probable that at the same time the Charter revision process can award to the improved world parliament a governmental power in several international jurisdictions such as these. Perhaps this is the most that a Charter Revision Conference can hope for. If so, it will be an enormous gain. It will tip the scales toward peace. And, significantly, we see that an international parliamentary power to manage a few principal problems which are common to all humanity will touch hardly a hair of the head of the internal sovereignties of individual nations.

The creation of an effective agency for peaceful solutions will set in motion a continuing evolution of peace. An inevitable result will be the progress of international organization toward the disarmament of individual nations and the maintenance of international law and order.

Chapter 6.

E Pluribus UNum

It will be obvious to the reader that CURE's studies seek to deal with the underlying causes of world unrest, and their democratic solution, rather than merely with their superficial symptoms in terms such as a "prohibition" of war or a prescription for "disarmament". It is equally apparent that CURE has dealt less with the scope and nature of the military or police powers which it may be necessary to give to an international government, than with the democratic controls which are to be placed upon the exercise of such powers.

The creation of a democratic legislature at a world level will result in fundamental changes in the world power balance. These will not be just shifts of power from nation to nation, but a basic concentration of limited but crucial powers toward the center.

There is no lack of proposals for the creation of enormous power at the world level. Bernard Baruch spoke for the United States government in offering an atom control plan of vast and sweeping implications. President Eisenhower urged world arms curbs which would radically reduce the war-making capacities of the nations. Though the American Legion professes to oppose world government, it endorses world police powers which nothing less than a world government could administer. CUREspondents Grenville Clark and Louis B. Sohn, in their *World Peace through World Law*, recommend a 12 to 16-year program of "complete, universal and enforceable disarmament" and the replacement of arms expenditures by a global welfare program going far beyond CURE's majority suggestions.

Cynical statesmen have come to regard the whole subject of disarmament as a fit field for propaganda. Disarmament discussions too easily fall into a vein of wishful thinking. But peace cannot be faked. It would be a cruel swindle upon the hopes of men to pretend that armaments can be abolished simply by bargaining to junk bombs, missiles and submarines. Talk of arms limitation in this vein is no more realistic now than it was in the naive era of Locarno.

Only 38% of participants in the Conference Upon Research and Education in world government see any real likelihood of success in current international disarmament negotiations. Instead, there must be world government before disarmament is possible, conferees insist by a 77% majority.

"Disarmament will not be the cause for security but can only be the result of it," declares Maurice R. Cosyn, Boitsfort, Belgium, Secretary General of Union Fédérale.

"Disarmament," echoes Louis B. Dailey, Maplewood, New Jersey, lawyer, radio commentator and past President of New Jersey State Branch of United World Federalists, "is neither the cause of peace nor realistically possible without first or simultaneously establishing an effective world government based on just and enforceable law."

American offers of disarmament such as the Baruch and Eisenhower proposals were meant to be rejected, Science Editor William Lawrence of the New York *Times* wrote in his book *The Hell Bomb*. Reporter Lawrence thought that the United States Congress, jealous of American atomic "secrets", would not have accepted even if the Russians did.

Most Americans probably feel that Russian offers to halt bomb tests are mere propaganda, but that their own government makes arms limitation proposals in good faith. Half of CURE's conferees think that the United States would go through with agreements if the Russians accepted. It is easy, however, to imagine the consternation in the American State Department, the fluttering in the bureaucratic dovecotes and the festoons of additional American provisos, which might greet a Russian announcement of acceptance all down the line.

Patchwork proposals such as neutralized buffer zones, "open skies" air inspection or cessation of atom bomb tests voice man's deep-seated urge to discover first steps on the path to peace. But these fringe proposals, insofar as they do not go to the heart of the matter, simply divide unreality into smaller packages.

"Neutralized buffer zones cannot stop long-range missiles," Alfredo Rodrigues Brent reminds us, "and any zone smaller than our globe can be negotiated by modern airborne troops within 48 hours. Safeguardings in terms of World War II offer no protection in a 1960-or-so war. Open skies inspections," he adds, "do not disclose what happens underground in mountainous districts where a mining industry already offers enormous coverage."

Governments will continue to rely upon arms as a last resort of national policy until the nations replace them by a better means of settling rivalries and disputes. As long as armaments represent some shred of security, no nation will give them up for less security. Nations can gain greater security by the surrender of their arms only if they relinquish their weapons as a contribution to a pooled security, to an international organization offering a more stable enforcement of peace.

"I feel sure that nations will never give up their arms but to an international government," prophesies Glenn P. Turner, Middleton, Wisconsin, retired lawyer and former member of the Wisconsin State Assembly.

The world's great antagonistic power centers, Russia and the United States of America, each hold in their hands weapons designed to demolish the other. Two hundred American missile bases on foreign soil threaten the Russian heartland. Four hundred Russian submarines, each a potential missile carrier, menace America's cities from the sea. Both adversaries vie in a desperate race to replace long-range bomb-carrying aircraft by long-range bomb-carrying rockets.

Each opponent views the other's weapons as being in irresponsible hands: the hands of an enemy. Each of the adversaries would be equally well defended from attack if the same arms which it now possesses were commanded by international peace forces in the name of humanity; and each would be much safer from an onslaught by the other if the other's extraterritorial forces were under a neutral international control.

Russians might feel quite justified in eradicating American missile and plane bases as long as they are poised as a hostile threat to the Russian homeland. Such enemy outposts will be prime Soviet targets in the event of hostilities. But the Kremlin would be much more reluctant to launch a blitz against encircling bases if the act were to constitute an aggression against the whole of humanity.

On the other hand, America cannot in good reason abandon her close-range bases for the containment of Soviet ambitions while Russia continues to disclose her recurrent initiatives in futuristic weapons. But the internationalization of American bases on foreign soil would be a cheap price to pay if it gained the neutralization of Russia's submarine fleet. By such an arrangement both these arms, with their costs still paid by the contributing nations, can pass under a United Nations command whose personnel are drawn chiefly from smaller countries.

Where disarmament as such would, at best, leave a power vacuum between Russia and America, by contrast the pooling of a decisive force of arms under United Nations command would interpose law between the two great adversaries. The difference is, in military terms, that a pooling of effective close-range weapons under the command of an international organization will render futile any attempt at sneak aggression by uncontrolled long-range weapons. The advantage, in this way, will pass from attack to defense. Pooling of arms will bring greater security to both the big antagonists, as well as to all the innocent bystanders. Neutralized buffer zones have less meaning with each year's advance in technology; as time passes, a pooled peacekeeping power has increasing significance for the welfare of the world's citizens.

We see now why an increased competence of the United Nations as a world parliament, enabling it to accept not only a responsibility for international justice but also ultimately for the command of pooled peace forces, will eventually make possible the disarmament of nations and the reduction of our present enormous weapons expenditures to a nominal level.

The issue is "to find means which give security to all peoples," affirms R. Madec, Caudéron, Gironde, France, Secretary General of the League of World Citizens.

Security cannot come from merely reducing the power of

hostile arms: it can come only from strengthening the inter-
vening power of peace.

Cutting the Veto Down to Size

When nations enter a diplomatic conference, each nation
takes its sovereignty along with it in the form of a power of
veto. In foreign affairs no nation really has a sovereign power
of decision. A diplomatic sovereignty, at most, consists of the
right not to agree.

At San Francisco, during the writing of the Charter of the
United Nations, smaller nations recognized that they could not
withstand the united will of five major powers. Five of the
largest nations, which would have found it difficult to coerce
each other, each received a veto power in the Security Council
of the United Nations. In the philosophy of the United Nations
Charter, every nation is sovereign, but great nations are more
sovereign than small.

"The veto is, under existing conditions, a safety valve,"
argues John Logue; "don't get rid of the safety valve until
you've done the major reconstruction job which will make it
unnecessary."

CURE's planners have avoided any proposal to usurp the
sovereignty of nations in their domestic affairs. Even in international matters, Conference members consider it unlikely
that the great powers would yield their veto rights in a world
legislature which attempted to govern by the present one-nation-one-vote rule.

"In order to even consider elimination of the veto," states
Neil Parsons, "it will be necessary to make the United Nations
a government of peoples instead of a League of Nations." The
veto "must be retained unless the voting system is changed,"
agrees Mary N. Temple, Chicago, Illinois, staff member of the
American Friends Service Committee.

The veto is a protection of minorities. The British House of
Lords long possessed a power to delay legislation by defeating
bills sent up from the House of Commons. The Senate of the
United States, with its virtual veto by the device of filibuster,
is a sanctuary of American minorities. A majority of United
States senators sometimes permit themselves to be outargued
by a sovereign minority consisting of a single long-winded col-

league. The President of the United States has an executive veto which the Congress may override only by a two-thirds majority, and the governors of most individual states have similar prerogatives.

"Since we are a small minority of the world's population, we cannot expect to protect ourselves by our own armed might," warns Stanley K. Platt. "Minorities can be protected only by the development of just law. Law and order are essential to the survival and advance of democracy. Without it we leave a vacuum into which the anarchy of force and violence will move."

"To be effective, a constitution must represent not a compromise, but a balance of the social and economic forces at the time of its creation," Neil Parsons writes. "While it may provide for decisions by the majority, it must provide protection for each minority."

Democracy cannot go too far in tying up the will of a majority. A society or a government has to be able to get something done. Nor is it always wise to protect every minority interest by a veto privilege.

"What minority will use it to protect themselves, and against what?" asks John Holt.

"The filibuster and the House of Lords have continually been used to obstruct the kind of social and economic reforms that most of the world's people need and will demand," Mr. Holt asserts. A veto may thwart efforts to make the United Nations more effective, he says; it may be used "by the wealthy minority of the world, notably the United States, to frustrate any scheme that would require us to use our wealth and productive power to help less fortunate people, or that would tend to distribute the world's resources more fairly among the world's people.

"A government made in that image does not seem to me to have a chance of winning that kind of fervent popular support that alone can make it an effective competitor to the challenge of Communism."

The United States, though a minority in fact, needs no veto in the United Nations as long as it can muster support by a majority of nations for its viewpoints. Russia, consistently outvoted in the United Nations, as consistently defends its interests

99

by invoking its veto privilege. Someone who does not need it cannot force an abolition of the veto upon someone who does need it. Limitation of the veto, even in chosen jurisdictions, is a two-way street; the relinquishment must be possible for the minority, as well as desirable for the majority.

Recommendations of the Conference suggest various ways of eliminating the obstacle of the veto. The creation of an Assembly of Peoples in the United Nations, and the establishment of a graduated scale for the better representation of large nations, will diminish their reliance upon the veto privilege. Further, to the extent that we limit the responsibilities of an international government to jurisdictions which do not infringe upon the domestic sovereignties of nations, we render the veto problem more manageable. And the inherent structure of parliamentary government, with its blocs and "veto groups", offers to minorities a substantial measure of built-in protection against the encroachments of others. The governmental structure which we contemplate will give the largest nations good justification to limit their veto rights.

Some sort of a limited veto might remain. Let us suppose that a revised Charter of the United Nations will provide that a measure must ordinarily receive a simple majority approval in each of the two chambers of the world parliament in order to become law. In the event of a negative vote cast by certain great powers, the statute might require that the passage of a measure will require a two-thirds vote by both chambers. The nations which are to retain such a limited right of veto might include China, India, the Union of Socialist Soviet Republics and the United States of America as well as possible future federations like a United States of Europe. In part, this privilege will serve them as compensation for the reduced proportionate voting power which great nations will receive in a graduated scale system of representation.

Suggestions of this nature are speculative. We can perceive, nevertheless, that it is possible by such means to design a world government possessing a workable system of checks and balances.

"In seeking to remove misgivings, we must recognize that it is inherently impossible to form a workable federation in which any nation (or even any small group of nations) can veto something to which they are opposed," maintains Vernon Nash. "But it does seem probable that we can devise methods by which a given category of peoples can be assured that they will not be dominated by any other rival group, and at the same time have a practicable government for world affairs.

"When a plausible case can be made for this hope," he adds, "most of the repugnance toward a federated world should disappear."

Once we have created the conditions for its solution, the problem of the veto begins to appear a good deal less formidable.

Areas of World Federal Sovereignty

Though we limit the legal jurisdictions of a future United Nations so that they do not intrude on national sovereignties, neither do we forbid it to deal with matters of more local interest at least on the level of discussion. In particular a chamber of governments in the United Nations parliament may continue, among its other functions, to serve as a permanent diplomatic conference among nations.

It is probable that the great powers will not accept majority rule in diplomatic areas of deliberation, concede 79% of CURE's consultants. Nevertheless, many foresee a useful role for an Assembly of Nations in wide vistas of conciliation. In matters on a diplomatic level, the Assembly of Peoples may have an advisory role, giving expression to public opinion on negotiations which are not subject to world law.

United Nations legislative powers in economic, atom and colonial matters, in jurisdictions over the high seas and ventures into space will free a sufficient array of international functions from the shackles of unanimity so that the new Charter can wield an unprecedented influence for stability.

"Powers to prevent war on a world scale necessarily imply quite a lot of power," Alfredo Rodrigues Brent argues. "This has little to do with the old minimalist-maximalist controversies among Federalists because the views expressed in that discussion were and are purely theoretical, taking as a base such powers as are exercised by national governments and transferable or not, according to the view of the speaker, to a supranational government.

101

"The practical issue necessitates dealing with such powers as are *not* or only nominally exercised now, by any government.

"For over a hundred years now technology has advanced at a great and ever increasing pace whilst the amount of anarchy in international and transnational dealings between private corporations as well as between states is by now staggering and so-called international law is about the most backward of all underdeveloped regions.

"Even if transfer of jurisdiction from national to world government is limited to gladden the heart of the most cautious minimalist, the number and the extent of affairs to be ruled by a world government will still awe and appall the most fervent maximalist."

Mr. Brent discovers illumination on this subject in his reflections upon the basic principles of government.

"The concept of 'sovereignty' has been the subject of many studies in many languages by professors of political science. In the end they mostly come to the same conclusions, mostly negative conclusions on this evasive 'Kompetenz-Kompetenz' or 'compétence de la compétence'.

"The more you go back in the history of peoples all over the earth, the more you find sovereignty to be a sacred and/or religious concept. It is a magic force attributed to either one chief or to a small group of medicine-men or witchcraft-priests. In advancing nations, sovereignty is gradually transferred to the king or the caliph or the pharaoh, who then becomes 'the sovereign' directly appointed by God or by the gods. Still later, sovereignty is vested in the king 'by the grace of God'. There is an exception in totemist societies, where sovereignty, still sacerdotal in character, is supposed to be diffused among all members of the clan. In the modern state sovereignty is supposed to be vested in the state.

"This concept is still in the metaphysical or, if you will, religious realm, because it takes sovereignty to be a force received in its entity by that state and for its structure as a whole. In this conception sovereignty is not the outcome of self-government but its base. In other words it is still not a political or a juridical but a metaphysical concept. The picture changes only when the position is reversed, self-government is taken as the base and sovereignty is regarded as the outcome. However, if you take that position, sovereignty is less a force than a function."

Carl Ross, Grass Valley, California, retired lawyer and a writer on world affairs, explains that sovereignty is then a function exercised by a people who *can* exercise sovereignty because they *are* self-governing.

"In the thirteen original states, the people acting as the sovereign adopted the state constitutions. In so doing they surrendered nothing," Mr. Ross reasons. "They went ahead, joining with the people of the other states in creating the United States. In so doing they surrendered no sovereignty, they merely exercised their sovereignty. They can go and join the people of other democratic nations and create a new government and when people of enough nations join, it might properly be called a federal world government, yet the people would have surrendered none of their sovereignty, they would merely have exercised their sovereignty again.

"The only way people in the United States can surrender their sovereignty," concludes Mr. Ross, "is for them to yield to some totalitarian government."

If the international government which we contemplate is to base its authority upon the consent of the governed, then the only freedom which we will relinquish will be the option to commit world suicide; a real enough choice, but one loathesome to our religions, to the ethical systems of man, and to the life forces which create us.

Where Persuasion Is Better than Force

Since laws are a charter of freedom, then it is logical to expect that a world law will prove to be a charter of world freedoms.

The Constitution of the United States guarantees "a republican form of government" to each member state. But a federal form of government allows a good deal of latitude in the governments of its member units.

"Our country was a federation, half slave and half free, for seventy years," comments William A. Wheeler.

"We should insist that the world government, itself, be democratic in form and in all its procedures," advises Henry C.

103

McIlvaine, "but we should not require that other member states be democratic in their own form of government."

"To exclude any nation on the basis of its internal governmental structures would be an arbitrary and unwise extension of our 'knowledge' of what is good and bad," feels David E. Bodner, Middletown, Connecticut. "It is still easier to achieve peace with an unco-operative member than with an 'outsider'."

A federal government, by this line of reasoning, should be ready to set standards, yet reluctant to enforce them.

The establishment of democratic standards in the constitution of a world government will tend to weed out despots from the governments of member nations, in the opinion of 58% among conferees voting on this question.

The elimination of tyrants from member governments will follow, predicts Donald Hensel, "because there would be an international standard which the local opposition to the despots could continually use as political ammunition.

"Whether we consider the political philosophy of natural rights valid or wishful mythology, I believe the concept's importance lies in the creation of absolute standards.

"The standard is a source of power in itself."

Rather than attempt to assure to each member state "a republican form of government," a world constitution may well guarantee to the peoples of each member nation the right to a continuing choice of their own form of government.

92% of correspondents urge that revisions to the United Nations Charter should place a maximum emphasis upon nations' own responsibilities. Our prime reliance should be upon persuasion. Enforcement by world authority should be a last resort where flagrant disorder imperils populations.

"No person of consequence, and no organized group," according to Vernon Nash, "proposes that a supra-national state now or later should be given any authority over matters which constitute the prized particularities of a people."

There are limits to the freedom of states, as of individuals. There is a point beyond which abuses of populations cannot go, a point when federal authority must intervene.

"I don't like starting off with strings to world government— 'government for world affairs alone.' Yes, and 'world affairs' has no beginning and no end," Alec C. Beasley, Winfield, British

Columbia, Canada, remarks of this problem. "Some 'demons' will figure they are outside world affairs; those with abominable tribal customs might think they were going to continue with the green light.

"People will have to give up wrong 'tribal' practises."

Among conferees a 65% majority prefer to propagate democracy by means of favorable incentives offered to politically backward cultures rather than by attempts at hard and fast legislation.

"The question whether a democrat—believer in democracy —can stand idly by while anti-democracy takes over elsewhere is a major question of philosophy which is largely unsolved here today," writes Kenneth R. Kurtz.

"My tentative thinking is that the general position should be,

"(1) that democracy is not an armchair faith but one that calls for active participation on the part of each adherent;

"(2) that therefore an American democrat must make some effort to help his one-world brothers suffering under a tyrannical foreign government; but

"(3) that he must always hold open the possibility that his brothers made that choice (albeit unwisely) and that they accept it, and

"(4) that therefore the *method* by which he seeks to supplant the tyranny becomes the most important."

Because it exerts a subtle and indirect pressure for democracy everywhere, the proposition of an Assembly of Peoples in the United Nations appeals to many Federalists who are averse to direct meddling in the institutions of individual nations.

What Is a Minimum Government?

"I am afraid of government, too," confesses CUREspondent J. W. Walker; "but we must educate ourselves to create and operate a government which is an instrument of the people and not their master. Impossible? Hopeless? We can face that way or we can face toward oblivion. There are no alternatives. Which do you want?"

Some advocates of world law have attempted to minimize their proposals by stating them in terms of a world police force which would prevent conflict, while matters in dispute would become the subject of arbitration by courts or commissions. But participants in the Conference find this view unsound. It is politically naive to see world government primarily as the world's biggest policeman, in the view of most conferees.

A world government with power to prevent war must necessarily govern in many other fields than armaments, in the opinion of 72% of CURE's voters.

The minimal definition of a world government as one with "powers necessary to prevent war" has as its purpose, in the view of Henry McIlvaine, "to get a foot in the door."

"We are all minimalists," one Federalist has said; "the question is what constitutes a minimum!"

Wars do not arise from the pure cussedness of men. They arise from disputes. A world authority able to prevent wars inevitably involves the responsibility to arbitrate the matter in dispute, or to administer the disputed area or activity. A court or agency which handles such jobs, if it is not to make its own laws, must act upon legislation by a world parliament. And the real prevention of war begins long before a conflict is imminent.

"A world government organized for a restricted aim of preventing war might come into being, but it could not long endure with so negative an aim," Dr. Mortimer Adler, one of the distinguished group of Federalists who drafted a model world constitution at the University of Chicago, has explained. "The functions of government must be positive and progressive. Government must serve the ends of justice and human well-being which are the substance of peace; not the prevention of war, which is the mere shell of peace."

A power necessary for the prevention of war is "inextricably bound up with the even more important 'powers to work good'," believes Harry E. Stanley, West Chester, Pennsylvania, Chairman of Chester County Chapter of Atlantic Union Committee.

"If the world government is to prevent war it should have the power to make laws on the subjects which lead to war," insists Glenn P. Turner; "people must be led to back the government because it does give justice."

Among the most important contributions of the United States Constitution to the science of government is its principle of checks and balances. One element in this system is the division of powers between the legislative, the executive and the judicial functions in government.

In other nations having parliamentary governments, where the executive is more directly responsible to the legislative body, there is a temptation under conditions of stress for the lawmaking arm not only to gobble up its executive cabinets at frequent intervals but also to treat its judicial colleague as a minor and inferior member of the partnership.

The relative stability of the American model gives special significance, in the words of Quincy Wright, to a structure of "federalism judicially controlled."

The power of American courts is solidly rooted in their established jurisdiction over questions of the constitutionality of laws adopted by the Congress and by state and local legislatures. It is no accident that those American influences which seek to begin a trend toward authoritarianism are forever complaining of the power of American courts to interpret the meaning of the United States Constitution. This very power of the courts to decide the constitutionality of legislation is what makes the American system of checks and balances the most effective ever devised, and is its stoutest bulwark against a usurpation of powers by other elements in the government.

A review of laws by a supreme court is essential to any government under a written constitution, believe 81% of forum participants. This applies equally to a world government.

"A World Court, not only with compulsory jurisdiction in the formal sense, but with jurisdiction, at least in an appellate sense, over individuals as well as states," says British barrister James Avery Joyce, is one of the "bare essentials" necessary "to the growth of a truly world law."

Studies by scholars of government indicate that a world judicial system will need more than the single International Court of Justice which has existed at The Hague since 1901 and is now incorporated into the structure of the United Nations. A world federal judicial system will necessarily include local courts with original jurisdiction over matters of international law, and perhaps appellate divisions in various parts of the world, with the world court providing the final resort for an appeal of decisions.

Police On a World Beat

A necessary function of an international government is the enforcement of its decisions. The United Nations Charter provides for a crude and primitive form of enforcement by means of the use of military forces under a world general staff against the armies of recalcitrant nations.

Speaking for many of CURE's conferees, Rachel Welch denies that "the perpetuation of the war system in the United Nations" is truly government.

Yet it may lead to government, others maintain, because it asserts the authority of mankind as a whole to govern disputes between nations.

"Just whom are you kidding when you imply that the very existence of a United Nations police force of any type" does not "in fact limit the sovereignty of all nations?" demands Dale M. Hiller, Wilmington, Delaware, member of the Atlantic Region Council of United World Federalists.

Any United Nations force does limit the sovereignty of nations to their internal affairs—where it belongs.

The experience of Korea pinpoints the danger of enlisting United Nations police forces from the armies of large nations which are likely to be major antagonists in world disputes.

An international expert in the brainy game of bridge and writer on problems of world order, Ely Culbertson, has proposed that a world police body should recruit its forces mainly from the less powerful members of the United Nations. A United Nations armed force whose personnel are mostly drawn from lesser nations, he reasoned, will more loyally represent the international organization in its role as a mediator between great powers.

In order to build a world police force whose primary allegiance is to the United Nations, 82% of conferees recommend that the Charter be amended to permit the enlistment of individual volunteers. Accepting the suggestion of Mr. Culbertson, several consultants wish to set a quota limit upon the number of volunteers which the United Nations police force can accept from any one nation. Leaders representing war veterans in Belgium, Canada, France, Greece, Italy, the Netherlands and the United States, a four-fifths majority of those replying to an inquiry by the Special United Nations Subcommittee of the American Veterans Committee, approved the enlistment of volunteers into a permanent United Nations police force.

"When the United Nations was established, it was envisaged that the Security Council would have armed forces at its disposal," Frank Witkamp, Vice-President of the Association of Former Non-Commissioned Officers of the Royal Dutch Indies Army, stated. "Even the Soviet Union, for example, suggested the formation of an international air force."

Popular representation is the logical key to greater United Nations responsibilities, and non-military administrations will logically pave the way to actual enforcement powers. But such logical patterns do not necessarily characterize real events. Historical perspective shows that a government may begin with the naked exercise of authority, and subsequently accept restraints upon its power. Whether in such cases a process of liberalization occurs, as we have seen, seems to depend largely upon the degree of security from foreign interference which the government enjoys.

Everyone who observes the United Nations recognizes its need for police powers. But United Nations forces will remain armies, and United Nations enforcement will remain a war system, as long as nations place their final reliance upon the sovereign power of their arms as an instrument of policy. Only when the armed forces of the United Nations become subject to the authority of a democratic world parliament will it become possible to replace the war system by police enforcement in its true character.

Men may not be willing to transfer ultimate power into the hands of a world legislature at the same moment they plan its creation. There may well be a period of transition while an international parliament becomes secure in its functioning and its competence. If it is useful, it will grow. Whether we attain the enforcement of peace at once or later, the disarmament of nations will be essential to a stable peace. In a conference for the revision of the United Nations Charter, if political commissions succeed in drafting improvements in the composition of the world legislature and in increasing the authority of the legislature to govern in key international jurisdictions, other commissions can have real hope of success in planning for a phased program to pool armed forces under the United Nations and to reduce the armaments of individual nations.

Power must reside somewhere. If it does not find its lodging in growing international government, it will grow, dangerously to our lives and progressively throttling our freedoms, in the uncontrolled stockpiles of dreadful weapons waiting only a touch of insanity for everyone's destruction.

As a world-wide buffer state created by all the world's peoples, the United Nations will insulate the great national powers from the frictions which cause wars. Like a cosmic glue, the new United Nations can overcome the hostilities which threaten to disintegrate all civilization. If it has the inward power to give justice, we may be sure that a world government will deserve and receive from mankind the external power to make justice prevail.

Chapter 7.

Europe First

In 1943, while the United States was busy building ships to replace the fleet sunk at Pearl Harbor, and while the Germans held undisputed possession of the European Continent, the writer of those parts of this book which are not in quotation marks addressed the first in a series of memoranda in English and French to statesmen of the Allied nations, to Roosevelt and Churchill, to Schumann and to scores of others, urging that a postwar United States of Europe be based upon a common ownership of the great industrial complex of the Ruhr and the Saar.

How inadequate a merely European solution would have been to stabilize the peace of the world became apparent with the atomic destruction of Hiroshima in 1946.

But how prophetic was the suggestion that the best opportunities for new government lay in Europe became evident during the first decade after World War II, with the emergence of the Schumann Plan, with the proposals for a European Defense Community, and with the organization of the European Coal and Steel Community, the Council of Europe, Euratom and the European Common Market Agreement.

A United States of Europe has been a long time in the making.

The Roman philosopher Seneca, condemning the frontiers which separate people from people, urged citizens to regard the world as a common dwelling-place of all mankind.

In the year 1310, Dante Alighieri gave written life to Europe's most melodious language. In the first Italian literary work, his *Inferno*, Dante told how Beatrice sang of a European empire, divinely ordained to establish peace.

During the fifteenth century George Podebrad, King of Bohemia, won the support of Hungary and France for a proposed European Assembly of Princes, with a court and a treasury, all designed to support a holy war against the Turks.

The Dutch scholar Erasmus, the Italian Pope Leo X and the English Cardinal Wolsey in the sixteenth century suggested that European nations adopt arbitration, a universal treaty and collective sanctions, for defense against the Turks and for peace among themselves.

In the seventeenth century Hugo Grotius, a Dutch jurist, declared that international law should bind sovereign states in the same way that municipal law binds individuals; and the Duc de Sully recommended that the nations of Europe should be constituted into a "Very Christian Republic".

William Penn in 1693 published a plan dedicated "Toward the Present and Future Peace of Europe by the Establishment of a European Diet, Parliament or Estates". He hoped that this federation would reduce "the very great expense that frequent and splendid embassies require, and all their appendages of spies and intelligence." As one of the principal colonizers of the New World, Penn was also the first to propose that the colonies of North America should be joined into a federal nation.

The Abbé de Saint-Pierre published in 1728 a *Plan for Perpetual Peace*. Many Europeans took up his idea enthusiastically, including the French romanticist Jean-Jacques Rousseau, who declared that a "European Republic" might logically be based upon the interdependence of nations.

The establishment of the North American republic offered a new inspiration to such plans for human harmony. "I am a citizen of the Great Republic of Humanity," wrote George Washington to the Marquis de Lafayette. "I see the human race united like a great family by brotherly ties. We have sown a seed of liberty and union which will gradually spring up throughout the earth. One day, on the model of the United States of America, there will be created the United States of Europe . . . the Legislator for all nationalities."

Renewed proposals for European federation were thrown

into the vortex of European strife by the Englishman Jeremy Bentham in 1793, who proposed that Britain and France unite and emancipate their colonies, by the German philosopher Johann Gottlieb Fichte in 1795, and in the same year by his countryman and fellow philosopher Emmanuel Kant, who pled for a republican federation of free states in order that Europe's citizens could decide for themselves grave matters of war and peace.

The German religious philosopher Karl Christian Friedrich Krause became the first theorist to distinguish between the concept of European federation and the organization of world-wide government. Krause, in *Das Urbild der Menschheit*, written in 1811 and translated into English in 1900, proposed regional federations of Europe, Asia, Africa, America and Australia. The European federation was to use the German language and to have its capital in Berlin; and, like the other regional republics, it was to be a constituent part of a sovereign world republic whose capital would be located in Polynesia.

As the Napoleonic wars drew to a close in 1814, the Comte de Saint-Simon proposed that European federation should commence with a union of France and England, the most democratic powers, to be joined gradually by other nations. The following year at the writing of the final peace, Czar Alexander I of Russia organized the Holy Alliance led by Russia, Austria and Prussia. Alexander's intention was to obligate all nations to the arbitration of disputes. "On principles such as these one could proceed to a general pacification," he wrote, "and give birth to a League of which the stipulation would form, so to speak, a new code of the law of nations."

As an ironic postscript to the hopes of this period, Napoleon Bonaparte declared in his *Mémorial de Sainte-Hélène*, written in 1816, that the final goal of all his wars had been nothing else than a federation of Europe.

In reality there followed a generation of Prince Metternich's despotism, and another generation of Prince Bismarck's power politics.

"An immense hatred fills the horizon. It seems a strange moment to speak of peace," wrote Victor Hugo after France had been defeated in the War of 1870, "and yet . . . peace is our inevitable goal. Mankind ever proceeds toward peace, even though it be through war . . . We shall have the European Republic."

The world republic, too, continued to kindle European imaginations. Parliamentarians William Randal Cremer, British labor leader, and Frédéric Passy, French economist, in 1886 organized the Inter-Parliamentary Union, composed of legislators from many countries. Their embryonic world parliament prompted the establishment by the First Hague Conference in 1899 of the Permanent Court of Arbitration, later incorporated as the World Court into the League of Nations and into the United Nations. In 1904 the Inter-Parliamentary Union, meeting at St. Louis, Missouri, by invitation of the Congress of the United States, proposed more formally "an international congress which should meet periodically to discuss international questions." At their suggestion, President Theodore Roosevelt in the wake of the Russo-Japanese War urged Czar Nicholas II to convene another conference at Holland's Den Haag. The Second Hague Conference, meeting in 1907, adopted thirteen conventions dealing with peaceful settlement of disputes and other matters, but failed to create the proposed world congress.

After the First World War, though America disowned President Woodrow Wilson's league of the world's nations, the movement to unite Europe sprang up with renewed fervor.

For several years the construction of a European federation was the official policy of France, led by a far-sighted group of men who included Aristide Briand, Alexis Leger, Amé-Leroy and Count Richard Coudenhove-Kalergi. In 1930, as French Foreign Minister, Briand prepared a "Memorandum on the Organization of a Federal Order of European Union." Briand cited "the danger threatening the peace of Europe, politically, economically, and socially, by reason of the lack of co-ordination in the general economy of Europe . . . the lack of cohesion in the grouping of material and moral forces in Europe." He spoke of the necessity for "subordination of the economic problem to the political problem." Briand told Europeans that they could determine for themselves their own destiny. "Unite in order to live and prosper!" he urged them. "I am absolutely decided to stick to my determination," he said, "that so long as I remain where I am, there will be no war."

Twenty-five nations responded to Briand's note. England and Switzerland objected that his scheme would overshadow the feeble powers of the League of Nations. Several states desired that other nations, not members of the League of Nations, should be included in the European framework. Most European politicians were more interested in immediate economic measures than in a fundamental program of political reconstruction. As a result of long debate, the Assembly of the League of Nations set up an economic "Examining Commission". For a couple of years this group struggled ineffectually against the dark tides of world-wide depression.

And once again, like Charlemagne and Napoleon before him it was Adolf Hitler instead who by conquest of arms briefly welded a European empire.

Germany As an Asset to Peace

"You will never know," said the Hollander Franz den Vilders, "how near Europe came to accepting the Nazis as well as being overrun by them.

"They came promising freedom within the walls of a federation of European nations. Within the federation, Holland would govern itself, so far as domestic affairs go. So would Belgium. So would everybody else.

"There was to be a central government to which each nation province would elect deputies in proportion to its population, and the central government would function only in matters relating to the common good. Customs barriers would be destroyed. We would become one big family, each branch running its own affairs, and this would happen as soon as our saviors had disposed of their archenemy across the Channel!"

Reporter Leslie Roberts of the *Saturday Evening Post* listened as Mynheer den Vilders, owner of the leading motion picture theater in Eindhoven, turned to a young fighter pilot from Texas.

"If you think of your own United States, you will know what we were promised, the United States of Europe, and it would surprise you to know to how many Dutchmen the idea appealed," he said. "It still appeals to many of us as the only solution to the violence of Europe. The Nazis," he added, "didn't mean it. But we must come to something like this, or Europe will perish by the sword."

The German conquest proved crude and cruel. In war there is little decency. War is a huge and savage indecency. The delinquent children of an ungoverned world, Germans exhibited a capacity for mass murder which gave to Hitler a place in history alongside such mass slaughterers as Genghis Khan and Napoleon.

Germans have great capacities for good and for evil. If we contemplate a stable and governed world, our appraisal of Germans must hinge not upon their capacity for evil but upon their capacity to serve the useful purposes of civilization.

The record of Germans in America indicates some of this. Plenty of German descendants are good Americans. German-populated Milwaukee and Cincinnati are famed for democratic government, sound finances and polite, efficient police. Governor John Altgeld of Illinois, Theodore Dreiser and Wendell Willkie were great American liberals of German stock. To the free world Henry Kaiser gave ships as Wernher von Braun gave satellites.

German names stud American war rolls. In the Pacific Ocean during World War II Admiral Nimitz headed naval forces which included among their senior officers Admiral Mitscher, Admiral Shafroth and General Geiger of the Marines. Among top officers of the United States Air Force under General Carl Spaatz were General George Stratemeyer and General Paul Wurtsmith. Under General Dwight Eisenhower's command were such generals as Albert Wedemeyer, Walter Krueger, Robert Eichelberger and Wilhelm Styer. A boy who began life as Karl von Tscheppe-Weiderbach grew up to be the tall Yankee commander, General Charles Willoughby, who received the surrender of Japan's soldiers on Okinawa.

It is hard for foreigners to understand the character of Germans in Germany. Perhaps it is even harder for Germans, whose language contains no word to translate the term "character". An anti-Teuton once said that the lack of this word in their language indicates that the Germans themselves have no character; but Germans retorted that the word is unnecessary to them, because to be German means to have character.

The truth is, of course, that there are far greater divergences

116

of character between the individuals within any given group, than the difference between the average of that group and of any other group.

The musical talent of Germans has produced the logic of Bach, the clarity of Mozart, the mellow romanticism of Brahms; and it has resulted, too, in the homosexual bombast of Wagner.

Wagner's music offers a clue to a disease of German character. Richard Wagner's great technical gifts found expression in a music whose themes pass through no logical development, but instead reiterate insistent motives or mottos. Adolf Hitler passionately loved Wagnerian music-dramas of racial egotism. Frau Winifred Wagner, the composer's daughter-in-law, told an American visitor to the Wagnerian shrine at Bayreuth, "I am extremely proud to have had the opportunity of being an intimate friend of the Führer." In Wagner was much of the beauty of music; in his music, too, was much of Germany's sickness.

One warm afternoon during the early thirties in the outskirts of Munich I had an opportunity to study Hitler at first hand. There was a brave parade of brownshirts. One squad of big plug-uglies led a long column of younger boys studying to be plug-uglies. What Hitler said at the rally was not remarkable: it concerned the failure of a rival party to win a recent election in Suabia. As he spoke, tossing his head, the homemade haircut fell awkwardly about his face. Whenever he paused, with a snakelike, narcissistic sweep of his left hand Adolf Hitler brushed the dark, lank locks out of his eyes, a gesture which spoke more eloquently than his words of a disturbed personality.

Children brought up without parental love and security often develop into persons with traits like those of Hitler's Germany. Lacking emotional stability, accustomed to bullying and fear, such persons become instinctively hostile to others, wearing airs of omnipotence when opposition is weak, yet likely to grovel when dominated by others who are stronger. Persons suffering from this psychological disorder blame their troubles upon everyone else but themselves. Psychiatrists describe such personalities as paranoid.

But German children are not, as a matter of fact, insecure

117

and unloved in their family lives. German parents are among the best in the world. No nation takes more trouble to assure the health and growth of its young.

The Hitlerian mental attitude was a mass paranoia of a nation, the maladjustment of a civilization. The domestic quarrels which bred German insecurity were the frictions and unrest of unrelated nations crowded together in the European household.

Today Germans are among the least interested of any Europeans in the reliving of past adventures, and among the most willing to build new guarantees of freedom and peace. This appears, for instance, in correspondence received by the Special United Nations Subcommittee of the American Veterans Committee from officers of war veterans associations in Germany.

"As Germans we know what the last war meant for victors and for losers," declared Fritz Rabe, Information Officer of the German Association of Repatriated, War Prisoners and Dependents of Missing, an organization which can muster at national rallies as many as a quarter of a million members. "It is our interest in Germany to carry on active participation in the political education and the political motivation of our young democracy."

"German victims of wars are, naturally, also interested in a strengthening of the influence of the United Nations," affirmed Gerd Brinkmann, Executive Director of the Association of War Cripples, Survivors and Pensioned, whose rolls carry over one and one-half million members. "The Federal Republic, as you know, is not a member of the United Nations," he added, expressing the hope that this "will be the case one day for our united German fatherland."

Anyone who knows them realizes that the constructive talents of Germans can be a valuable asset to world organization.

The British Contribution to World Order

Such peace as Europe has known during the past few centuries has been at least partly due to the precarious success of Britain's balance-of-power policy, based upon her insularity, her sea might and her hostility toward the emergence of any dominant Continental rival. Like the deaf man who can hear when it is convenient, England, at will, could be European or non-European. For British statesmen, the Straits of Dover were a magic moat of variable width. No Continental nation could match Britain's aloofness when she chose. When Britain intervened in Continental affairs, she found her allies anywhere in Europe: Spain or Prussia, France or Poland. In wartime British ships strangled enemy sea trade, and British troops had the pick of Europe's ports for their landings. As recently as the Second World War, the British Isles were a citadel from which the Allied armies launched their sortie against Germany; once more, in that instance, a ruler of the Continent found England's shore too near for comfort, and yet too far for conquest.

In the distant past, England maintained her outposts of defense on the Continent of Europe itself. For more than a century, English kings ruled parts of western France. The seapower of Britain at the beginning of the seventeenth century smashed the Spanish challenge, at the beginning of the eighteenth century overwhelmed Holland, at the beginning of the nineteenth century defeated France, and during the first half of the twentieth century twice stopped the Germans. During these many generations, Englishmen have fought the rise of any dominant European power as an intolerable threat to themselves.

Through the years while Britain neutralized the Continent at her back door, her seaborne sphere of influence spread over the whole globe. As empires go, her rule was humane. During the Civil War in America, when Great Britain had an opportunity to cripple the growing vigor of the United States, British mercantile interests and British military ambitions both urged that the British Navy break the North's sea blockade and rescue the South; but English moral opinion could not support a fight to maintain human slavery. As a result of President Lincoln's Emancipation Proclamation, the British government withheld its aid from the Confederacy, knowing well that Britain thereby lent her assent to a restoration of American unity.

Elsewhere, during the decades, the men of Britain's ships entrenched her power in distant outposts. The Mediterranean Sea became a British lake. At Gibraltar an English garrison stood sentry over the entrance to the Mediterranean. At Malta, England's mid-Mediterranean link held fast even against the fury of the Luftwaffe. At the Suez Canal, Britain guarded the northern passage of the torpid Red Sea. At sun-baked Aden, the Royal Navy commanded the southern portal of the Red Sea and its juncture with the Indian Ocean.

To an extent hardly realized by landlubbers, the British empire held entrances of every great ocean. The British Isles themselves lie in one of the most strategic positions of the globe, at the northeast corner of the North Atlantic controlling the entrance into North Sea, Baltic and Scandinavian waters. In Canada, the deep, landlocked anchorage of Halifax guards the Atlantic's northwest corner. Britain's island possessions command ocean routes of the central Atlantic from Gibraltar and Madeira to Bermuda and to Barbados at the very gates of the Panama Canal. The Union of South Africa rings the eastern entrance to the South Atlantic with harbors at Cape-town, Port Elizabeth and Durban. At the western corner of the South Atlantic, where her Falkland Islands lie athwart the approaches to Cape Horn and the Straits of Magellan, Britain's World War I navy sank Graf Spee's squadron and cleared the sea of the Kaiser's maritime raiders. In the Pacific Ocean Great Britain's pattern of possession is fainter but still discernible. At Vancouver a Canadian harbor outflanks the Pacific sea lanes of the United States. The port of Hong Kong served as a barrier between Japan and its onetime "Greater East Asia Co-Prosperity Sphere". Australia, New Zealand and Singapore dominate passages between the South Pacific and the Indian Ocean.

The First World War sowed the seeds of disintegration in the British Empire when, in order to secure the belligerent support of her major overseas possessions, England promised to them a future status as Dominions. After World War I, Great Britain, her grip loosened upon the former big colonies, emerged as the chief loser on the "winning" side; while Germany, with her rivals and neighbors weakened, proved to be the chief winner on the "losing" side.

By the time of the Second World War, the onetime major colonies owed to England little more than a common crown and a common language. When Marshal Jan Smuts proposed the formation of a Commonwealth parliament intended to link the Dominions into a federal union, Canada's government coldly rejected the South African's suggestion. For purposes of military defense Washington had replaced London as the effective capital of the English-speaking peoples. As a political organization, the British Commonwealth had deteriorated to a sentimental bond and a league for free trade.

Today the inhabitants of the British Isles move between four different systems of gravity.

For a generation they have been receding from the security which they once felt as the lords of a great sea-flung empire.

More recently, Britons have begun moving away from the dependence upon America which cast them in the role of an island outpost of the Atlantic defense system.

The navigators of Britain's destiny are recalculating the attractions of a united Europe. They realize that what they can no longer prevent they must join. They are discovering new formulas to reconcile a Continental role with their links to the Empire, to their American allies, and to the United Nations.

The British foresee that it will be possible for their isles to become a European state as Europe itself will become part of a global polity, and that Britain herself will stand in a special relation to both. The many strategic possessions remaining to the British crown will be a major asset to an international federation's responsibility for the freedom of the seven seas. And the calm, unhurried political skills of Scots and Britons will be a great personal asset to new, bold enterprises of government far removed from the Thames.

Many signs attest a recognition among Britain's people of her new global orientation. A poll in Nottingham, England, taken by the Business and Professional Council for World Government of that industrial city, showed an overwhelming 95% of British citizens in favor of a United Nations World Development Authority, and 81% for direct election of representatives to a world parliament.

The hundred and more members of the British Parliamentary Group for World Government are more active than European or American counterparts in advocacy of their purpose. "The technique that has been used to great advantage in Great Britain has been delegations to the Prime Minister or Foreign

Minister. Such delegations usually consist of Members of Parliament along with the Secretary of the Parliamentary Group, the Secretary of Federal Union and perhaps one or two experts on the subject under discussion.

"Another technique used in Britain which undoubtedly affects legislation, although rather indirectly, is that members of the Parliamentary Group take advantage of foreign policy discussions in both Houses of Parliament, on almost any question, to bring in the world federalists' point of view," reports Ralph Lombardi, Amsterdam, The Netherlands, Secretary General of the World Association of World Federalists.

According to British historian Arnold Toynbee, civilizations survive or fall by their response to the challenges of history. Perhaps better than any other people, the countrymen of Toynbee know how to adapt themselves to history's challenges. Britons surmount defeats and recover from errors. Modern Elizabethans stand firm for freedom.

Europeans Seek Security

While Britain muddles along brilliantly with her loyalties divided between four different orbits, and Germany, split by the Iron Curtain, feels three separate demands upon her allegiance, the French, preferring simplicity, seek to merge their colonies' economic fate with that of the European Common Market.

France's major overseas possessions are a different proposition from those remaining to Great Britain. Not so much strategic, they are primarily economic assets. More nakedly, France's colonial conflicts are those of exploitation; and her native colonial populations resent it the more fiercely. The very government of France reels under repeated blows to her old imperial order. By kicking their problem upstairs, the French will give Europe a headache; but the solution of France's colonial difficulties in a broader frame of reference may help make a united Europe possible.

Other European nations have fewer colonial distractions on their hands. But some Europeans find it difficult to relate themselves to both a Continental union and a world union.

"What has been presented and accepted in Europe as The Great Proposal is Euro-Federation," writes Alfredo Rodrigues

122

Brent. "This movement is very intolerant and particularly hostile toward the movement for world federation. Nevertheless the idea of world federal government is slowly gaining popular support."

In response to an inquiry by the American Veterans Committee, some spokesmen for European war veterans have doubted the possibility of transforming the United Nations into a parliamentary government, seeing a United States of Europe as a more feasible alternative. Vice-President Dr. Luciano Bolis of the National Association of Liberated Prisoners (Italy) explained that his organization "is an adherent of the European Federalist movement," and that he himself is Secretary of a Pan-European organization which has a United States of Europe as its goal. President Octave Lohest and Secretary René Geraads of the National Federation of Combatants (Belgium) reported that their group's policy "is strongly attached to an effective European organization."

The First Congress of the World Association of World Federalists (then called the World Movement for World Federal Government) at Montreux, Switzerland in 1946 brought to prominence the divided views of Europeans on this problem of priority. Some Federalists there felt that a United States of Europe should become their pilot project, intended to pave the way for world union. Others held the opposite belief, claiming that only a world government could provide the security in which Europe will be able to govern itself as a continent-wide federation. This controversy, as we have made evident, still exists; but the passing years have brought an increasingly compatible relationship between European union and world union in many Federalist minds. Both undertakings are allied in the general plan for a self-government of man: each makes the other easier. There is agreement among 90% of participants in the Conference Upon Research and Education in world government that European federation will be an asset to world stability.

Many signs point to acceptance among Europeans of broader systems of security in general.

The national constitutions of France, Italy, Western Germany and The Netherlands already contain specific sanction for their governments to enter into an international federation.

A poll in Italian provinces won a fantastic majority vote for the proposal of applying for statehood in the United States of America!

There are differences between European and American concepts of government, just as there will be differences to distinguish the constitution of a United States of Europe or a revised Charter of the United Nations from the basic laws that prescribe the American form of government. And Europeans know, perhaps better than Americans, that adopting constitutions is only a part of the job to be done.

"We in Europe are far less trusting than Americans that international bodies will stand by their pacts and charters and that the interplay of governments will be anything like cricket. Ever since 1933 one people after the other on the European continent has suffered from too many sordid experiences in this respect," writes Hollander Brent. "If confidence in international or so-called supranational institutions and pacts could be rated at say 60% in the United States, it would come to barely 20% in Europe.

"On the other hand, Europeans are far less concerned with any problem of 'giving up sovereignty' than Americans appear to be," he notes. "In fact, the concept of national sovereignty has lost most of its meaning in Europe."

The Roman and the British law underlie the great traditions of European liberty. On the meadows of Runnymede beside the River Thames in the year 1215, two thousand British barons forced the arrogant King John to sign an agreement in which he promised to account for his royal expenditures, to limit his drafts of soldiers, and to try offenders against his laws before a jury of their peers. The contract which the English king signed that day was the Magna Carta, the Great Charter of English freedoms, whose echoes resound in the American Declaration of Independence, in every modern day constitution and bill of rights, and even in the Atlantic Charter.

The voice of the Magna Carta will speak once again in a constitution of Europe. Citizens of Europe's nations are among the foremost of those who know how to cherish government of, by and for the people.

Chapter 8.

The Russians: Are They Human?

"A specter is haunting Europe—the specter of Communism!"

In the century after Karl Marx and Friedrich Engels began the Communist Manifesto of 1848 with these words, Communism has ripped its own vitals with purges and feuds. Yet now, in its second century, the Communist specter haunts the whole world.

Marxism, as a philosophy, offers a potent pattern of emotional persuasions. To the exploited, it whispers of revenge against their bosses. To the persecuted, it encourages the overthrow of their rulers. To the frustrated, it hints that the social revolution will make all men brothers. To the disillusioned, it grants new saints and dogmas. It outbids rival forms of socialism by combining the appeals of all. It promises everything.

The scriptures of the Communist religion are more vengeful than those of the Old Testament. More than the prophets of any other living faith, Marx and Engels preached hostility toward non-believers. The Communist Manifesto of 1848 called for class war, for world revolution, and for the abolition of marriage, attacking in a venomous crescendo the church, the state, the aristocracy, the middle classes, and most bitterly of all the prophets of rival sects of socialism.

But Karl Marx made no plan for a government.

"Marx did not undertake the task of discovering the political form of this future state," Nicolai Lenin explained long afterward. "Marx waited for the experience of a mass movement to produce the answer . . . as to the exact forms which this organization of the proletariat as the ruling class will assume."

After the fleeting and tragic Paris Commune of 1870, the Communist oracles began to think about the institutions of government which would rule their future polity.

"The proletariat can use only the form of the one and indivisible republic," decided Friedrich Engels in 1902 with his own native Germany in mind, demanding "the abolition of all local and provincial authorities appointed by the state." The working class, he wrote, must "safeguard itself against its own deputies and officials by . . . two infallible remedies . . . by election on the basis of universal suffrage . . . with the right of . . . recall . . . and in the second place, all officials paid only the wages received by other workers."

Whatever might have happened in Germany, in Russia a cruder form of Communism took shape, influenced by Nihilism and Anarchism. The Russian revolutionists pictured to their gullible followers a perfect brotherhood arising in the wake of their seizure of power, dispensing forever with all restraints of law.

"Two institutions are especially characteristic of . . . bourgeois society: bureaucracy and the standing army," wrote Lenin on the eve of his accession to power in Russia. "World history is undoubtedly leading . . . to the concentration of all the forces of the proletarian revolution for the purpose of destroying the state machinery," he prophesied. "There will vanish all need for force . . . since people will grow accustomed to observing the elementary conditions of social existence without force and without subjection."

In October, 1917, the Bolsheviks launched their revolutionary dream upon the swirling waters of a world at war. The ship of state which they set upon ominous seas was of a frail and improbable design.

The Dream and the Reality

Russians threw the vigor of their revolutionary enthusiasm into the remaking of a civilization. In a moving memoir Alexander Barmine has described the labors of a typical young soldier, diplomat and industrial commissar in the early Soviet state, when an earnest generation sought to create the world to which Marx, Engels and Lenin had looked forward. In the Russia of the 1920's a ferment of ideas struggled for expression. Party congresses rang with ideological debate. As late as

1936, Russia adopted a Constitution in which Article 125 guarantees freedom of speech and press, and Article 134 decrees universal suffrage by secret ballot in elections for the Supreme Soviet of Russia as well as the Soviets of the various Republics and the Soviets of local regions. Education was a first goal. Under Communism illiteracy became a thing of the past even, as Richard Lauterbach found, on the steppes of Samarkand. "Every cook must learn how to govern," said Lenin: an ambition which any society may cherish. Newspapers like *Pravda* and *Izvestia* give little space to comics, advertisements and slayings. The Russian masses are avid with hunger for such information as they are allowed to have.

But the stir of political freedom in Russia wilted under the menace of Hitler's rise in Germany. The early liberty of Communist ideological debate disappeared under a rising tide of repression. In 1937 Stalin's state slaughtered a handful of "confessed" traitors together with thousands of Old Bolsheviks and tens of thousands of inoffensive citizens whom it termed "rotten" liberals. Millions more were condemned to labor under conditions of virtual slavery.

"I came to have a deep respect and affection for the Russian people," wrote United States Ambassador to Russia Joseph Davies, praising the Russians' "aspirations to better the conditions of life of common men." Yet the lawyer in Davies took alarm at the arbitrary manner of proceeding against men accused of treason in Russian courts. "The right of the accused to counsel upon arrest" he found lacking, as well as "the right to refuse to testify against oneself, the writ of habeas corpus," and "the right to require that the state shall prove guilt instead of the accused being required to prove innocence."

How unlike the dream of Marx, Engels and Lenin has grown the Russia of reality! In an ungoverned world, Soviet tyranny is the same spawn of insecurity as were the tyrannies of Napoleon or Metternich, of Mussolini or Hitler. Russians who have battled foreign troops to prevent the restoration of the Czars, whose soldiers have died by millions to repel from their soil the Nazi invaders, who face a world of hostile "containment" and "preventive" missile bases, have no longer much time for dreams of liberty. Russians, like their opponents, are prisoners of power politics.

Instead of abolishing force in government, Russia has built a standing army to the most monstrous proportions in human history. The Soviet steamroller has enslaved neighboring populations by tens of millions. Everyone in the world knows that Russians do not elect their leaders, as Engels promised, or live without force or subjection, according to the prophecy of Lenin. Rather than end bureaucracy, the Soviet despots have enthroned a creaking machinery of bureaucrats in arbitrary rule over the people, under commissars who enjoy villas on the shores of the Black Sea, and who in turn tremble at the frown of the Politburo.

In the environment of an insecure world only the grimmer tenets of the Communist gospel survive. Russia's political philosophy rests on the class struggle, the materialist dialectic or conflict between the socialist and the capitalist economic systems. In the Russian book, everyone's background determines his being: a capitalist is the creation of his money, a socialist the creature of his state. In deterministic terms, any member of one economic class who pretends to see the other fellow's point of view does so only in order to victimize his opponent. The Communist dialectic foresees no accommodation with an implacable enemy. It dares think of no resolution save that of its own complete triumph.

The language of Russians is strange to us, not only in its syllables but in its sentiments. It has its own grammar, its own vocabulary and its own logic. According to its alien syntax, Westerners, far from being "free", are prisoners of a capitalism doomed to decay and extinction, exploiters who will try to drag Communism down with them in their death struggle. In the Russian discourse we can hear elements of shrewdness alongside elements of absurdity; traits of dangerous neurosis side by side with instincts to avoid major catastrophe. Because it believes world revolution and the triumph of socialism to be inevitable, Communism expects to overwhelm capitalism without resorting to the aggressive itself in a major war. Russia hastens her destiny by endless pressures, but invites a minimum of real risks.

Only 16% of CURE's counsellors see a sneak attack by Russia as a principal hazard to her enemies. Instead, 88% view blundering into war as the chief threat to Russia's peace and to that of her adversaries alike.

The design of the Soviet state is shaped to the environment of pressures and hostilities in which it exists. If it did not have something to oppose it would fall over. Asking Soviet rulers to change this cherished pattern would be requesting them to abolish their own jobs. It is the basis of their being.

Exploiting the Communist Weakness

"We have today a situation in which Russia will automatically oppose almost any proposal we make in the United Nations, and vice versa, because both sides are convinced that whatever the other is for, is bad," CUREspondent John Holt sums up the deadlock between East and West.

The Russian pose of opposition appeared promptly when the United Nations took up a possible revision of its Charter, according to United States Ambassador to the Security Council of the United Nations Henry Cabot Lodge, in his testimony before the Subcommittee on Review of the United Nations Charter of the United States Senate Committee on Foreign Relations.

SENATOR ALEXANDER WILEY (CHAIRMAN): "It has become apparent that the Soviet Union vigorously opposes any discussion of Charter Review."

AMBASSADOR LODGE: "Oh, yes; with amazing vigor, I may add. I was quite surprised at how vigorous they were. I thought they might wait a little while and not look so terribly arbitrary. They might take a position, 'well, we are willing to have it discussed, but we are not willing to make any changes.' But right at the very minute the thing came up, they were up on their feet opposing any discussion of it even."

This attitude is of peculiar interest to the free world, coming, as it did, at a time when no one had advanced any serious proposals for revision of the United Nations Charter, beyond some rather general talk about reapportionment of the voting strengths of nations in the General Assembly or a limitation of the veto.

Procedures for amendment of the United Nations Charter provide that Russia may veto any amendment which it does not approve. Russia cannot, however, veto a proposal for the convening of a United Nations Charter review conference;

nor does she hold a veto power over the proceedings of such a conference or its formulation of specific recommendations for Charter changes. The negative attitude of the Soviet hierarchy toward the very existence of a conference to review the basic statutes of the world polity, therefore, betrays a Russian fear that the democracies may turn a conference of this nature to substantial advantage.

Why do the Soviet leaders find Charter review so disquieting a proposal? What has Charter revision got, from a Russian point of view, that disarmament hasn't got?

Russian rulers have displayed no reluctance to talk about disarmament. They have made disarmament proposals, in fact, their favorite sounding board in bidding for world approval. Obviously disarmament is a propaganda issue whose unreality lends itself to Communist exploitation. But proposals to strengthen the United Nations Charter might not prove so easy to manipulate to Soviet benefit.

The non-Soviet world has little enough idea, as yet, how to go about harvesting the gains which might accrue from a review conference; nevertheless, the negative posture of Soviet emissaries did help the free nations to decide upon casting their own votes in favor of initiating the necessary preparations.

The proposal of a Charter review confronts Russia with a new threat of hostile "containment". Given an opportunity to alter the status quo and to shift the world power equation, Russians fear that other nations may seize the occasion to gang up against them. Some pundits of the free world see the United Nations primarily as an expanded arena for power politics. From a Russian point of view, those citizens of Western countries who advocate a world law to keep world peace, but who are vague about who is to make the law, offer only a more devious approach to the same encirclement. "Law" in the sense of impartial justice has no place in the Soviet glossary. In all such suggestions Reds sniff danger. Communist nostrils detect the odor of a capitalist conspiracy in any plan to create irresponsible new power. Uncontrolled power is always a menace to someone; and each individual sees it as a menace to himself. One of the Kremlin's nightmares is the image of a United Nations concocted by hostile governments in the form of an anti-Soviet bloc. The concept is correspondingly explosive.

A proposal to place an increasing share of world decision in the hands of the world's peoples is something else again. It is more difficult for Soviet propagandists to brand a plan for world democracy as a capitalist power play. A movement toward world democracy will not be a mere formula thrown on the table by a diplomat. In the eyes of Soviet leaders, it will not have the automatically bogus character of a proposal from the official enemies of their state. It will speak from the peoples of the West and from the neutral nations and populations of the world directly to the populace of the Soviet realm. It will speak straight to the very real yearning which the Soviet peoples have for peace. And it will speak to the friendliness which every visitor testifies the Russians feel toward the common peoples of other lands.

Democracy in the United Nations can frighten only those who fear the people. Russian opposition to a United Nations Assembly of Peoples will prove awkward to Soviet leaders who claim for themselves a spiritual leadership of the world's masses.

No one need expect that the Russian government will actually welcome a trend toward world democracy. Even if a conference for a review of the United Nations Charter could achieve an ideal justice and security equally benefitting Russia and everyone else, the consequent gain in world stability will not necessarily make the position of Soviet rulers more secure. On the contrary: where fear now serves to unite the Russian people more securely with their government, the real advent of peace will of necessity weaken the grip of autocratic regimes.

In formulating suggestions for United Nations Charter amendments, the West will be well advised not to make proposals which it would be dangerous for Russians to accept, but to aim at proposals difficult for Russia to veto. The West's proposals for amendment, in the 87% majority opinion of CURE conferees, may logically include measures whose veto would put the Russian government on the spot in world public opinion.

"Russian policy is directed primarily to prevent failure of

Communism. The restraints of even limited world federation are so inconsistent with Communist ideology that they will never be willingly accepted," comments Clare A. Davis, Oak Park, Illinois, Chairman of the Public Affairs Committee of the Chicago Area Council of United World Federalists.

United Nations Charter review discussions offer democratic nations an opportunity to appear before the world as champions of freedom and peace: a role convincing because it is real. Sufficient grounds for uneasiness of Soviet rulers appear in the possible emergence of such proposals as those we are studying in this book. Popular representation in a world legislature is a step whose rejection by any single national government would offend world public opinion. Russia's veto of an Assembly of Peoples in the United Nations, should this occur, would rank with her rape of Hungary as a gesture of contempt for fellow human beings.

Such reasoning leads 58% of the Conference Upon Research and Education in world government to believe that the government of the USSR will not reject in principle the proposal for an Assembly of Peoples in the United Nations.

Acceptance in principle would not, of course, immediately bring democratic elections to the Soviet Union.

"The Russians might set up their customary 'slate' for election, which is definitely non-representative yet has the form of popular government," surmises David N. Freeman, Mill Valley, California.

The Russian government "might accept popular elections to the United Nations chamber of peoples and rely on lack of freedom of the press and radio and intimidation of families and friends of the candidates" to control the elections, speculates CUREspondent John W. Schneider.

Such expedients would be in keeping with the Soviet use of the appearances, if not the realities, of popular freedom. "Popular" elections of Russian representatives in a United Nations Assembly of Peoples would simply add a new dimension to an old illusion. Deep in the heart of Communism's illogic are embedded its seemingly grotesque counterfeits of democratic procedures. "Elections" to the Supreme Soviet of Russia are not, however, a perfunctory joke, but an important occasion for the ratification of their leaders' acts by the Russian people.

Everyone votes, under strong persuasion that voting is his civic duty. Every March and October the resulting "parliament" of the Soviet Union proceeds to "approve" by a unanimous vote each resolution brought before it. The Communist philosophy is now so well established, its apologists claim, that there is no longer any need for parliamentary debate. All citizens agree on all laws, and this the Soviet Constitution, the "elections" and the "parliament" are supposed to prove.

The important lesson for outsiders to observe in this rigmarole is not the degree to which it is false by Western standards, but the degree to which by Western standards it is valid. Russian charades upon democratic institutions acknowledge a real need for popular sanction. Soviet rulers place great emphasis upon the appearance of popular support precisely because of the mischievous potentialities which a visible loss of popular support might hold for their regime. Any admission that its own masses suffer under forcible subjection would shatter the entire premise of the Soviet "peoples' democracy."

Nor is the Constitution of 1936 just a joke. 76% of CURE's consultants think that the provisions of the USSR Constitution for the civil rights of Soviet citizens are potentially embarrassing to Soviet tyranny.

"There is substantial evidence that the Russian and satellite peoples resent their regimes. But they will move toward liberation only if it offers a good and respected way of life for them as individuals and as nations," writes conferee John Logue. "They will act only if convinced that freedom does not mean a new class, or foreign, domination.

"But, if convinced, they have and will use techniques of civil disobedience which will overthrow those regimes. The Russian people have a capacity to suffer in a good cause. Their own revolution and their fight against the Nazis are not the only examples. They can look outside to India and the example of the Indian independence movement. The satyagrahas of Gandhi and his followers are inspiring examples of what can be accomplished by a co-ordinated, popular and sometimes heroic disobedience.

"The Russian regime must change its present totalitarian character. It would be foolish and suicidal to attempt to *force* a change upon her," Mr. Logue concludes. "The change can only come about by persuading the Russian people and some of their leadership that there are great gains to be had by changing their regime and joining a world federation."

Change in the character of the Russian regime is a generally accepted goal of these discussions. Yet 74% of CURE conferees feel that a change in the Soviet government need not be a prior condition to its participation in a world government.

When Doctrine Bows to Circumstance

There is no obstructive power in the world entirely insensitive to public opinion.

On this point let us return to the hearings of the United States Senate Foreign Relations Subcommittee on Review of the United Nations Charter.

SECRETARY DULLES: "At San Francisco . . . there was a gentlemen's agreement, so-called, between the nations which presented the Dumbarton Oaks proposals, that neither would depart from these proposals without the agreement of the others, and in that sense the Soviet Union had a veto power over any changes from the Dumbarton Oaks proposals. Nevertheless, it agreed to a number of changes, although these changes were not of the kind which it liked at all.

"There is a measurable response in the Soviet Union to world opinion. There seems to be in many quarters a feeling that the Soviet rulers, because they are dictators and despotic, do not pay attention to world opinion. Actually they pay far more attention to world opinion than most of us realize. They spend probably ten times as much as we spend on that, and they realize full well the importance to them of world opinion. They are always putting out proposals and statements as to how they love peace, and so forth and so on, to win world opinion, and they don't want openly to break with world opinion, so that I am not discouraged at all at the possibilities of having some changes (in the United Nations Charter) if they seem reasonable and if they have a strong backing from world opinion."

The United States Senate Subcommittee on Review of the United Nations Charter held hearings for two years. The Subcommittee broke precedent by travelling all over the country to get local views. Its testimony filled two thousand pages of printed record. There were not lacking witnesses to predict that proposals of Charter revision would result in Russian veto or withdrawal. But like the reports of Mark Twain's death, these opinions of the United Nations' frailty are probably exaggerated.

Within the United Nations, the Russian position is strategic. Russians are a minority capable of infinite filibuster. The inept United Nations machinery gives world majorities little hope of overcoming Russian obstructionism. Russian isolationism impedes any move to adapt the United Nations to true governmental functions. People sometimes wonder why the Soviet Union remains a member of a world organization in which it seldom co-operates. It would be more of a wonder if the USSR withdrew from a position so advantageous for the frustration of possibly antagonistic majority action.

To see this, we need only imagine what would become of the United Nations if Russia should withdraw. The USSR's "walkout" during debates on the Korean crisis enabled the remaining nations to act with unanimity. A severe setback to Communist ambitions resulted. The lesson went home to Soviet leaders. A United Nations without the Soviet Union and its satellite nations would constitute a global alliance for the containment of Communism, restrained in some degree by neutralist elements. A transformation of the remaining organization into a federal union of democracies might become the next and logical trend.

This is a specter which may well haunt Russia's leaders. Russia's present attitude toward international organization includes a fear of being left out. Today a Russian departure from the United Nations could occur only under circumstances in which her continued presence no longer inhibited anti-Russian unity. In this negative and left-handed way, the Russians, too, find some security in the present United Nations.

In the opinion of 88% of conferees voting on this question, the Soviet Union is not likely to walk out of the United Nations for any reason connected with Charter revision proposals by the United States or by anyone else.

The Soviet Union may be expected to oppose steps toward a Conference for the Review of the Charter. There may be dark talk of a boycott. But if the other nations are prepared to go ahead without Russia, then Russia is not likely to let them do so.

"I have the feeling," says Glenn P. Turner, "that if an empty chair at the table was reserved for Russia she would occupy it very shortly."

Success in strengthening the Charter will depend primarily upon the wisdom and popularity of plans which the free world initiates and supports at a Review Conference. Russia may resist, but cannot ignore, the combined opinion of the rest of the world. Legally the Russians can easily decline to ratify amendments to the United Nations Charter. Morally it will be more difficult.

Because the voice of the people is sovereign, those who work to give it expression need not assume that United Nations Charter revision will be impossible simply because of the opposition of any existing tyrannical government. Russia's power of veto over Charter amendments is not absolute. Popular pressures for an international government will not end with the casting of a veto. There are ways in which the world's yearning for peace may flow around vetoes, seeking an outlet through "reinterpretations" of the existing Charter, through a veto-free reorganization of the present world body, or through the initiation of a new international organization.

"Although the Charter does contain a provision that Charter amendments must have the approval of the five permanent members of the Security Council, this is not an insuperable obstacle," Stanley K. Platt reminds us.

"The United States Constitutional Convention in Philadelphia pointed the way.

"Although the Articles of Confederation contained a provision that amendments must be approved by a unanimous vote of the 13 states, the Convention decided that the Constitution of the United States would become effective when nine of the thirteen states ratified it. George Washington took office as the first President of the United States before two of the states, North Carolina and Rhode Island, had ratified the Constitution; but those two states found it to be prudent and desirable to ratify soon thereafter.

"The perspective of history suggests that repetition of the

same logic may again produce similar results, particularly when the weapons of modern war impose a vital common need for international peace and security."

"The Russians didn't join the Atoms for Peace program until the other nations decided to go ahead without Russia," notes David M. Stanley, Muscatine, Iowa, former member of the Executive Council of United World Federalists. "The same will undoubtedly be true of world federation."

It is useless to complain that Russian obstinacy prevents progress toward world peace. Russia stands immovably athwart our path only as long as we lack an understanding of what our goal should be.

By whatever means mankind approaches world order, to seek victory for one's ideas runs the risk of violent opposition. Russia's leaders, if cornered, may be in a mood for desperate measures. But Russian leaders are not likely to embark upon a war in which Russia's peoples have no interest. The one tactic which can win for the West is a campaign to enlist the peoples of the earth in a design for world law, order and democracy. To have the peoples of the world on our side, we must be on the side of the world's peoples.

It is through the people of the world that the West can best and most subtly reach Russia's masters. The tenets of the Russian dialectic remain sacrosanct only as long as they are expedient to Russian purposes. A dialectic neurosis does not feed upon air: it feeds upon actual antagonisms. We cannot argue with a neurosis. All we can do is to try to reach the human being within the neurosis. Men are only in a superficial sense the product of doctrines. Doctrines can make men difficult and dangerous to handle; but more basically doctrines are the product of men and the situations in which men find themselves. Any doctrine which rules men blindly becomes suicidal once its justification no longer exists. The principle of self-preservation dictates even to the dictator.

And we may continue to hope that there persists a salvageable humanity within the dialectic neurosis.

"What has for centuries raised man above the beast is not the cudgel but the inward music: the irresistible power of unarmed truth..."

Soviet author Boris Pasternak penned these words in

Doctor Zhivago more than forty years after the Bolsheviks began their rule of Russia.

Security Is a Two-Way Street

Perhaps the most sensible way to look at Russia is to realize that United Nations Charter revisions which tame the military and political and economic conflicts of the nations will shrivel the power of tyrants who thrive by strife.

A virtually unanimous 96% of respondents agree that a more secure world will "soften" tyrannies.

And according to 85% of opinions among conferees, there are ways in which the free world can offer increased security for Russia's peaceful development. Some steps toward co-existence need not wait for United Nations reform: freer trade, admission of Red China to the United Nations, and the relaxing of passport and travel restrictions are examples. But more basic measures must wait upon a more basic world law.

Christopher Meredith, Stanmore, Middlesex, England, suggests that "by reducing the hostile encirclement of atom bomb bases, so-called 'defensive' alliances (NATO, Baghdad Pact, SEATO) and propaganda, we can do much to reduce the fear of attack which is very strongly felt by the people and government of Russia."

"Obviously," Henry C. McIlvaine points out, "Russia feels insecure while encircled."

"The Pentagon can make an impressive case for our overseas bases as the world is now," adds Vernon Nash; "but imagine how we would feel with such Russian bases in Mexico, Cuba, Newfoundland, the Aleutians and Hawaii."

"The Russian people like us but fear what our leaders will do. This feeling greatly aids their leaders in keeping dissatisfaction down," CUREspondent James M. Scarritt, Kansas City, Missouri, graduate student at the Woodrow Wilson School of Political Science of Princeton University, reports after a visit to the Soviet Union.

At first sight it might seem that a Western acceptance of Russia's position in world power would abandon her satellite peoples to a fate of slavery. But most conferees do not interpret assurances of security for Russia's peaceful development as a betrayal of Russia's vassals. 78% who express an opinion do not feel that greater security for Russia's peaceful development will deprive the subject peoples of hope. Instead, the majority believes, security for Russia will relax the bondage of the captive nations about her borders.

"If Russia felt greater security, she would allow the satellites more freedom," contends Ruth Askew, Chicago, Illinois, seconded by Clarence L. Pickard, Indianola, Iowa, a retired Professor of Agricultural Economics, who says, "if she felt such security she would not need satellites."

Russia's subject neighbors "can have no valid hope based on military intervention," points out William Bross Lloyd, "for it would be destruction for them."

Much of the hostility between Russia and the United States springs from the mental hazard of fear on both sides rather than from any drastic conflict of interest.

"I think that the circumstances under which either Russia or the United States would attack the other are not likely to arise within the next fifty years. Further than that—who knows?" muses John Holt. "By then neither Russia nor the United States will be much like what they are today, and the chances are both will be much alike. Probably they will be in each other's laps with their arms around each other, worrying what to do about China and India. Sooner or later Russia is going to realize that she is one of the rich."

Prosperity and respect for each other's scientific, cultural and economic prowess are preparing Russians and Americans for the realization that there is room in the world for both nations. A growing third force of world law will strengthen the self-confidence of each country. An increasing security will diminish the fears which inhibit a more constructive relationship.

People to People

It would be naive to suppose that security could actually soften the hearts of tyrants.

"The essence of driving motivation of leaders in all totalitarians is personal power, and would not be changed appreciably by greater external security," declares Vernon Nash.

Dr. Elliott R. Goodman, Providence, Rhode Island, Professor of Political Science at Brown University and author of *The*

Soviet Design for a World State, concurs. "Moscow represents a revolutionary power, which by its very nature is incapable of reassurance or satisfaction, save at its own price, which is the creation of an exclusively Communist world government."

"Neither the USA nor the USSR want to be offered assurances of security," contends Patrick Armstrong, spokesman for the British Parliamentary Group for World Government. "Their governments want to go on believing in their expensive national defense systems. Like a man who has bought the most expensive kind of car, only to find that there is so much traffic it is quicker to go on foot; but he will still keep the car, because the neighbours have one. Time may bring sense; logic won't," he adds.

A psychological approach seeks to "soften", not the hearts of tyrants, but the fears and hostilities of the Russian citizen. Ivan, in contrast to his masters, has nothing to gain from a public state of fear. He would like to be rid of his fears, and quite possibly of his masters too. Assurances of a secure position among the world's nations will not alone suffice to end tensions between Russia and the rest of the world. But a system of security running alike to Russian benefit and to that of other peoples is an indispensable part of any program ʿor that purpose.

The "inscrutable" Russians react in an intensely human way to other peoples' attitudes.

"You see," says Eliza Doolittle in Bernard Shaw's play *Pygmalion*, the source for the musical comedy *My Fair Lady*, "really and truly, apart from the things one can pick up (the dressing and proper way of speaking, and so on) the difference between a lady and a flower girl is not how she behaves, but how she is treated."

Participants in CURE's conference are inclined to agree that adequate assurances of a good life for Russia, as for others, are not possible by any steps short of "re-organizing the United Nations," in the words of Dipl.-Pol. Günter Krabbe, Bonn, Germany, President of Internationaler Studentenbund-Studentenbewegung für übernationale Föderation (ISSF).

Germany's rightist fascism did not arise from a racial wickedness peculiar to Germans, nor does Russia's leftist fascism stamp Russians a nation of evil men. If we accept Russians as human beings, we must offer to them, not a contest of propaganda maneuvers, nor an intensified rivalry in power politics, nor the mutual suicide pact of an arms race, but the reality of world democratic law, the peaceful means to contain world competition within constructive channels.

Given the security of acceptance by mankind as citizens of a governed world, Russians can get along with other men, because they are the most human and practical of people, desiring peace and the dignity of the individual no less than ourselves.

Chapter 9.

The Meek Shall Inherit . . .

Such success as the United Nations has enjoyed during its initial years stems in large part from the emphasis which the one-nation-one-vote system gives to the good offices of smaller nations as mediators in disputes between great powers.

The great armed nations cling to their nuclear weapons in the hope that these arms will somehow preserve their sovereignty. Lesser nations know that the use of such weapons by great nations is likely to result in an increased domination by the strong of the weak. But lesser powers do not draw their importance from their potential possession of atomic bombs. They are important because they do not possess weapons to destroy anyone.

Nations lacking major weaponry are a majority of the human race. Most of humanity is already disarmed. A pre-eminent moral prestige among postwar world figures has accrued to Prime Minister Jawaharlal Nehru of the Federal Republic of India, leader of the largest relatively unarmed population on earth.

The role of mediation is welcome to less powerful nations. "A little child shall lead them," said the prophet. The citizens of powerful nations, too, may hope that for purposes of keeping the peace, the least shall be the greatest.

Democracy is, among other things, a process of distributing power to the less powerful. Seen in this light, the enormous and growing populations of relatively unarmed countries are both an asset and a potential liability to the establishment of world democracy. They are an asset because they constitute a "third force" which reduces the struggle between great powers to a perspective in which it appears faintly absurd and unnecessary. And they can become a liability, not because of their political inexperience, but because the explosive growth of backward populations, if it continues unchecked, can rob mankind of the fruits of peace and prosperity.

It is a moot question whether population control is a problem of technology, one of religion, or one of psychology.

Birth control is least likely to remain in the realm of religion, as is plain to see in the example of Ireland, one of the most Catholic countries on earth, whose population is steadily dwindling despite the hopes of the Church for unrestricted propagation.

Scientists see population control as a problem in technology. In Ceylon, the chemical substance DDT wiped out malaria within three or four years, with the direct result that the population will double within the next thirty or forty years. If science cuts the death rate, technicians reason, science will have to cut the birth rate too, in order that the world's resources may not become overwhelmed by a veritable plague of humans.

Every fifteen months the population of China increases by twelve millions, a number equal to the total of inhabitants of Canada. The Chinese Communist government has adopted drastic means to curb birth rates. Towns have established free birth control clinics, according to reporter William Kinmond of the Toronto *Globe and Mail*, and thousands of mobile birth control units tour the countryside. A realization of her hope to enjoy the benefits of five-year plans for industrial expansion will depend upon China's success in limiting population increase as well as in developing more ample supplies of foodstuffs and of manufactured goods.

The population of India grows by five millions each year, with only famine as a control. Calcutta alone has increased from three millions to five millions within the past fifteen years. Any foreigner who sees the swarming misery of a Calcutta slum must comprehend that its inhabitants seek no increase in their number. In India, China, Japan, Java, Bali, Thailand, populations are growing faster than any hope of increased food supply. Technology must tackle both ends of this dilemma in order to raise living standards to a reasonable level.

143

The psychological aspects of population control, of which least is known, are possibly the most important. During the frontier years of America, when children counted as a labor asset on the farm, a good-sized family consisted of a half-dozen youngsters. Later, with the countryfolk drifting to cities, an average American family shrank to two or three children. But when the threat of war interfered with the normal decline in birth rates, a completely unexpected bulge in child production took place. An instinctive human reaction to danger increased the rate of procreation; the fear of atomic devastation is, apparently, responsible for the shortage of American schoolrooms.

"The very high birth rates at Los Alamos during the A-bomb development indicates this to be so," states Rutgers University entomologist Dr. Martin T. Hutchinson. "In times of stress, all organisms tend to push reproduction to the limit."

Similar reactions have occurred in France and other countries where populations previously had been assumed to have reached their maximums. Faced with a basic challenge to their existence, a reinforcement of populations appears as the crudest psychological response. Instinctively, peoples closest to the peril are breeding to replace their future dead. But such a reaction is likely to be self-defeating: it is likely to precipitate the very conflict which it anticipates.

And, of course, it may be that the poisoning of the human genes by increasing levels of atomic fallout radiation will serve as a crude limit upon population growth. This is not exactly attractive to contemplate. It is particularly unattractive to those members of highly developed cultures who need birth control least, who are the most likely to start wars, and who will be the first to become poisoned and die out.

There are more desirable ways to limit population than by starvation or by poisoning, by disease or by war.

World security will ease the psychological pressures which impel the human community to prepare for depopulation by catastrophe. And a governed world will release enormous resources and energies for economic aid, for improvement in subsistence levels and for education in birth control. On these grounds, it is reasonable to suppose that an increase in world political stability will, among its other benefits, be a good way to set the stage for world population stability.

144

Every Man May Love Liberty

Peoples lacking armaments may love liberty as truly as citizens of well-armed powers. And the people of impoverished countries can desire a better life as eagerly as their wealthy neighbors. A plan for world law which hopes to win the support of less developed nations cannot be one designed to freeze world relationships in their present status: it must offer a peaceful path to progress.

"It is a mistake to assume that power begets freedom," says William A. Wheeler. "The war of ideas will be won by those who can show the way to the defeat of disease, poverty, ignorance, overpopulation. There can no longer be islands of plenty in seas of chaos."

The gulf among the world's peoples is not so much between the freedom-lovers and the freedom-haters as between the "haves" and the "have-nots", maintains John H. Davenport, Levittown, New York, a former Instructor in Political Science at the University of Miami: "I think it very unprofitable to discuss world affairs in the rigid context of the Soviet-American power struggle."

"The great problem of our time is the problem of the world's dispossessed—the black, brown, yellow and other colored peoples of the world, sick, ignorant, oppressed in one way or in many," affirms John C. Holt.

"The strongest government ever devised could not hold a lid forever over the mass of conscious inequalities and injustices that today beset our world," writes correspondent Mary Hays Weik. "Colonialism is a striking current example.

"Human rights have a way of towering above laws that tend to constrict them. We must recognize that in the so-called 'internal' problems of colonial bondage and racial inequalities within countries today, we face, legalistically, much the same situation as did the American government of pre-Civil War days, when it endeavored to treat the institution of slavery as one of property rights.

"As the Egyptian delegate to the United Nations, Omar Loutfi, said during the attempt to bring the 'bloodstained Algerian problem' into general discussion in the United Nations Assembly, 'the question of the rights of man can no longer be regarded as the exclusive affair of states'."

Direct trusteeship by the United Nations over territories emerging from colonialism will enlist support among native peoples if it offers a more direct path to personal freedoms than the national administrations which it replaces, in the opinion of 93% of Conference voters.

"If the trustees are colonial powers," warns John Holt, colonies might win only a status "like the current independence of Liberia, in which practically everything worth having is owned by Firestone and perhaps a couple of other rubber companies. There are all kinds of independence."

It is the near-unanimous conclusion of participants in CURE's conference that provisions to promote colonial freedom in a revised United Nations Charter will be an asset before world opinion.

All about us, as we watch, the peoples' desire for freedom has surged over old or new restraints. Many instances bear witness to the fierce independence of the human spirit: South Korea's freed Communist prisoners who refused to return home to tyranny, East Germans who revolted against Red oppression, Hungarians who revolted to throw off their Soviet shackles, Algerians who rebelled against French rule. Each day's newspapers bring us fresh tidings of the self-respect of the human individual.

The New Voter

Only one-tenth of the world's people possess long-established democratic governments. In a hearing of the United States Senate Subcommittee on Review of the United Nations Charter, Senator Alexander Wiley, the Subcommittee Chairman, cited this fact as an indication that only a tenth of the world's populations desire self-government. But he missed the meaning of the statistic which he quoted: there is abundant evidence that many more people want liberty than are accustomed to it or get it today.

"The revolution which is in the air in the Middle East is prompted by the same spiritual values as the American Revolution," Turkish spokesman Nuri Eren has told the West. "The new consciousness of political freedom has been aided by the continually improving economic status of the area."

Ventures of inexperienced populations into unaccustomed democratic responsibility alarm some observers.

146

"Election through mass franchise, though a high ideal, in backward and undeveloped countries will afford an opportunity to the ruling sections of parties to engineer the election of the candidate of their own choice," declared D. S. Thakar, General Secretary of the All-India Gorkha Ex-Servicemen's Welfare Association, in discussions initiated by the American Veterans Committee.

Taking into account the large proportion of illiteracy in India, election ballots carry such symbols as a star or a rooster to identify the parties for the benefit of voters who cannot read or write.

"Despite all the talk of giving the colonials complete independence I think in most cases we had better step softly; non-Western peoples seem to have had a difficult time in self-government," asserts Harry W. Malm, Chicago, Illinois, lawyer and past Chairman of Near North Side Chapter of United World Federalists. "A trusteeship gives them a face-saving device and at the same time acts as a check.

"I now feel," he adds, "that the years that India struggled for independence were not wasted as it gave India an opportunity of developing leadership and, thanks to England, the best administrative set-up of any of the new constitutions of the world today."

However, as we have seen, it is not inexperience, but more often insecurity, which poses the chief threat to younger democracies. There is a considerable trend of confidence among CURE's conferees in the democratic capacities of populations around the world.

Admission of populations inexperienced in democracy to an international parliamentary federation will be "the best possible means of their learning what democracy means," reasons Henry C. McIlvaine. Jr.

"The 'common man' needs only guarantees of freedom," agrees W. Thetford LeViness, Santa Fe, New Mexico, Librarian for the New Mexico Department of Public Welfare.

Vernon Nash concurs. "Extensions of democratic responsibilities to electorates without previous experience in them (as in the ending of property qualifications in our history) have always been accompanied by forebodings which were not justified," he observes. "Human beings rise to such 'tasks'."

147

"The new democracies are doing very well," comments Dr. Stringfellow Barr, Princeton, New Jersey, Professor of Humanities at Rutgers University and originator of the "Great Books" curriculum during his term as President of St. Johns College at Annapolis.

"We often find that it is the so-called backward countries," notes Neil Parsons, "who send the most able representatives to our international conferences. We may well expect the same result in an international government."

Neutrals Want World Law

In other chapters we are considering briefly the climate of feeling toward a stronger United Nations among peoples who are part of such security groupings as the European community, the British Empire, the Moscow-ruled Communist empire, and the United States of America. Nations outside such partial security systems must place their undivided reliance upon the peace-keeping powers of the United Nations. There is doubt among such peoples of the ability of the great powers to agree on an improved organization for world security. But there is little question in the minds of spokesmen for less powerful peoples that such an improvement is desirable. And there is little hesitation among them in airing their opinions, even when they speak in the very shadow of Communist expansion.

Exploratory discussions initiated by the Special United Nations Subcommittee of the American Veterans Committee between spokesmen of the World Veterans Federation, comprising 20,000,000 ex-servicemen in 135 organizations of 34 free nations, find evidences of widespread desire for peace among the war veterans of less powerful nations.

Improvement of the United Nations as a parliament of the world is "desirable and necessary," declared Lieutenant General Charoen Suvanavisutra, General Director of the War Veterans Organization of Thailand. However, "because it might imply change in the sovereignty of the various nations," he said, "all nations might not agree" to the inclusion of representatives of peoples in addition to representatives of states in the United Nations.

"An international body composed of elected representatives

of each country will be very much more dignified and trust-worthy than a body of government nominees from different countries," D. S. Thakar predicted, speaking for Indian Gorkha veterans. "Every sovereign state, large or small, must find representation in the world parliament irrespective of its social or economic system. But the greatest snag will be 'what determines the number of representatives'. It will be extremely difficult," he prophesied, "to get the European and American states to agree on the basis of population."

Each delegation of the present United Nations organization "was appointed and sent out by the government" of its origin and acts "under the instructions of their government and in compliance with their country's policies," observed Sang Bong Kim, writing as President of the Korean Disabled Veterans. At present, he said, delegations often cannot vote as members wish. "It is our idea," he declared, that the present organization "would not achieve the world peace and welfare of mankind" which is the principal objective of the United Nations. Therefore, he concluded, "we wish to have a world organiza-tion with the delegations elected by people directly, which would discuss and decide freely for the world" matters of peace and human rights.

"A lot of things can be done" to improve the United Nations as a parliament of the world, "not only for necessity but for practicality and progress," wrote Colonel Pham Van Cam, (Ret.), Acting National Commander, Vietnamese Vet-erans Legion.

Colonel Pham commented that the present United Nations is "shaky", that even smaller nations ignore United Nations actions if they choose, and that there is danger that the United Nations may fall apart like the League of Nations.

"With our experience of World War II, greater precaution is not only extremely necessary, it is indispensable if the world we presently live in is to survive.

"In the present set-up, whereby the representatives are appointed by the governments of various nations, these rep-resentatives are bound by country loyalty. Their country first, before the world, is their primary aim, and the world's wel-fare an incidental or secondary aim. These representatives cannot commit their country for whatever the United Nations decides would be beneficial to the world, without informing their government first. How about if their government refused to commit themselves with the United Nations' decisions; who loses? No country in the world, even if she is the most powerful, can stand alone and look with satisfaction upon what is happening to the countries around her."

Eventually, he added, a country which ignores the problems of other countries "will be involved with a result too catastrophic to imagine."

Colonel Pham predicted that enhancing the United Nations by a Chamber of Peoples will add to its dignity and effectiveness. "The greater the number, the more will be the voice to defend the rights of small men, to denounce aggressions of hostile countries and to make every country feel that she is part and parcel of the world existence," he declared. "In peace they all have one enemy, WAR."

In the eyes of these men we see the vision of a democratic world government as the antagonist to war and the answer to tyranny.

The Debate on Revision

The less powerful countries saw imperfections in the United Nations Charter at the time of its framing. At the insistence of smaller countries, Article 109 of the Charter contained a provision to hold a Conference for the review of the Charter at the end of ten years.

The lesser nations, resentful of the veto privilege accorded large powers in the Security Council of the United Nations, were frankly skeptical that the unanimity of the veto powers would last long. For that matter, they were skeptical of the real power of some of the five veto nations. How right they were is apparent today when one compares the actual powers of Formosa and France, both holding "great power" veto privileges in the Security Council, and the present power of Great Britain with those of the United States of America and of Russia. Within a decade the "equality" of the permanent members of the United Nations Security Council had become a legal myth.

At the tenth anniversary of its adoption, Article 109 of the United Nations Charter placed the subject of a revision conference upon the agenda of the General Assembly. The changing fortunes of the handful of veto nations became a favorite theme of the smaller nations during the week-long debate which followed.

The delegate from Iraq stated the position of many nations on the imperfections of the present Charter.

MR. AL-JAMALI: "At that time, there were slightly more than forty Members at San Francisco; today, we are sixty Members and we hope to be almost eighty Members. Thus, the Charter represents the views of those of us who were at San Francisco, but not the views of many who were not Members at the time.

"In San Francisco, we were sharply divided on the issue of the veto, and I must say that the majority were opposed to the veto. But when we were confronted with a dilemma—either the veto or no United Nations—we had to accept the idea of the United Nations with the veto."

From inequalities of voting the Iraqi spokesman went on to examine the injustices which exist between peoples.

"International conscience is more alive today than ever to the cause of freedom, to the cause of the liberation of peoples," he said, and stated as basic principles of the Charter "that there shall be no subject people remaining in the world and that all peoples shall have the opportunity to exercise freedom and liberty.

"In this respect, certainly, the Charter needs improvement. Many of us believe that the colonial issue does not fall within domestic jurisdiction; others, however, believe that it does ... Let us assume that a state decided to persecute within its own boundaries the people belonging to a certain race or religion. Would that persecution be regarded as a matter of domestic jurisdiction? Or is it not true to state that such a policy would have repercussions in other countries, where persons of the same race or religion would sympathize and suffer with the persecuted people?

"Are we going to realize that the sovereignty of humanity is greater than the sovereignty of the state?"

In his turn, the Delegate from Peru made it plain that he believed the strengthening of the United Nations Charter to be a matter of life or death.

MR. BELAUNDE: "How are we to solve the acute problems which occur in the United Nations year after year? How ... can a Charter which was signed in the pre-atomic age still

151

stand today? Does not this awaken enough instinct for reform of the Charter?

"If errors and flaws and deficiencies of the past require a revision of the Charter, then the Charter will have to be brought up to date. If the Charter is to be brought up to date, then the Conference will have to be called and we shall have to study all the precepts that may have to be changed in order to guarantee continued life to humanity.

"I am of a religion and of a type of thinking which may be characterized by those who think otherwise as too conservative. But I repeat: 'From the giving of some things and the taking of others is the harmony of centuries born!'" And the Delegate from Peru spoke the sentence again with emphasis. "You may say that I am quoting something from Hegel or Comte. That is not so. This quotation is a trifle older and a trifle more glorious—it is Saint Augustine speaking."

A Conference to review the United Nations Charter will have to begin on an exploratory basis, observed A. K. Brohi, Delegate from Pakistan.

MR. BROHI: "There is nobody in the twentieth century who is so unsophisticated as to say that the economic or political situation of ten years ago continues to be the same now . . .

"These considerations compel a rational mind to look at the present Charter and ask one simple question: Are the assumptions on the basis of which the Charter was drawn up . . . still valid? If we ask ourselves the question, is that concept still good, the answer can be: no, it is not good. But there can be another question also: have we got a better one? I doubt that; but certainly what I cannot grant is that such a concept cannot be found.

"Nobody knows that in the Conference the Members, sitting together as honorable men, will not discover another assumption which is less pretentious, perhaps, but which is of greater pragmatic relevance for the purpose of building the edifice of the new Charter. The review conference can therefore be of an exploratory character, where the many minds can converge and come into common focus and where world opinion can be consulted."

The Delegate denounced the tendency toward changing the purposes of the Charter by "re-interpretation" of its provisions.

"The Constitution of the United States of America, as actually interpreted by its judges, is radically different from the type of constitution which its sponsors thought it was likely to be, and this has been frankly admitted. But the redeeming feature is that the supreme authority of the highest court in the United States backs up the final interpretation, and there all controversies come to an end ...

"But when we come to the law of the Charter of the United Nations, which is a written law and which has not at its back the supreme authority of any organ to compel the recognition of that law, this type of approach is disastrous. It would be encouraging everybody to flout the definite provisions of law in an attempt to find out some solutions by back-door devices; not amending it, because amending procedure is difficult, but yet mutilating the provisions of the Charter, misconstruing them, misapplying them, and triumphantly turning around and saying: because of the fact that I was able to violate the previous law, that is how the law of the international community is advanced.

"The moral conscience of humanity cannot but view with disfavour any such devices of misapplying the law of the United Nations ... whether it is the resolution on 'Uniting for Peace' or action in Korea, or with regard to the appointment of the Secretary-General, or even with regard to the accommodating character of the North Atlantic Treaty ...

"There is a contest on this issue ... The only thing to do to wash it away is to secure a forum in which that contest can be resolved.

"I have come across a great deal of literature on the subject, where the private organizations are coming up with useful suggestions ..."

Mr. Brohi then described to the General Assembly the studies of CURE.

"I shall read out to you two paragraphs from the hearing on the review of the United Nations Charter which was held by the Sub-Committee on the United Nations Charter of the Committee on Foreign Relations of the United States Senate. These paragraphs are from a statement by Mr. Millard who represents the Conference Upon Research and Education in world government ...

"'... Our studies give proof that human ingenuity can

153

quite possibly find ways out of the cold war without destruction or appeasement ... There are two possible sources for additional strength of the United Nations. One is a direct grant of power in certain carefully chosen areas of sovereignty. Such grants can be in power vacuums where existing national sovereignties are not effective anyhow ... Direct trusteeship of former colonies and prominent trouble spots ... An economic development authority somewhat on the order of a world lend-lease bank ... A world atom agency intended to prepare for the time when the nations can agree on armament control ...

"'A second potential source of strength for the United Nations will be the direct participation of the people, not only the people who today exert great influence in world affairs, but also the colonial, the coloured, the poor of the earth ...'"

The recommendations growing out of CURE's studies, mentioned at this point by the Delegate from Pakistan, as it happened were the only proposals from any source—governmental, organizational or individual—cited during the week's debate in the General Assembly as examples of the task which faces a Conference for the review of the United Nations Charter. But Mr. Brohi made it clear to the General Assembly that CURE's suggestions are only one of several possible approaches to the problem of establishing a stronger world organization.

"I do not say that this concept will bear examination, but it is a concept which has to be considered," he observed. "There are many such concepts that are available in relation to which international order in international relations can be brought about."

The Delegate from Chile, who spoke on the following day, saw the debate in a perspective of history.

MR. ORTEGA: "Let us remember that it will be our sons and grandsons who will, rightly, hold us responsible both for what we have done and for what we have failed to do ..."

On the last day of the week, Delegate Carlos Romulo of the Philippine Republic rose to address the General Assembly.

MR. ROMULO: "Whatever the disagreements of those who have spoken on this question, there has been no dis-

154

agreement about one fact of towering importance. That fact is that existence of the United Nations must not be jeopardized or weakened or enfeebled. Both the advocates and opponents of Charter reform stand as one in their desire to save the United Nations and to serve the cause of world peace through world organization.

"The Philippine delegation does not question the sincerity or good sense of people who arrive at different conclusions after stating that their principal desire is to uphold the United Nations . . . We are not working with slide rules here . . . We are working with the measureless flow of history itself. Yet there is at least one fixed point on which all friends of the United Nations should agree . . . The United Nations has its mandate only nominally through the actions of governments. Basically and primarily, the United Nations derives its ultimate power from the will of the world's peoples. It derives its total strength not from the discussions on this floor, but from the determination of the world's peoples to keep it alive . . . And if there is anything more powerful in the world today than nuclear weapons, it is the opinion of the human community.

"Woodrow Wilson, who in many ways really was a founding father of the United Nations, used to say that his clients were the next generation. Our clients are today's generation. Unless that generation is well represented, it is possible that there will be no other.

"Is there any doubt in the mind of any representative here that the world's peoples expect the United Nations to fulfill the promise made in the Preamble to the Charter: namely, that the purpose of the United Nations is to do away with the scourge of war?"

The peoples of the world will not tolerate a failure of the United Nations, the Philippines spokesman declared.

"I believe that peoples everywhere are profoundly worried by what has been happening to the world in general and to the United Nations in particular. They are worried because they know that an atomic armaments race is on, and they know where armaments races lead. They are worried because they know that if the United Nations fails to prevent war, the probable effects will be measured in the extermination of man at worst and the poisoning of the human genes at best.

155

"There is a sense of the ultimate in the concerns of men today.

"If we take soundings—which is to say, if we find out what our constituents in the human family are really thinking—we will learn that the biggest and not the smallest things are expected of us. As public men and representatives of our governments, we are perhaps over-enamoured at times with the small, single steps at one time; but the large strides are what the world's peoples want and deserve...

"All our yesterdays are littered with Locarnos, and we are expected to abandon the habit of error..."

Diplomats, like everyone else, Mr. Romulo remarked, tend to get into a rut, a habit of taking things as they are.

"Perhaps the great expectations that still exist among our clients make us uneasy because we are so well versed in the difficulties and the complexities. Indeed, we may know them too well. We have been living so intimately with our day-to-day problems that the historical vistas tend to become somewhat blurred. We are apt to be impatient with those who seem unappreciative of the tangles and confusions that surround us and confound us. And so we counsel patience and more patience, hoping that the world will be convinced that we are doing our best.

"But the great danger is that we ourselves may lose our perspective and a true sense of the historical panorama. The difficulties in which we are enmeshed, and our razor-sharp awareness of the day-to-day complexities may cause us to put our working problems ahead of the basic problem.

"It may well be that the view of the people is the only correct one.

"It is because of this, and because I feel that it is time for us of the United Nations to bring our own perspective in line with that of the human community we represent, that I advocate a long, hard look at where we have been and where we are going..."

The Philippines Delegate stressed the need for the United Nations to provide not merely a meeting place for mediation of the nations' foreign policies, but to develop policy making powers of its own.

"A review conference is far from the be-all and end-all of a solution to all our problems. It will bring to pass no miracles in world organization or world peace. But at least it will set a time and place for full and appropriate consideration of our ability to do our main job.

"I do not hold with the argument that a properly constituted review conference would result in a break-up of the United Nations. If the United Nations is so weak that it cannot stand honest self-examination, then it is living on borrowed time indeed. It is precisely because I believe the world's peoples own the United Nations that their voice becomes mandatory.

"We are representatives and delegates, true; but in an even greater sense we are custodians—the custodians of the greatest idea yet to be conceived by the mind of man—that the violence among nations in the world may yet yield to the courage and imagination of men in constructing a world of law, and that our modest-sized planet may in time and in fact become the good earth . . ."

In the voting which followed, only Syria of the less powerful nations opposed a decision to convene a conference for the review of the Charter.

India, Yugoslavia, four Scandinavian nations and three Middle Eastern countries abstained from voting.

Other than these, the less powerful nations of the world cast their ballots to initiate a Charter review conference, and to set in motion events which, in time, could strengthen the parliament of man.

Chapter 10.

Appraisal of Americans

Americans, too, owed an obligation to United Nations Charter review. The major powers holding veto rights in the Security Council of the United Nations had, in effect, given their pledge for a Charter review conference when, at the insistence of lesser powers, they consented to the terms of Article 109 of the Charter at the time of its drafting. During the General Assembly's debate on the subject of a review conference ten years later, Delegate Laird Bell presented the views of the United States government.

MR. BELL: "The United States believes that a review conference should be held. The United Nations has become a new and vital force in world affairs. Now a period of trial has elapsed and a body of valuable experience has been built up. Much good can come from a collective scrutiny at the proper time of the role, accomplishments, shortcomings and potentialities of this great instrument. We do not conceive of the task as merely the narrow consideration of specific verbal changes. Neither do we conceive of the task as one of re-writing the Charter or changing the basic character of the organization ...

"The United Nations, a decade of experience has shown, derives its greatest strength from the support and understanding of the peoples of the world ... It is in the words of the late Senator Vandenberg 'the Town Meeting of the World'. It is our belief that a Conference to review the Charter could greatly strengthen that understanding ...

"The farseeing men who drafted the Charter at San Francisco had no illusions that it was an immutable document.

158

The provisions for amendment were obviously put into it for a purpose. The Charter and the procedures under it have served remarkably well. We recognize to the full that there are dangers in any attempt at revision, but we do not see such dangers in a review to determine whether there are any changes that could usefully be made in the Charter or in the procedures that have developed under it."

The United States, Britain and France cast their votes as did most of the lesser powers in favor of the Conference. Russia's "nyet" could not veto the provisions of Article 109 of the Charter. On November 21, 1955, by a ballot of 43 to 6, with 9 abstentions, the General Assembly adopted the first step in preparation for Charter review.

A comprehensive survey of American official thinking up to that time, and an important background to the development of CURE's report, appears in *Proposals for Changes in the United Nations,* by Francis O. Wilcox, Chief of Staff, and Carl M. Marcy, Consultant to the Committee on Foreign Relations of the United States Senate.

American initiative seems to have exhausted itself, however, with this endorsement in principle of a United Nations Charter Review Conference. During the following few years the Western nations have deemed the time "inauspicious" for basic steps toward peace. Yankee leadership, whether shrewd or crude, has lapsed into occasional proposals of arms inspection, leaving the way open for the subtle or the brutal initiatives of Russian aggression. The West tries to block Russian thrusts, and complains of Russian perversity; but the kindest thing that can be said about a basic American foreign policy is that none exists.

"Hatred of Communism has paralyzed the United States," asserts John Holt. "Ask a foreign affairs expert what our foreign policy would be if the Communist menace collapsed. All you'll get will be a blank look."

Disraeli once declared that the British built their empire in a fit of absent-mindedness. Without really meaning to, Americans in their turn built the most powerful nation in history. Just as Russians are the captives of the Communist conspiracy, so too are Americans to a large extent prisoners of their own power.

"One of the obstacles to our nation's emergence as a world

159

leader is a limited concept of power and a curious attitude toward its acquisition and use. It appears to be inherent in the American character to seek power with considerable energy and determination and then, having attained it, not to have any clear idea how to put it to use," James P. Warburg wrote in *Agenda for Action*. "One might call this almost purposeless acquisitiveness—a pursuit of power more because of a keen competitive instinct than because of any wish to possess and exercise it."

Nor is there any more reason to suppose that the Soviet rise to power bespeaks a determination to rule the world on the part of the average Russian citizen.

From Colony to Colonial Power

Because the homeland of the United States is many times vaster than that of the British Isles, American power rests in a lesser degree upon the possession of overseas territories. Nevertheless, the colonial empire of the United States forms a burden upon its conscience and upon its foreign policy. The most serious errors committed in the name of American foreign policy are likely to be those which support European rule over colonial peoples. When America underwrites the disintegrating colonial empires of other nations, the ostensible reason is to help friendly governments, but plenty of people suspect the real reason is to protect the imperial rule of the United States over some of her own territories.

"A courageous American foreign policy would long ago have brought out publicly the suggestion of United Nations administration of the Suez Canal," point out William Bross Lloyd; however, he adds, "parallels with the Panama Canal have probably sufficed to scare Washington off."

During the many years while the United States Congress procrastinated in the admissions of Hawaii and Alaska to statehood, America's colonial interests, though of relatively little importance to the mainland's economy, have repeatedly proved themselves an obstacle to the long-range role of the United States as an apostle of freedom. Such inhibitions are no more logical abroad than they are at home. American encouragement for United Nations trusteeships of restive colonies would not result in the surrender of friendly European nations to

Communist control, but would actually protect their legitimate overseas investments. An American attitude which strengthens the ascendancy of democratic elements among colonial populations will at the same time strengthen the forces of world order.

With each passing year, America's exclusive possession of strategic territory at the militarily obsolescent Panama Canal zone is less essential to her defence of the Western Hemisphere. United Nations trusteeships or full statehood for the entire range of American colonial possessions, if matched by similar contributions from other colonial powers, would cause scarcely a ripple on the American mainland; yet as part of an American formula for the overall organization of peace, such an earnest of good faith would carry incalculable weight.

This American colonial problem is just one example of the basic and even radical revisions of attitude necessary to an American initiative in the achievement of a successful government of man.

Because of the fundamental nature of the changes involved, participants in CURE's forum are skeptical whether Americans will successfully seize a leading role in United Nations reform. Only 43% see a realistic possibility that the United States' policy toward United Nations Charter revision might go so far as CURE's proposals. It seems even less likely that the United States will seek a stronger form of world government than that which we outline here; only 23% of conferees see this as a realistic possibility.

The United States government might adopt CURE's proposals "if given a substantial public opinion push," in the typical opinion of Niels T. Anderson.

A Conflict of Interests

Psychological problems often seem even more insuperable than physical obstacles. "One of our main troubles is that we are trying to convince politicians that they should give up some of their power to world politicians," Ralph Lombardi has written. "I doubt whether many are willing to do this unless they can be the world politicians." Maybe our politicians have not yet grasped the patronage possibilities open to the postmaster general of a world government!

161

The psychology of the United States presents to the world an extraordinary spectacle. As the Quaker said to his friend, "Everyone's daft but thee and me—and methinks thee is a little queer!" Each of us suspects the other is a candidate for psychiatry; but in the pathology of nations, the behavior of none is more irrational than that of the American community.

"Whom the Gods will destroy," said the old Greeks, "they first make mad."

Consider the fact that the democratic federal government of the United States is the model for human freedoms, the revelation of liberties for all those people who since 1789 have won self-government under law. Consider that the people of the United States know full well an arms race is, by definition, a one-way ride to ruin. Consider that Americans have more power, more friends and more material prestige than any other nation in history, with which to help shape the architecture of a new world order.

With these assets, what is the record of American leadership in the present crisis?

Each year the United States reduces its efforts to enlist men's allegiances by means of information services, by mutual enterprises of economic development, or by construction of a parliamentary apparatus for world decisions. The budget of the United States Senate Subcommittee on Review of the United Nations Charter, for example, was about one two-millionth of America's annual expenditures for war-connected purposes. And individual Americans devote just about an equally small proportion of their serious thought and effort to the achievement of a world law. The advocacy of a world government has acquired a "crackpot" tag in the popular mind. We hear of few proposals for establishing an Academy of Political Science for the nuclear age. No one starts a crash program for the ultimate breakthrough toward a world organization.

An America which we can picture placing its maximum emphasis on the short-term physical "security" of weapons and technology, while giving minimum attention to the long-term political security which can come only through organizing the allegiances of men to a world democratic law, is a vision to chill the heart of any thoughtful person.

Perhaps one of the most serious obstacles to world government in America's unconscious psychology is the vested interest which many elements within the United States have in a condition of world chaos.

The United States spends sixty billions of dollars a year upon armaments, military services, pensions and hospitalization, and other costs of past and future wars. Over three-fourths of the national budget goes to war expenses. The cost of arms unbalances the American budget. Everyone who owes money gains as the resulting inflation gradually cheapens the American dollar. All debtors have an intrenched interest in maintaining a war budget, as do all those into whose pockets flows some small part of the vast public expenditures for war costs. For many segments of the American economy, an outbreak of peace would be disastrous.

"To say that a concord with Russia now would solve all our problems is fantastically unrealistic. What would happen to our war economy? We just have to take a look at the budget— a very quick look—to see what proportion of our physical effort as a people is invested in maintaining this threat as it is," points out correspondent Harvey Frauenglass, Iowa City, Iowa, a member of the Special United Nations Subcommittee of the American Veterans Committee. "Because we are booming as it is, nobody, but nobody, wants to upset the whole business with a war. Would it be possible, in this confused state of affairs, to let Russia know we want her as a threat, but not as a shooting enemy? Does this sound too cynical?"

An outbreak of peace is the only possible way in which a serious threat of deflation could confront Americans. The proposal of a world government poses the peril of a world depression. As absurd as it seems to drag it out into the open, this may be a deep-seated psychological impediment to any earnest American peace effort. In the light of this consideration, we see the necessity to include in plans for world organization some definite commitment for the replacement of war spending by peace spending.

"Let's have some new, TOTAL thinking, please!" pleads Mr. Frauenglass. "For example, — how to phase out military spending, phase in things like Point Four on a *major scale* . . ."

A massive array of psychological allegiances bind Americans to a war-ready status quo. In addition to the vested interests of many Americans in war spending, we face the ingrained and inevitable resistance to change which is characteristic of any community of habituated creatures. But there exist opposing and equally valid emotional incentives which urge men to establish a stable peace. There are many Americans who are prepared to change an old way of life in those respects in which it is growing increasingly onerous and hazardous to them.

Every creditor is on the side of a balanced budget. Every wage earner, every bank depositor, every pensioner is against inflation. Practically everyone, without exception, wants lower taxes. Reduced taxes mean greater spending power and higher standards of living. Diminished armaments costs mean increased international investments. Putting the brakes on inflation will result in an enormous new flow of money for bonds, for savings and for pensions, of mortgage money for home construction and of commercial credit for industrial expansion. Funds spent in aiding the less fortunate populations of the world to raise their living standards will offer almost limitless means to build foreign markets and to sustain the domestic economy of the United States.

Obviously those arrayed for and against war spending, inflation and world chaos are not two separate factions of Americans. Most citizens of the United States have selfish interests on both sides of the fence. If Americans have the wit to adapt themselves to a changing environment and to survive into a new world society, the instinct of self-preservation will be an overriding factor in their decision. It will be a decision not entirely of a conflict between antagonistic groups, but in some degree of conflicts within each individual.

World stability will demand drastic readjustments of the American economy and of the American psychology; but if it should come, Americans may have confidence in their ability to master the problems which peace will bring.

The American Mission

Some years ago the writer of this book conducted a series of nationwide surveys of winter sports resorts in order to determine the effectiveness of safety-release ski bindings in reducing leg injuries. It quickly became apparent that skiers using release bindings, which permit the foot to come loose in a fall, suffered only one-half to one-quarter as many broken or sprained legs as skiers using non-release bindings. Despite these statistics, there appeared among skiers a predictable resistance to change. Some ski instructors, rescue patrolmen and ski racers opposed the introduction of a safety device as though they possessed a vested interest in danger. If skiing became safer, they seemed to feel, anyone could ski; and the glamor of their dangerous sport might pale. But new skiers had no such prejudices. After a few years most ski bindings on the American market became release types, and accident rates dropped markedly lower than previous levels.

Few people are such showoffs that they consciously delight in the danger of broken legs or of war. Nevertheless, hidden urges to invite danger lurk within the best of us. Basic pitfalls of the human character lie concealed within America's psychological commitment to the status quo and to a war-ready economy. We must not underestimate the very real self-destructive traits which Americans rationalize in their acceptance of inflation, in the blame which they place upon the Russians for a continuing state of world chaos, or in an "inside-dopester" belief in the inevitability of war.

Other psychological obstacles appear in the nature of the proposed remedy: that is, in certain of the practical consequences which people can foresee in the organization of international peace. It is disconcerting to find, for instance, some evidence of resistance to the idea of a popular chamber in the world legislature on the part of those citizens of the United States who fear that the United Nations may permit large numbers of colored races and of humble people in general to vote.

"A world government will be run, on the whole, by poor and colored people," comments John Holt. "If they ever get world government, they are going to use it to attack two things. One is race prejudice, in all its forms. The other is poverty—the maldistribution of the world's wealth. They are going to take the two-thirds of the world's wealth that is now enjoyed by five percent of the world's people, and spread that wealth around a bit more evenly.

"To say that these events will make changes in our way of life is putting it mildly. The average American, and even Federalist, who is deeply if unconsciously prejudiced against all colored people, as against all poor people, as against almost all

165

foreigners, takes a dim view of these changes. In fact, they scare the hell out of him.

"What he wants from the world are (1) all the raw materials he needs, and (2) peace and quiet. He wants to be left alone, and under world government he is not going to be. Therefore, he fears it."

At more rational levels of their psychology, American businessmen realize that the world needs enormous inputs of Yankee dollars, products and skills to raise its living standards. The pattern of foreign investment by private citizens of the United States will grow vigorously if there exist conditions of increasing stability which protect his return of profit. The American industrial colossus can function even better as the world's biggest banker, the economic heartland of humanity, under a new world system than under the old lack of system. Americans realize this intellectually. But it may be hard for them to accept emotionally the changes which are necessary.

"Their mission, the whole point and climax of their history, is to use their wealth, talent, energy and idealism to attack the world's poverty, ignorance and suffering, and to release the human potential in all mankind," Mr. Holt declares. "Let an American see that this is his country's and his job, what we are meant to do, and it will not be long before he sees the need of world government."

The Charter and the Constitution

"The basic principle of Federalism is so simple and so elementary that people don't realize that they have learned anything by just hearing the principles expounded," says Neil Parsons. "The *method* or the *process* is all important to Americans."

The public mind lacks a clear picture how much independence each citizen would actually give up in forming a world government. People fear the unfamiliar. Here understanding will point the way. An argument is half over when we decide what we are talking about.

"I hear many Federalists preaching about 'giving up' sovereignty to get world government," observes labor union official Byrl A. Whitney. "Do they believe that little Nevada is less

166

sovereign or more sovereign by having joined the federal union known as the United States of America?

"The only sovereignty worth preserving is the sovereign right of the individual which says that neither the sovereign state of Illinois nor the sovereign United States of America can take away my sovereign right to worship as I please, to speak as I please, to assemble as I please, to do all the precious things the Bill of Rights guarantees me as a sovereign individual."

An essential condition to acceptance of a strengthened United Nations in American public opinion will be the democratic nature of the proposed world institutions, in the opinion of a 71% majority of participants in CURE's forum.

"I would feel bound to resist to the utmost all proposals for the United States to delegate any real powers to the United Nations as the United Nations is today, and as long as the United Nations has fundamental structural defects incompatible with the American concept of sound government," declares Col. R. Frazier Potts.

The preamble to the United Nations Charter begins "We, the peoples of the United Nations . . ."; thereafter "the peoples" are mentioned only a half-dozen times in the Charter and only in descriptions of purposes of the world organization. The Charter leaves the method of selection of its delegates to the choice of each individual nation. Even in the Charter as it is at present, there is nothing to prevent any nation from electing by popular ballot its delegates to the General Assembly or even to the Security Council.

It is not the United Nations Charter, but the United States Constitution, which at present fails to make any provision for direct elections by American citizens of their representatives in the proposed Assembly of Peoples of the United Nations.

Article 2, Section 2, Paragraph 2 of the Constitution of the United States directs that the President ". . . by and with the consent of the Senate shall appoint ambassadors. . . and all other officers of the United States whose appointments are not herein otherwise provided for." The United States Member of the Security Council of the United Nations holds ambassadorial rank under this provision, and the delegates and alternate delegates of the United States to the General Assembly

167

of the United Nations receive their appointments in the same way.

"It has been argued therefore that election of United States delegates to the United Nations would require a constitutional amendment, a difficult and time-consuming process. However, this can be avoided by having the election results merely advisory and leaving the final choice to the President and Senate," points out John W. Schneider.

Mr. Schneider notes that "the party primaries in many states which are not binding on delegates to the national party conventions" offer a precedent for such advisory elections.

In advisory elections of United States delegates to the United Nations, Mr. Schneider observes, it might be objected that "the President could disregard the election and appoint someone else. Such defiance of the public will, however, would certainly arouse public hostility and would make it difficult for the President to get Senate approval for his nominee. Moreover," he adds, "even if confident of Senate approval and willing to disregard public opinion, he would probably be reluctant to nominate someone not elected, because of the resultant low prestige of the United States delegates to the United Nations and the great propaganda advantage to enemies of the United States."

For such reasons, a 73% majority of CURE conferees believe that "advisory" elections of United States delegates to the United Nations, if such a procedure is adopted, are likely to become real elections. Under the United States Constitution, the Electoral College chooses the President and the Vice-President; but the real choice is by the people at the polls. Similarly, in the election of United States representatives in the United Nations, the nominal appointment would be by the President and the Senate, but the real selection would be in the hands of the voters.

It is undoubtedly possible to elect United States delegates to the United Nations by such means without first amending the Constitution. But is it wise to do so?

Close votes in the United States Senate on various isolationist amendments of the Bricker type indicate, writes Stanley K. Platt, "that it may be politically wise to be careful to avoid any implication of acquisition of fundamental powers by the United Nations by other then constitutional processes."

A good many Federalists are in sympathy with the general objectives of the various amendments to the United States Constitution proposed by former Senator John W. Bricker of Ohio, which would place severe restrictions upon executive agreements and treaties in the conduct of America's foreign affairs. In the present state of world disorganization, agreements and treaties are not part of an enforceable law system, but are "extra-legal" or diplomatic in their nature. Federalists agree with isolationists that treaties and agreements are not a proper way to conduct international affairs.

These thoughts might well tempt the Machiavellian instincts of Federalists. Bricker-type amendments would, in effect, repeal those provisions of the United States Constitution which place the conduct of foreign affairs in the hands of the chief executive. They would render the United States government almost powerless to conduct international relations by usual diplomatic methods. As a result, Americans would necessarily depend even more upon the United Nations as a means of international decision than they do today. Under these circumstances, public opinion in the United States would increasingly demand the development of the United Nations into a competent world government.

The immediate predicament in which a Bricker amendment would place the United States government is too real and too perilous, however, for serious consideration. This is good reason for most Federalists to shun an irresponsible tactic such as the support of a Bricker amendment or the formation of a cynical alliance with isolationists. The United Nations is not yet ready to accept responsibility for American foreign policy.

A better way to begin this change is to build the new world structure before demolishing the old. If, for purposes of proper procedure, an amendment to the United States Constitution seems desirable, it should be one which aims to strengthen the United Nations by providing for the election of American delegates in a world Assembly of Peoples, rather than one which weakens the United States by tying the President's hands in his conduct of foreign relations.

Americans cannot evade the struggle for a democratic world law. Uncle Sam is in the position of a mountain climber who, having reached the point of no return, has nowhere to go except to the top. He cannot back down. If he tries to stay where he is, he may well end in death by exposure. Although it is possible that his friends can offer him a helpful hand, in the main he must rely upon his own efforts. He has no way to enjoy the fruits of his great accomplishments other than to make an even greater effort for future achievement.

Yankee Initiative

"It is being recognized by farsighted Americans that the United States is becoming ever more dependent on the United Nations rather than the other way round," notes British barrister James Avery Joyce.

A recent poll showed that 85% of United States citizens rely upon the United Nations to control the explosive elements in the Near East powder keg, just as one instance of Mr. Joyce's theme.

The indebtedness is mutual. In the past, the democratic institutions of the United States have inspired the liberalization of the British constitutional structure, as they sparked the French Revolution and provided impetus for all the other peoples' governments which have since sprung up in Europe and elsewhere in the world; and now the latest and potentially the greatest descendant of the United States Constitution is the Charter of the United Nations.

Americans often underestimate their principal political asset, which is their own experience in self-government. History and logic both prove that it is an exportable asset. This does not mean that Americans can impose upon others the forms of their own political institutions; it does mean that people will listen today when Americans advocate what they feel is best.

"Americans need not hesitate to urge upon a prospective world federation the basic principles of their own experience of democracy, and even the most useful features of their own political institutions; which have, of course, a valuable contribution to make to world democracy," advises Mr. Joyce.

Citizens of the United States have a great stake in achieving the right kind of world government.

"If Americans fail to do this, the United States itself will be the greater loser, for world government *is* coming," Mr. Joyce admonishes.

In many of its features, the Constitution of the United States gave expression to principles invented by earlier scholars of the science of government. In other respects, American history has added a vast store to the practical experience of men in the conduct of government under democratic institutions. In some particulars, America's Constitution introduced new concepts. One American contribution to the principles of government was the bicameral legislature with one house representing populations and the other representing component states. Another novelty contained in the United States Constitution was its provision for orderly amendment. On an international level, the usefulness of a bicameral world parliament and of a veto-free amendment procedure will be too obvious to need any apology. Both these provisions seem wise to urge upon the framers of a new United Nations Charter. In such matters the United States may hope for the support of a world majority.

Economic Co-Existence

The United States has a valid right to seek adoption of its own best institutions in the design of a world government. An equally fair-minded attitude toward institutions favored with some logic by other peoples will help to gain acceptance for a world constitution containing provisions which Americans think essential.

"Every nation has something to contribute to the world order," remarks Mrs. Kenneth G. Carpenter, West Hartford, Connecticut; "we should meet others as our peers, not as underlings."

One of the most urgent instances of the need for international conciliation lies in the general field of economics. In ecnomic matters, too, America has taken many pioneer steps, not only in such areas as its techniques of production and methods of management, but in such legal concepts as the anti-trust laws, unique to the United States, which help to limit the excessive concentration of monopolies and cartels. Citizens of the United States have a justifiable pride in the achievements of their economy. In economic matters, as in politics, Americans cannot impose their practices upon other peoples; but they have a great deal to contribute.

The attitudes of Americans toward the economic practices of other nations are strongly tinged with the prejudices of

171

wealth. Anything suggesting socialism excites suspicion in the land of the Yankee dollar. But Americans would perhaps be more able to tolerate socialism in others if they were better acquainted with their own history. During the early nineteenth century, America was the world's principal testing ground for primitive Communistic experiments, ranging from New Harmony in Indiana where Robert Owen anticipated by a generation the teachings of Karl Marx, to the multiple-marriage colony at Oneida, New York, whose descendants make Community Plate silverware.

The logic of having a nationally operated postal service is evident to most modern Americans. In the United States, as in other countries, other inherently monopolistic industries such as railroads, utilities and communications are no longer truly "free" enterprise. Non-competitive capitalism is commonly tamed by government supervision in the public interest. The difference is of degree. Many European states have socialized their power, railways and telephones, and sometimes other enterprises such as tobacco shops or the steel industry where the logic of public ownership is less convincing. Sweden and other Scandinavian countries prefer the "Middle Way" of partial socialism which combines extensive public ownership with consumer co-operatives. At the other extreme from capitalist nations stand the Communist nations which permit private ownership only on a self-employing basis in family shops.

It is a reasonable view that throughout the world future economies will not be exclusively socialist or solely capitalist. The world trend is toward mixed economies, modified by government controls where they are needed. A mixed, flexible economy has many advantages over a single economy, whether a raw capitalism or a regimented form of socialism.

"Because I believe our mixed system of private ownership, co-operative ownership, regulated private ownership and public ownership is best," states Glenn P. Turner, "I will take a chance on competition with Communism."

Where backward nations have little private capital of their own, world security can help international private enterprise to provide capital for development. Totalitarianism seems necessary as a discipline for the formation of state capital only when better ways are unavailable. The best missionaries for capitalism are dollars. Capitalists of the Atlantic world are ready enough to perceive this logic once the political conditions are favorable.

A difference in economic structures or a disparity between forms of government of various nations is not an argument against international government. On the contrary, one of the best reasons for having a world government is the need to reconcile the varying philosophies of government and of economy among its member nations.

Learning to Live With the World

Attitudes depend upon circumstances.

"Persons once uncongenial as members of competing groups find themselves in accord when an act of union makes them members of the same fellowship," notes Dr. Vernon Nash. "Radical changes in attitude can come suddenly. There was general indifference toward a weak Russia before the Second World War, then prevalent good will toward 'valiant comrades in arms,' followed by growing hate and fear as the USSR emerged from the war as a powerful and expanding empire. Communism was the same vicious perversion throughout; attitudes towards proponents of it shifted as relations between them changed."

In the United States, race relations are a laboratory of changing attitudes. Within recent years, as one example, Americans of Japanese descent have taught Americans of European descent some useful lessons in respect for one's fellow man. During the Second World War, Japanese-Americans of the 100th Infantry Battalion and the 442d Infantry Regiment were the most decorated men of all United States troops in Italy. These Nisei outfits had more than 9,000 battle casualties. Their only AWOLs were six men missing from a hospital who had returned without permission to the front line. Americans of European descent might well envy the Nisei record of devotion to duty in the battle for freedom.

During World War II, in an investigation of interracial morale, the Department of Information and Education of the United States Army took a poll of white officers and noncommissioned officers assigned to command of Negro troops. Most of the white officers admitted that at first they had disliked their assignment. Three out of four, however, reported that

173

during their tour of duty their respect for the Negro had risen. In the end, white officers and noncoms almost unanimously agreed that their Negro soldiers performed "very well" in combat and were "just as good" as white soldiers.

The result of the Army's experience in wartime led to the racial integration of United States armed forces during the postwar period. And inevitably the experience of integration in military service is eroding the barriers of ignorance and fear which long delayed an equality of status for Negro citizens in American civilian life.

Thomas Jefferson believed that knowledge is the greatest of forces for good. "Above all things," he wrote in a letter to James Madison, "I hope the education of the common people will be attended to; convinced that on their good sense we may rely with the most security for the preservation of a due degree of liberty." And Jefferson did not limit learning to books, for he said that forty years of experience in self-government was worth a century of reading.

Within the last forty years, since the end of World War I, education has changed American life almost as much as in the first forty years of the nation. The advancements of science have far outrun the growth of political understanding, which is an older and more difficult wisdom; but other arts have progressed too. It is less than a century since Theodore Thomas tried to interest American audiences in a Beethoven symphony. Today there are seven thousand symphony orchestras in high schools of the United States.

"The general spread of music and song establishes the general atmosphere of peace in the people," said Confucius, the wise old Chinese teacher, long ago. "When the violent elements of a nation are kept quiet, the different rulers come to pay homage, the military weapons are locked up, the five criminal laws are not brought into use, the people have no worries and the Emperor has no anger, then truly music has prevailed."

Political skill, like music or philosophy, consists of resolving discords into a harmony which is not static, but which lives and moves. The wisdom by which Americans can adapt their attitudes to the rhythms of the coming epoch is elementary: it is to know that the best thing about the American way of life—the dignity of the individual—is, in fact, the common heritage of all mankind.

THE CONCLUSION

Chapter 11.

The Search for Solutions

Since the day of Hiroshima the human race has stood under a sentence of death. The odds are against survival. Let no one doubt that an ungoverned world can breed terror, and then tyranny, and finally a flaming hell to engulf our lives.

The future has burst upon man with bewildering abruptness. He must adapt himself, or perish. The average man senses that survival is out of his hands. Individuals feel powerless. Most of us watch with fascinated horror as events drift out of control.

The human race, despite its many achievements, is still in many respects close to savagery.

"Millions of people who think they are civilized still have in common with the primitives that they would rather ascribe the evils that beset them to specters of their own making than find out rationally what should be done and do it," comments Alfredo Rodrigues Brent.

It is unfair to compare the human being with the ostrich, world federalist Brock Chisholm has said. The comparison is unfair to the ostrich, who does not hide his head in the sands: only man is so foolish.

Measured in the scale of the challenge, man's efforts to extricate himself from catastrophe seem puny indeed. You may find it depressing to read the history of world federalism, something like watching stranded insects struggle for life on the shore of a relentless sea; or, perhaps, you may find in these humble and yet indomitable efforts of your fellow man some glimmers of hope for a world order.

"For our own federal union to become stable, it was necessary not only to have a Constitution and a Congress, but also for the great mass of Virginians and New Yorkers to come to think of themselves as Americans first," says Everett Refior, Whitewater, Wisconsin, Assistant Professor of Economics at Wisconsin State College. "Gradually, as more confidence in the national government developed, it was entrusted with more and more functions. World government and world loyalty must develop side by side in the same way."

The efforts of Federalists to awaken the conscience of their fellow citizens have taken many forms. Among them are campaigns aiming to condition people for their opportunities and responsibilities in a new world. One program seeking to develop world consciousness is the symbolic registration of individuals as "world citizens," initiated after the liberation of Europe by former leaders of the anti-Nazi underground Resistance.

"The first primitive man who looked up at the stars felt a kinship with the universe about him that stretched far beyond his family and his tribe," reflects CUREspondent Mary Hays Weik. "Two thousand years ago, Socrates wrote, 'say not I am a citizen of Athens, but say I am a citizen of the world!' And down through history, every truly great nationalist leader — Mazzini, Tom Paine, Gandhi, Sun Yat Sen — has urged his people to remember also their responsibility to mankind.

"The concept of world citizenship — of being a part of the whole world as well as of one's own city or town or nation — was as old as man himself. The idea of registration, by a symbolic 'passport' common to citizens of every land, was a new and striking one."

The program has reached into many nations. "More than 300,000 citizens of 78 countries were registered as World Citizens," Mrs. Weik reports.

A program of this nature does not seek to take legal steps toward world order. "While nationality is still determined by the happenstances of national legislation, so that some people may have triple nationality while others are stateless, world citizenship is merely a phrase," points out Frank E. G. Weil. The concept of world citizenship, he adds, is not legal but psychological in its value.

Such values are quite real, other contributors note.

"If this is one world and we are working for law, order, justice and freedom in this world community, then logically we are interested in world citizenship," affirms the Reverend M. Everett Dorr, Des Moines, Iowa, Minister of Trinity Methodist Church. "I do believe that I am a citizen of the world."

A 79% majority of CURE's consultants are of the opinion that world citizenship is a concept of value to the world federalist movement.

If individual citizens can promote the "one world" idea by means of symbolic citizenships, so, too, can communities adopt a symbolic world status.

"It was this same elemental need felt by men and women who had learned by bitter experience the helplessness of nations to protect their citizens in time of world-wide catastrophe that led to the postwar movement in Europe for mundialization," continues Mrs. Weik. "Begun in 1949 in France — where recently the 178th village in one southern province alone, Gard, was mundialized—this citizen movement has extended to more than 400 communities in France, Germany, Belgium, Holland, Italy, Denmark, India, Australia and the United States. By overwhelming vote of their inhabitants, these towns and villages have declared their welfare indivisible from that of all the world's citizens."

In other instances town councils have taken the initiative by declaring their communities "world territory whose security is bound up with that of all the world's communities". Action by town councils has given Japan 47 mundialized communities, totalling ten million inhabitants, and including such large cities as Hiroshima, Okayama, Amagasaki and Kyoto, in addition to the mundalized prefectures of Okayama, Toyama and Nagano.

"The mundialized community may provide the basic unit of a world society," speculates René Wadlow, Far Hills, New Jersey, past Chairman of the Young Adult Council of the National Social Welfare Assembly, who notes that it is "more compact and rooted in a culture than the individual, but not as large and centralized as the Leviathan."

A two-thirds majority of CURE correspondents believe that the mundialization of communities is a program of value to the Federalist purpose.

A Peoples' Constitutional Convention

Other Federalists see little need to prove a necessity for world order which is already so overwhelmingly obvious. Instead, they aim their efforts at the legal solutions which will make its accomplishment possible.

Some of them advocate research into the practicable features of a world constitution. A panel of experts at the University of Chicago have made the most elaborate proposals in this direction. CURE conferees Grenville Clark and Louis B. Sohn have prepared a far simpler plan to modify the United Nations Charter into a rudimentary world constitution. On the whole, however, the human community has seemed almost pathologically shy of entering into constitutional explorations. In nearly every small town someone tinkers with home-made rockets; but seldom is heard, even in great nations, the awesome swoosh of trial drafts for a world law.

One of the first ideas which occurred to Federalists was to combine the political and legal approaches to the construction of a world law.

"In a democratic government, and even to some extent in a totalitarian government, people will find a way to get done what they want done, no matter what constitutional guarantees may stand, or attempt to stand, in their way," declares John Holt.

History tells us how quickly the American nation became aware that the Articles of Confederation and the Continental Congress were inadequate to govern its affairs. The schooling of American colonists in this matter was brief and effective. Within a few years they replaced their first imperfect government with a Constitution whose creation seems almost miraculous to the eyes of posterity.

Similarly, from the first sessions of the League of Nations in 1920 its flaws were evident. Critics of the League soon suggested calling a world constitutional convention to draft a more efficient document than the loosely worded Covenant of the League. If the governments of the nations failed to take the necessary steps, suggested Federalists Rosika Schwimmer and Lola Maverick Lloyd in 1924, the peoples of the nations might themselves convene a world constitutional conference, using so far as possible such official means as the electoral machinery of states and nations to select the persons who would be its delegates.

"The necessary world institutions will be acceptable only if they have a democratic basis," declares Jacques Savary. "We think that such an integration could not be made without recourse to the people in whom sovereignty resides, and who alone are qualified to create new institutions on the world level. How, indeed, could a world community develop, how could it survive, if it were not based on some factor common to all the nations and independent of them, some common element which transcended their particularities? This common factor is the human being, the citizen."

"According to many of the proposals for United Nations amendment, the changes needed to transform the United Nations into a *democratic* world government are of such a thoroughgoing nature as to require the drafting of an entirely new Charter. If this is so, then to speak of United Nations amendment obscures the true nature of the job: what is required is a world constitutional convention, disregarding the present United Nations Charter altogether," maintains Philip Isely. "This is not just a question of theoretical principle. Practical results are at stake. In this field of human endeavor as elsewhere, the general principle of ends and means also applies: i.e., the means used will condition and largely determine the end product. In this light, it might be well for advocates of United Nations reform to re-analyze that approach. Practically speaking, is it reasonable to expect our present national governments (which are encumbered with domineering military programs and innumerable other considerations of vested national interests) to create a world government designed to operate as the direct agency of the world's people—rather than as a vehicle for the chicanery of foreign office diplomats?"

Jacques Savary does not believe so. "We are therefore relying, on one hand, on the great scientists and thinkers, who are able to think and act as members of the world community," he explains, "and then upon the 'man in the street', whose human instinct and desire for peace lead him naturally and inevitably to recognize the validity of our aim: the recognition of the right of people to self-government and to participa-

179

tion, through their elected representatives, in the management of world affairs."

In theory, the construction of an international government by popular action could take place entirely outside existing institutions. Some enthusiasts for popular initiative visualize the growth of a peoples' government by way of unofficial "voluntary" elections. Others find such a self-appointed electorate unrealistic. Even in the process of founding a world government it is a question whether the people could carry the ball on their own without the use of governmental channels. It is doubtful that anything the people really want would fail to influence their leaders.

Proposals for a self-contained constitutional crusade win little support among conferees. Such plans "betray political naiveté," thinks John H. Davenport: "more promising results might be gotten by enlisting the co-operation of existing civic, church, farm, labor, business, professional, veterans' and other interest groups in securing popular response or state legislation."

CURE writers point out that delegates to the Constitutional Convention of 1787 in the United States were *not* elected by citizens of their states.

Delegates to the Constitutional Convention were elected by their state legislative bodies, "as is clear from the texts of their credentials printed in *Documents on the Founding of the Union*," Edith Wynner writes. "But many of them doubtless were part of the inter-state lobby for a stronger union and had lobbied themselves into this appointment. Many of the most active members of the Convention had prominent roles in the break away from Britain, held important posts in their states and probably were delegates to the Continental Congress at some time."

It seems unlikely that there will be any hard-and-fast distinction between popular action and governmental action toward a more stable world order. Officials are not likely to act without popular pressure; but in the event that Russian vetoes or other obstacles block revision of the United Nations Charter, the world's peoples may well take a direct hand in the creation of a new world legality through other means.

Federal Union among Democracies

One possible way to create an international union is to form a federation of a pioneer group of governments. This type of proposal grows naturally out of a desire to strengthen defensive military alliances.

In the 1930's as the League of Nations tottered during the invasions of China and of Ethiopia, during civil war in Spain and the conquest of Poland, the free nations increasingly felt a concern for their own safety. Talk of a federal union of democracies became a matter for serious discussion.

On the eve of French defeat in 1940, Prime Minister Winston Churchill dramatically offered to form a constitutional federation between Britain and France as a basis for carrying on the fight. But it was too late; no government remained in France able to accept his invitation.

The proposals for a nuclear Atlantic Union or for a Federal Union of the Free can claim the support of a substantial minority of American public opinion. Public opinion polls show that some eight million American citizens think a federation of democracies is a desirable step toward greater security. A resolution in the United States Congress backed by 157 members of the House of Representatives and a similar proportion of the Senate proposes that the democratic nations hold an exploratory conference on the subject of a federal union. There is substantial backing for the proposal in Great Britain, but its support, like that of NATO, the North Atlantic Treaty Organization, appears to dwindle as we move farther east toward its proposed European frontiers with Russia.

Proponents led by Clarence Streit cite the fact that democratic nations which might contemplate a limited federation, though they include only a minority of the earth's populations, possess some 80% of the world's industrial production. With this in mind, 87% of participants in the Conference Upon Research and Education in world government agree that the democracies would gain in a Federal Union of the Free, which would pool their power and resources, a greater security than they have at present.

"There is an obligation to stop the disintegration of the non-Soviet world by (1) integrating the Atlantic nations which are of sufficient homogeneity to federate, and (2) creating a unified common policy towards the non-Soviet areas of Asia, Africa, etc.," believes political scientist Elliott R. Goodman. "Only this holds any chance of frustrating Soviet ambitions. With considerable time, Soviet attitudes might mellow so that a common world government could emerge."

A federal union of free peoples "represents the only sure means by which the nations included may attain a period of peace, and make their maximum contribution to the world-wide development of mankind," agrees Evadne M. Laptad, Lawrence, Kansas, a Red Cross worker overseas in two world wars.

"Almost any imaginable federation of democracies would be a great step forward toward true world government; through force of example, and by virtue of providing a concrete case for observation in the world of today; whereas Federalists now must argue from premises of historical precedent and theoretical speculation," asserts R. Frazier Potts. "Federation is a political proposal, and politics is the art of the possible. Therefore that particular federation which is most susceptible of early realization is the one on which Federalists should concentrate the weight of their efforts."

Some proponents would limit membership in a Federal Union of the Free to those nations which possess a well-established history of democratic practice.

"We value the free way of life even more than peace," writes Justin Blackwelder, Washington, D. C., Executive Secretary of the Atlantic Union Committee. "This means we cannot accept a world government that is not soundly democratic in nature. A start should be made now with those people who are willing and who, by virtue of their own democratic institutions, have gained enough experience in democratic government to stand a reasonable chance of success. We do not, however, see anything to be gained by attempting to form a democratic federation among people who have neither the education nor experience to make a success of such a government."

Contributors to CURE's forum who hold this point of view express fear that universal membership in a world federation would be unworkable. Under a constitution including all nations, prophesies Col. C. A. Edson, "demagogues from the majority groups would soon seize control of the government."

This school of thought views a democratic federation as an initial nucleus, designed to progress toward fuller membership. "It would be much sounder to start with a geographically limited 'high quality' government, in confidence its quality would surely attract quantity growth," Col. Edson suggests.

"The Soviets have been quick to form and steadily enlarge their union," argues A. W. Schmidt, Pittsburgh, Pennsylvania. "Why should not the democratic nations of Western civilization do likewise while there is time?"

"To Americans living in, say, Illinois today, it is not a matter of any importance whether or not their state was among the original thirteen," says Justin Blackwelder. "We all now live under the same general set of rules. What is of the utmost importance, however, is that if thirteen had not formed a federation on a sound democratic basis, the United States would never have come into being."

A federation on a democratic basis makes a good deal of sense to members of CURE's conference. Few, however, would limit membership in a federal union to a select group of nations. Only 44% of conferees see a union of Atlantic powers—a federation of NATO countries—as an asset to world stability. 72% of Conferees feel that a federal union of free peoples should be open to all nations wishing to join. And a thumping 92% deny that universal membership in a world government would necessarily result in a seizure of power by Communists.

An invitational federal union will not serve a useful purpose, in the view of Vernon Nash, "if any who wish to join are excluded."

Any scheme for Atlantic Union or a federation of democracies will involve the complication of colonial possessions.

"Will Britain and France grant equal political representation to all individuals, whether white or black, in their African territories?" inquires William Bross Lloyd.

In the eyes of Asia, for example, an Atlantic Union "would only appear to be a union of super-imperialists," observes Dr. Elliott R. Goodman, "if it did not provide for self-government for the colonial areas."

The sponsors of the Atlantic Union proposal have made an effort to deal with this difficulty. "Federalization of the possessions, on the analogy of the United States Northwest Territory, is an important part of Streit's 'Union Now' plan," explains Col. R. Frazier Potts. But there would be an obvious inconsistency in "federalizing" the widespread colonial possessions of democracies in an allegedly regional union. And it would be equally illogical to accept former colonies as full members if a world-wide Federal Union of the Free excludes other nations which lack democratic experience.

And there are other difficulties. Even if a democratic federation is open to all nations, the idea has dangers. The whole thesis of partial federation comes under skeptical fire from many CURE debaters.

A union begun by the more mature political democracies "would be under suspicion throughout Asia, Africa and South America," objects Dr. Stringfellow Barr.

George Hardin, Philadelphia, Pennsylvania, Secretary of the Friends Peace Committee, fears that a Federal Union of the Free would be "a security pact rather than a peace plan, and not a federation based on law and order."

Such a partial union "would further crystallize our bi-polarized world," warns Rev. Ralph Fleming, Jr., Newport, North Carolina, Methodist minister and former National Student Chairman of United World Federalists.

" 'Atlantic Union' or a 'union of free peoples' would tend to perpetuate the East-West division and intensify the arms race," agrees Grenville Clark, "whereas what is required is the opposite."

"The very heart and core of Atlantic Union is the proposition that America is the spiritual leader of the Western world, and that the Western world is the spiritual leader of the world as a whole," John Holt observes, stating that in his opinion this may have once been true, but is no longer true now. "There is only one condition under which European nations would consider forming a federal union with us, and that is, not that they might make our leadership more effective, but that they might more effectively overcome it," he argues. In a wider view of world affairs, he continues, "much of the non-Communist world is now in revolt against the domination, political and economic, of the West." The effect on the neutral nations would be unfortunate, he adds, if the West were "to form a 'Rich White Men's Club', and to tell the two billion outsiders that they can come in when we think they are ready."

Partial federation of an anti-Russian character could win little allegiance from India or other neutralist nations, other debaters point out.

A partial union "is not a big enough solution to the problem posed," in the belief of David I. Gilchrist, New York, N. Y., former Executive Director of Connecticut State Branch of United World Federalists; "it does not measure up to the size of the challenge. I hardly think that sufficient impetus for by-passing the United Nations can be mobilized among those who by and large have to be counted in as movers until it has been demonstrated that it cannot be done within the United Nations."

"An alternative federal union is only proper when all hope of giving the United Nations law enforcing powers has been lost," declares George C. Holt, Hartford, Connecticut, newspaper columnist and Executive Vice-President of United World Federalists.

"The USSR may block Charter revision, and leave us— where?" counters Colonel Potts. The "obvious precaution," he says, is "foresight and intelligent preparation."

A preponderant 70% among CURE conferees hold that, lacking actual proof to the contrary, it is reasonable to hope for substantial improvements in the United Nations Charter. The possibility that the West might otherwise move independently toward a nuclear federation may help to soften Russian objections against Charter revision, many CURE observers think. Russian vetoes of Charter improvement might well spur the development of an Atlantic Union; and if negotiations within the United Nations prove impossible, 77% of Conference participants agree, proposals for a federation of democracies will be a useful resource to the free world.

The Charter Revision Approach

Since the end of World War II, the largest number of Federalists have hoped to build world law and order on the foundation of the United Nations. One very simple reason is that it exists. Another equally good reason in the minds of Federalists of this persuasion is that the United Nations begins on a principle of inviting the universal membership of all nations which are devoted to peace. Among Federalist aims, this concept claims the largest proportion of public adherence; polls show that some eleven million Americans favor this approach. Such powerful agencies as the American Bar Association are enlisted in its support.

Organizations actively urging a stronger United Nations in many countries include United World Federalists, the largest group of world government advocates in the United States. These organizations promote their goals by membership drives, discussion meetings and the distribution of literature and films, and by the influence which their members, as substantial citizens of the community, are able to exert upon leaders in political, civil and intellectual fields. Arguments by the advocates of world peace under law have helped to establish American policies in favor of United Nations Charter review, of a permanent United Nations police force and of peaceful uses for atomic energy and space travel. The underlying currents of human sentiment run much closer to this Federalist channel of thought than to the opposite shore of isolationism.

Yet, paradoxically, the most stubborn resistances, too, are those to the direct and simple thesis of giving the United Nations effective powers of peacekeeping and disarmament. These are, in truth, earth-shaking powers—the powers necessary to govern a world.

Citizens of free countries are not inclined to accept a government at a world level which is defective in democratic practices; Soviet leaders are still less willing to grant decisive powers to the majority decisions of an international tribunal in which the Iron Curtain countries are outnumbered. In many ways, 84% of Conference debaters believe, disarmament under the present United Nations would invade the vested interests of various world "veto groups". Universality of membership is necessary to a world government, but it is scarcely a sufficient condition in itself for a world government to exist.

This dilemma brought the Conference Upon Research and Education in world government into being. It seemed to the writer of this book that a desirable Federalist concept might combine the democratic principle in international government with the principle of universal membership. Twenty-one

186

members of United World Federalists joined the writer to invite new discussions with members of the Atlantic Union Committee and of Peoples' World Convention organizations, and other Federalists of every description as well as uncommitted scholars of world affairs in the United States and overseas. The Conference sought to compare doctrines, to eliminate the weakest and to combine the strongest features from each of the Federalist proposals.

There is nothing easy about the democratic approach to a universal world law. 61% of participants in CURE's forum think that various world "veto groups" will oppose the creation of an Assembly of Peoples in the United Nations as vehemently as they resist disarmament under the present United Nations. There will be differences, of course, in the identity and strength of such groups in each case. But there is no painless way. If this is the path of least resistance, it is still a rocky route.

"Our opponents are not stupid; they will recognize any approach to world government for what it is," acknowledges Dale Hiller. "Creation of an 'Assembly of Peoples' would be 'dangerous' because, whatever its specified functions or lack thereof, it would almost certainly grow in power and influence."

No Federalist wants a "super-government". A majority of participants in CURE's debates doubt that a revision of the United Nations Charter will immediately produce even national disarmament or a United Nations power to enforce world peace. Few foresee a sudden leap to a true world government in the sense of world federal supremacy. But most conferees feel that an approach which combines democracy with universality can set great events in motion. Communicants of CURE, by an 88% margin, expect that the proposals derived from their discussions, if adopted as United Nations Charter amendments, will facilitate other and later revisions.

Putting the People In the UN

Evanston Federalists sent out eighty invitations to their party. Eight hundred guests came. Evanstonians were delighted, for their "party" was a Model United Nations Assembly. Sir Leslie Munro, President of the General Assembly of the United Nations, came from New York to open Evanston's "Inside UN" at the local high school. Five sessions of energetic committee work, politicking and "resoluting" followed.

The Evanston, Illinois, Chapter of United World Federalists had asked various organizations along Chicago's North Shore to provide delegations representing the countries of the United Nations in the model assembly. The "Argentine" group were a local Lions' Club. The "British" were the Junior Chamber of Commerce. A North End Mothers' Circle spoke for Thailand, and a world politics class came as Russian delegates. Serious issues got serious attention. Chicago metropolitan newspapers carried half-page stories about the model United Nations in the sedate suburb. Evanston's model assembly advised Illinois Congressmen and Senators of its votes for a permanent United Nations police force, for admission of Red China upon her acceptance of disarmament legislation, and for United Nations administration of economic aid programs.

"This is not a 'mock' assembly; it purposes to be a 'model' assembly, in the sense that people were not there 'just to role-play', but accepted an assignment in the study of world government and attempted to present the views of another country, but not pretending that they were really people of India, etc., in a personal way; not 'acting', in the real meaning of the word (trying to get inside another person's skin) but simply to study the issues, to understand something of the problems of a certain country, in its geographic location, its economics at the moment, its historical attitudes and their shifts, and to present these without the emotional attitudes attached to 'role-playing'," explains Peggy Culler, San Francisco, California, past Chairman of the Evanston Chapter of United World Federalists and sponsor of its "Inside UN" program. "There is a difference here not of degree but of attitude. So Russians did not arrive complete with guttural accents or tirades, at all, but were quiet-type people trying (and succeeding in their aim) to tell only the 'facts'—what the Russians have said and are saying on disarmament — simply and clearly, much more so than the Russians do in the real United Nations."

The headquarters organizations of United World Federalists

and of Rotary International have prepared handbooks to aid other communities in conducting similar programs.

If we assume that a first objective of world federalists is the effort to improve the United Nations as a world parliament, the use of model United Nations assemblies is "rich in potential efficacy," believes Jacques Savary.

Model assemblies attract the participation of citizens and of organizations which are in no way visionary. Everyone can see their relation to reality. At the same time, they offer a promising avenue toward reform of the world political structure.

Consider, for a few moments of fancy, what the popular approach could become through such means as the model assembly. We may imagine an international organization of Model United Nations Peoples' Assembly Councils ("MUN-PAX", for world peace) to conduct these assemblies on a world scale.

In CURE's study of a possible large-scale program, three-fourths of conferees recommend that model assemblies could logically consider themselves to represent peoples' delegates rather than governments, and could use a formula of representation based on populations instead of the one-nation-one-vote plan of the United Nations General Assembly.

By these and other means, a program of this nature need not limit its aims to political education, but may dedicate itself to aid in the creation of an actual Assembly of Peoples in the United Nations.

The organizers of the projected "MUNPAX" councils, as a further step, may make provisional assignments of worldwide electoral districts for a world model assembly. Each district may then become the basic unit for a local assembly. To take an example, the "Eighth United States District" might comprise California. Each Electoral District, in addition to holding its own model assembly, may conduct annually the election of a delegate to a world assembly. Elections may take place initially by ballots circulated among members of participating organizations, printed as ads in newspapers, or distributed by various other informal means. Later, as the project gathers momentum, it will seek election of its delegates through the official machinery of balloting in cities, states and nations.

Initially, to fill the seats of missing nations, the world Peoples' Assembly may nominate volunteer advocates. A possible basis for their choice might be a competition to rate the most effective volunteer delegations at district model assemblies. With growing success, the world Peoples' Assembly will include an increasing number of delegates more or less officially elected in the districts which they represent.

"MUNPAX" planners will coax Russians to come, just as Russians urge visitors to attend youth festivals in Moscow. This will, to be sure, put Russia's rulers on the spot. Why not? This is the precise spot on which free peoples wish to place tyrants. With the participation of Russians in a world Peoples' Assembly program, the appearance of understanding will begin to take on reality, just as world government is the reality of peace.

The broader the constituency of each MUNPAX world congress becomes, the greater will grow its example and its influence as a voice of world opinion. The business of a world Peoples' Assembly will be the world's business: a crisis, a colonial problem, an economic need, control of armaments—yes, and the study of United Nations Charter revisions.

Popular participation in such activities offers a means to build and concentrate public demand for United Nations reform. A world Assembly of Peoples may spur national governments to convene the pending United Nations conference for the review of the Charter. Its leaders may request the Secretary General of the United Nations to certify the world Peoples' Assembly as an accredited advisory body to the United Nations, and in this way make it an official, if informal, part of the world parliament.

A world Model United Nations Peoples' Assembly can only recommend. But it can recommend with the most sovereign of voices, the voice of its voters. A voluntary Peoples' Assembly will hasten the emergence of a legal Assembly of Peoples in the United Nations. And an elected Assembly of Peoples in the United Nations will speed the growth of its power as an international government.

In this illustration we see how a seemingly uncontroversial activity can develop massive momentum within wisely chosen channels.

There are, of course, many other means by which men can hasten the evolution of a true world parliament. Proponents of United Nations reform have made relatively little use of free men's basic rights to assemble, debate and petition. Nor have Federalists made use of such a simple educational means as colored cartoon leaflets—a form of communication favored by 71% of the Conference—to tell the Federalist story in simple terms of everyday life. And other forms of persuasion which Federalists have used well in the past can be even more effective in support of an approach against which people have fewer reservations.

This chapter is not a chronicle of accomplishment. It is an account of some progress, and of much hope. At bottom, it is a confession that men of peace have their task yet before them. Resources which are available to Federalists can effectively promote the attainment of their goal. The possibilities of peace are limited only by men's will to attain it.

191

Chapter 12.

Govern unto Others . . .

Out of 100,000,000 Americans of voting age, a sample poll reveals that some 73% support the United Nations. About 35%, or 35,000,000 individuals, desire the United Nations sufficiently strengthened to enforce peace. By contrast, only 9% take an isolationist stand against all international organizations of any type, and a mere 7% have the defeatist attitude that war is inevitable.

But here is a curious paradox. The 35% who desire more world organization outnumber by nearly four-to-one the 9% of isolationists who desire less. Why, then, are the many who desire progress apparently helpless to advance against the few who oppose it? Why is there no motion, no evolution, no adaptive growth of the world political organism? What is holding up a Conference for the review of the United Nations Charter?

We may find it enlightening to examine this paradox in terms of the sociological theory of "veto groups", which explains how a minority in a democratic society can successfully defend a status quo in which it has a vested interest and a strongly felt commitment, while a majority can achieve changes only if it has an overriding emotional motivation for action.

The many persons who favor a stronger United Nations have yet to win the position which they one day hope to occupy. Their commitment is to something relatively vague: a hope, an ideal, scarcely a plan. War fears about which peacelovers can seem to do nothing, we have heard psychologists explain, have a paralyzing effect upon their will. We can readily see that what the psychologists call a paralysis of the will is approximately the same thing that sociologists identify as a lack of motivation. As long as they lack a program and a purpose, the "pros" appear to hold only lightly their conviction in favor of world law. Lacking push, they fail to move.

No such doubt or reluctance inhibits isolationists. The status quo is in their possession. In the terms of sociology, the "antis" hold their conviction in depth, so that everyone knows what they think and most people imagine them to be far more numerous than they actually are. Isolationists are a classic illustration of a "veto group" in operation.

These sociological reflections help to explain why the endorsements of politicians and other high-level personages for a proposition such as a governed world or for a federal union of free peoples are easy to obtain but relatively meaningless. The endorsement pleases large numbers of people who possess lightly held "pro" convictions, while the small number of deeply felt "antis", realizing that they are a minority, express little resentment against what any personage says as long as he doesn't try to do anything about it. In such cases the words do not lead to action: they are a substitute for action.

On the world level a similar situation exists. The Russians, as a world minority, comprise less than one-tenth of the world's peoples. And yet their opposition is so effective that other nations lack the courage to convene the United Nations Charter Review Conference authorized in 1955 by the General Assembly. The deadlocked "veto groups" of East and West allow little more to develop out of humanity's urge for peace than plaintive pleas for amity and understanding or pleasant but largely irrelevant cultural exchanges between Cold War adversaries. The "nay" and the "nyet" of numerically small veto groups paralyze action for disarmament, for world law and for a world parliament.

In a predominantly democratic society, structured into veto groups, there can be few major changes except those wrought by catastrophe or by the slow erosion of time. A reform as great as world government is unlikely to gain peaceful acceptance unless several interest groups which favor it can unite in a strong commitment to get something done.

Mankind's yearning for peace constitutes an emotional reservoir which, given favorable outlets, can power effective engines of change. Public opinion polls taken by the Gallup organization in ten consecutive years have reported that the prevention of war is the problem uppermost in men's minds. In order to employ these psychological forces to good purpose we must make use not only of their extent, but of their depth.

"Decisions will be made by someone," remarks Kermit Eby, Chicago, Illinois, Professor of Social Sciences at the University of Chicago, Minister of the Church of the Brethren and a former labor union official. "The real choice lies in the value-pattern which the decision-maker brings to the task."

The average man does not indulge in abstract reasoning. His work, his play, his politics are all tangible. Leaders must offer him specific objectives. For him, theory must take shape in concrete examples.

"I might say a word about this famous man in the street," observes Alfredo Rodrigues Brent. "Let's take a look at him. To begin with, and judging by the audiences in Federalist meetings and congresses, more often than not he is a woman. Not a woman of the streets, but of the home; and she has a few very definite ideas about the rights of her children, her husband and herself. On this issue she is intensely practical; and all her thinking is conditioned by this. She is little interested in technical procedures. If you tell her of the end you wish to reach she is no little suspicious of the means by which you propose to reach it. She wants to put names to persons who are to handle things. Does it all come to the same crowd of banqueting and speechmaking diplomats who were talking about peace and disarmament when her Johnny first went to school, and never got anywhere, so that now Johnny is called up for military service instead of sticking to that job he was making good at, and heaven knows where they'll be sending him next, making him play with guns and things? Thank you for your wonderful theories, she's not interested!"

The President of the World Association of World Federalists, Lord Boyd-Orr, put it bluntly to one of the association's congresses: "If you offer to the poor and starving millions of the world the choice between the Four Freedoms and four sandwiches," he told his fellow Federalists, "they will take the sandwiches!"

"To talk to a man dying from hunger or disease in the slums of Asia or Europe about the blessings of Western democracy, about Federal constitutions, voting systems, equity tribunals—that is not adding insult to injury; it is plain stupidity. He won't understand. If he does, he will be bored, or furious. He will listen to the demagog who exploits his misery with slogans and fans his hatred," warns Dr. E. L. Loewenthal, Nottingham, England, physician and President of the Nottingham Business and Professional Men's Council for World Government.

Kermit Eby, as a member of a post-World War II education mission to Japan, once asked a Japanese former Kamikaze flier his motives: "But the Kamikaze flew only one mission—to their death! Why did you do this?"

"To show the white race," the young Japanese answered, "that if I could not be equal in life, I could at least be equal in death!"

The most compelling of motivations come from the pangs of the hungry belly, from the self-respect of the individual, or from the yearning for security.

A Federalist who examines his beliefs must soon realize that a yearning for peace is not alone sufficient to his ends. The advocacy of concepts which appear to offer little likelihood of realization can lead only to lightly held commitments: to persuasions upon which the possessor feels powerless to act. The feeling that decisions are made by others suits only passive sects. It is essential that a faith seeking accomplishment shall offer to its adherents a way as well as a will.

The intellectual basis of a belief such as Federalism may shift and develop with changing circumstances. But the emotional commitment of its advocates, once gained, may remain firm. Only the convinced can convince.

"I am persuaded," says the Quaker.

"I believe," declares the Catholic.

"Have you been saved?" demands the Evangelist.

A willingness to suffer for one's faith is a witness not only to its depth, but to its influence upon others.

"These people have a realizable kingdom," comments Kermit Eby. "Concerned people speak because they must. They have a vision. They testify. They sing. They have fellowship and a sense of community."

How do we make people care? The answer must be one of heroic proportions if it is to override the vetoes of lethargy, of neurosis, of incomprehension, of cynicism, and of panic.

The Obstacles to Overcome

"There will always be plenty of men and groups impressed by the difficulties of advancing at all, often inclined to try for too little," writes W. W. Waymack, Des Moines, Iowa, formerly a Pulitzer Prize winning Editor of the Des Moines *Register and Tribune,* and a former member of the United States Atomic Energy Commission.

"Thorstein Veblen once observed that anything new is vulgar by definition," Dale Hiller reflects. "The idea of world government is still new to most people. Thus, to stand up and be counted for world government in public, among people who are unfamiliar with the idea, is to risk being publicly vulgar and ill-mannered. Most people sense this though they would probably not phrase it so concisely, and are therefore reluctant to risk it. This is compounded by the lack of goals that show immediate results. Few people like to risk unpopularity, which can come quickly, for the sake of what seems to be a very long range reward."

"Without nasty, unrespectable men to provoke it, we will never force the United States or any government to move toward world government," retorts Harvey Frauenglass. "To be a hero—we learn from the ancient Greeks—one must risk the wrath of the gods," he adds. "And risking unpopularity among mere mortals certainly isn't as dangerous!"

As at every crisis in men's affairs, the world awaits leaders who can discern the shape of the future.

"Our greatest obstacle to effective world law to prevent war is the lack of dynamic leadership—leaders with the vision, ability, courage and 'motivational drive' to move ahead to overcome inertia which is inherent in all change," declares Peter P. Cooper, Salisbury, North Carolina, Executive Director of the American Freedom Association.

But men have never been able to count on miracles. "Those who govern, having much business on their hands, do not generally like to take the trouble of considering and carrying into execution new projects," Benjamin Franklin observed in his

Autobiography. "The best public measures are therefore seldom *adapted from previous wisdom, but forced by the occasion.*"

History tells us that patriots Samuel Adams of Massachusetts and Patrick Henry of Virginia bitterly opposed a federal union of the American colonies, fearing to lose in it the freedoms which they had just won. And they had plenty of company.

"As to the future grandeur of America, and its being a rising empire under one head, whether republican or monarchical, it is one of the idlest and most visionary notions that ever was conceived even by the writers of romance. The mutual antipathies and clashing interests of the Americans, their differences of governments, habitudes and manners, indicate that they will have no center of union," lamented Dean Tucker around the year 1786. "They can never be united under any species of government whatever; a disunited people till the end of time, suspicious and distrustful of each other, they will be divided and subdivided into little commonwealths or principalities, according to natural boundaries."

Wiser men were able to prove Dean Tucker wrong. But today, once again, we have our negativists. Much of the pious quibbling and quacking of our supposed leaders is just poison in our cup of coffee. Big names utter little ideas. Doubletalk dulls the public sense of danger. It sometimes seems as though a substantial proportion of contemporary oracles have joined together in a conspiracy to deflect the subject of world law and order from penetrating into men's consciousness. These are, at least in spirit, the descendants of the same people who said Christopher Columbus would sail off the edge of the world; the identical fellows who knew men would never fly, and who promised us that the atom was indivisible.

"It can't be done," say those who are slow to learn but quick to resent change.

"Visionary," croak diehards who are instinctively hostile to new knowledge.

Is it any wonder when common citizens question the wisdom of those in authority?

"Even the brains of the United Nations are not clear as to what they want or how to get it," remarks lawyer Harry Malm. "Why should we on the grass roots level be any more clairvoy-

197

ant in this, the most difficult of problems that man has ever attempted?"

"There is more to this business than getting a lot of good-sounding phrases down on paper," confesses CUREspondent Charles C. Wilson, Danville, Illinois, Managing Editor of *Tax-payer-Consumer Research Reports*. "The political, economic and social problems are deep and vast and to surmount them will require the best brains from many countries."

"The difficulty with United World Federalists and several other world federalist groups in various countries is that they blithely embarked on a program of world reform, grossly underestimating the magnitude of their proposal," declares Alfredo Rodrigues Brent. "World government, introduced even in the most cautious way, is still a revolution. To make a revolution you need people who are revolutionaries by nature, most of the time quiet-spoken, well-mannered, rather 'nice' people, but warriors at heart," he goes on. "Your true reformer is endowed with Messianism."

Modern Federalists, like the architects of the United States Constitution, are mostly substantial, conservative citizens, many of them with patrician and university backgrounds. Politically speaking, it should surprise no one that world federalist organizations in America are top-heavy with Republicans. Citizens with many responsibilities are among the first to recognize a community's needs.

The educated man, says Kermit Eby, is "he who can see the consequences of his acts in the sum total of their relationships."

Federalists who spoke before the United States Senate Subcommittee on Review of the United Nations Charter were obviously persons of a higher educational level and community status than the spokesmen who appeared on behalf of isolationist groups. But the class of people who, by their background, are best fitted to gain Federalist convictions are not necessarily suited by their experience to impart their convictions to the average man.

"Organized peace groups led by prominent and respected citizens have a good deal of social prestige and are generally considered to be on the side of the angels," say the authors of the sociological study *Action for Peace*. "There are a number of signs that the objectives of these volunteer groups are approved by millions of Americans, yet the groups themselves, through the literature they distribute, reach only thousands."

One reason for this is that people dislike to be "told" or "sold" what to think.

"The idea of 'selling' concepts of thought and feeling as if it were merchandise, so dear to the hearts of Americans, is absolutely out of touch with reality," Alfredo Rodrigues Brent charges. "Whenever it comes to a meeting of ideosyncracies—whether of national, religious, rational or any other origin—you enter a market where there are only sellers and no one wishes to buy."

The authors of *Action for Peace* put this sales resistance on psychological grounds:

"Research has shown over and over how people evade arguments contrary to their views. They will not read arguments in many cases. If they do read such things, they refuse to believe them. Or they will express distrust for the authors. Or they will fail to comprehend the message. The ancient Egyptians used to slaughter bearers of unwelcome tidings; psychologically, we often do something similar by rejecting information and argument contrary to our beliefs."

Men prefer to buy their ideas on the open market. Therefore, an emotional appeal must be eclectic. Christianity challenged its rivals of the early day not only in its content, but in its willingness to be all things to all people. It took from Judaism, from oriental, Greek, Roman religions; it absorbed features of paganism, of the Isis, Gnostic, Mithraic, polytheistic worships; it outbid and devoured most of its competitors. He who seeks to please everyone is not necessarily fated to please none. It depends how many elements one's eclecticism can persuade into compatibility. To some men world government means law. To many it can mean food. To most it may spell peace; and to all it should convey the promise of freedom.

"The United States would probably not be in existence today had Hamilton and Jay formed a Federalist organization to solicit memberships," writes Neil Parsons. "Instead, they maintained the integrity of their ideas as powerful, personal proposals which, because of their clarity and logic, became the ideas and plans of many individuals."

An organization is a purpose. An organization should not think of itself as a self-contained movement; it should perceive its function as a party within a movement.

"The Federalist movement is behaving in a perfectly normal movement's way; organizing, extending, closing up too tightly for the comfort of many so that they split off, re-organizing . . . In the final stages the movement's principles are adopted by other large groups—political parties, churches," observes Alfredo Rodrigues Brent, and he cites the history of movements for abolition of slavery, for women's suffrage, and against child labor.

Education for Survival

"It is obvious that the schools have failed to educate us to think constructively on any subject that is not entirely personal," a tank sergeant wrote to the United States Army newspaper in the European Theater during World War II. "Apparently the schools and colleges have made government and current history so boring that it is a relief not to have to worry about it when you have completed your courses. How can you have ideas about internationalism and how can you expect a fair and lasting peace when the only reading you have done is Superman and the captions under the pictures of movie queens? If we were really educated, would we have allowed ourselves to be as unprepared for a war of this magnitude?"

Dramatic evidence of the West's psychological unpreparedness for survival came again during the Korean War. A comparison of the behavior of American and Turkish soldiers serving in United Nations forces who were taken prisoner by the Communists in Korea showed startling differences. Of 7,190 soldiers of the United States Army taken prisoner, a large proportion yielded in one way or another to Communist psychological techniques. These techniques were, for the most part, not the radical alterations of personality known as "brainwashing," but simply a demoralization accomplished by exploiting the immature emotions of average young American soldiers. Most shocking of all, 2,370 or 38% of the American soldiers died in captivity. The apparent causes were dysentery, pneumonia and starvation. Yet Turkish soldiers held prisoner under identical conditions did not suffer a single defection or a single

200

death. Eugene Kinkead's *In Every War But One* has told how Army investigators, puzzled by the unprecedented waves of American collaboration and mortality in the hands of the enemy, later spent literally millions of man-hours interviewing returnees to gather facts about these strange phenomena. According to Army studies, the real causes of death were lack of discipline among the American prisoners, lack of care for the ill by their comrades, and, in the last analysis, lack of the motivational will to live. The American soldiers, according to the Army's own evaluation, did not know what they were fighting for.

These and other instances are enough to show that psychological preparation for a world rule of law and order will require, as a minimum, rudimentary political re-education on a widespread scale. Many who might be, at best, willing to accept peace as a gift from the hands of others will have to learn how to earn it for themselves.

"We must make allowances," says Mr. Brent, "for persons to whom the acceleration of momentum is too dazzling for their powers of realization."

"Even a minimal world government may require more institutional change than people will accept even if the alternative is to live in a state of world peril," writes Emile Benoit, New York, N. Y., Professor of International Relations at Columbia University, author and former diplomat. "One reason is that the situation is continuously rationalized not to appear as perilous as it really is. National governments do this to avoid the repudiation by their electorates which would follow recognition of the actual danger in which they deliberately choose to live rather than to renounce any of their sovereignty. The public welcomes the minimizing of the actual danger in order to avoid anxiety, the most insupportable of emotions."

The subjects of tyrannical governments have little chance to face facts or to cope with them. Free peoples have a better chance to deal constructively with realities. On the face of it, the biggest potential block to United Nations Charter revision is an unwillingness of the free peoples themselves to face the facts and to do something about them.

Many of us tend to sweep realities under the rug—both the unthinking revisionists and the unthinking antirevisionists.

Many of us voice opinions formed long before the present crisis.

As Waldo Mead says, "there are too many Federalists today who have associated themselves with ideas that they have not attempted to criticize as the world situation changes."

Few of us tolerate the mental discomfort of reviewing and rethinking. To plan, to grapple with facts, to invent new solutions are forms of mental torture.

"There has been too much dependence upon the use of words for their ability to discomfit and harass and too little upon the power of the better idea to get itself accepted in the open market of ideas," admonishes Rachel Welch. "We must cease to consider 'democracy' as a sort of 'Lodge' secret which binds us into an exclusive society, and see it as a method by which ideas can be tested."

A motivation survey by the Chicago Area Council of United World Federalists shows that the average midwestern American has a favorable association with phrases like "government", "world government" and "federal government". Most people can define what a "government" is but have little concept of a difference between its internal sovereignty, where it rules by law, and its external sovereignty where it acts by force or by diplomatic negotiations. The average person likes the word "federal" but has only a hazy idea what it means. Most people associate federalism with *centralized* concepts. Few recognize the *decentralized* philosophy of a federal system which grants to the common government only the minimum of powers most necessary to the general welfare, while reserving to the governments of its territorial subdivisions as many sovereign jurisdictions as possible.

If people do not know what words like "sovereignty" and "federal" mean, their education for survival is, as yet, hardly begun. This simple lack of knowledge is also the measure of the educational opportunity before us.

The ancient Greeks had an excellent definition of education: "know thyself". The present crisis in Western education is not only a lack of schools and colleges, of teachers and scientists: it is, more fundamentally, that we have lost sight of who we are, that we lack understanding of the meaning of free institutions to world peace.

Some people are too uninformed to learn anything, but no one ever knew too much to learn more. Education campaigns, believe 87% of CURE conferees, should stir people to think for themselves. When the nature of the task is clear, plenty of people will be ready to deal with the imminent peril and the given opportunity.

"There are no shortcuts," declares Donald Keys, New York, N.Y., former Field Secretary of California State Branch of United World Federalists. "History hands us opportunities, such as Charter review. But only popular support can determine an outcome in favor of world government."

A Charter Review Conference will meet if, as and when people want it enough. No agency on earth but public opinion, the mass will, the desire of each man to live multiplied by hundreds of millions of men, can put the world on the road to governing its affairs.

How Government Sets Us Free

The twentieth century is a thrilling time to live. If men survive the scientific and political perils of the atomic age, the realization of new thought, of high achievement, of global citizenship may well awaken one of mankind's greatest ages.

"What a privilege to be alive and well enough to make even a small contribution towards this exciting challenge!" exclaims CUREspondent Louis B. Dailey.

The matchless blaze of Hellenic culture resulted from man's discovery of his own mind. The magnificent art of the Renaissance, the clear trumpet-voice of Elizabethan England, accompanied man's exploration of the physical globe. What may not follow the literal accomplishment of man's brotherhood? What nobler ways of life may not derive from the increase in democratic wealth, from new sources of energy, new modes of travel and the closer impact of differing traditions? What drama, what art will mark the end of tyranny?

For world government is an escape from the tyrannies of local nationalism. No one need confuse the size of a government with its severity; indeed, experience and judgment lead us to expect that the greatest of governments will be the most liberal. The trend of Conference opinion, by a 74% majority, is that a federal world government will not enforce a greater conformity upon peoples.

"Lack of government above the nation states creates the tensions which demand uniformity and more governmental regulations," in the opinion of John A. Mathews, Dayton, Ohio, a Lieutenant Colonel in the United States Air Force and a Director of the Atlantic Union Committee.

And 86% of CURE's advisers agree that individual citizens will be subject to less total government in a federated world.

"In a federated world," predicts Glenn P. Turner, "taxes will be much less than in the present world which depends upon national protection."

A world constitution will establish, in principle, civil rights for citizens of the globe: free speech, a free press, freedom from racial discrimination, freedom of religious belief, the secret ballot, trial by jury, habeas corpus and the other guarantees of individual liberty which centuries of democratic development have proven to be essential in free countries. Even more important, world law will establish—in practice—an environment which allows men to progress toward the achievement of these ideals.

Let us listen as members of our Conference sum up their faith in a free and federal world.

George H. Lewis, II, Tallahassee, Florida, past President of the Florida State Branch of United World Federalists:

"Isn't world government necessary to a real rebirth of freedom to trade and to travel? Isn't it necessary, in fact, to any realistic guarantees of rights to life, liberty and the pursuit of happiness in the world today?"

Dr. J. David Singer:

"Eliminate the possibility of war and the peripheral problems of trade, civil rights and regional development will melt before a voluntary, co-operative effort."

Mary Hays Weik:

"The picture of a world government as a superpoliceman with the biggest stick in existence has never appealed to me. If you will look into the history of any productive and law-abiding country, you will discover that it was the basic respect for justice among its people which gave such laws authority, not the laws themselves that made such order and progress possible."

William Bross Lloyd:

"To some Federalists, nationalism is a dirty word. But they could well ponder the example of Switzerland, in whose political thought the term 'federalism' means what to us is 'states' rights': namely, the opposite of centralization. The value of both principles is recognized, as well as the normality of their frequent political conflict and the need for seeking a balance between them."

Alfredo Rodrigues Brent:

"The 'federal' principles advocated by world federalists imply decentralization and discontinuous power rather than the reverse. There is consent of the governed to more than one government; consequently a government of the world cannot be otherwise than both territorial and functional."

Stanley K. Platt:

"One of the important contributions of the Federalist concept is that it provided a plan under which the peoples of the world may live together in a world which can be safe for such differences as the people may cherish."

Dr. Vernon Nash:

"A future world federal union may move in time into some fields previously held to be strictly domestic by the nations, but such extension is likely to be very gradual, as it has been in our existing federations. Also, in all probability, such increases in its responsibility will be far more limited than they have been in our present federal unions since tendencies toward centralization have been largely created by a desire for greater national security.

"It is, moreover, a near certainty that mankind will never become as socially regimented as most federated nations have. Since diversity so greatly enriches life, it is most earnestly to be hoped that mankind will never become homogenized.

"With the establishment of a world federal government, the constituent governments of the member-nations whose armed forces have been reduced to those needed for the maintenance of domestic order will be very different in character and in power from what they are now.

"A few federal unions, broadly patterned on ours, have been sufficiently successful long enough to demonstrate conclusively that it is possible to maintain a common government for some designated purposes over peoples with extraordinary diversities of language, economics and culture."

By unity and political security the United States has progressed to broader standards of freedom and has built an ever-rising level of wealth.

The United States Constitution did not take liberty from the people of Connecticut and Virginia. Future federation will not enslave the Russian and the Swiss, the Kansan and the Kaffir. In the end, law will assure liberty to all men.

Democracy has the world to gain and nothing but fear to lose. We live on borrowed time; and the people are waiting for their leaders to catch up to them.

Conference Upon Research and Education
in world government

Majority votes or author's opinions expressed in this book do not necessarily reflect the view of individual participants in the discussions. Many conferees have engaged only in certain aspects of the discussions of interest to them, or on which they have been consulted. Biographical data, where known, appear as of the most recent date available from records of the Conference.

ABBOTT, Mrs. Arthur, Winnetka, Illinois

ACKLEY, Mrs. Stanford, Blacklick, Ohio

ADAMS, Mrs. Carl, East Concord, New Hampshire

AINSWORTH, John E., Washington, D.C.

ALLINSON, Brent Don, Highland Park, Illinois, former Associate Professor of History, Government, and International Relations, C h i c a g o Teachers College

ANDERSEN, Niels T., Kearny, New Jersey, automobile export executive; past President of New Jersey State Branch, United World Federalists; editor, New Jersey United World Federalists Newsletter

ANIXTER, Mrs. William, Highland Park, Illinois

APPERSON, John W., Memphis, Tennessee

ARMSTRONG, Patrick, London, England, Clerk to Parliamentary Group for World Government

ARNETT, Dr. John H., Philadelphia, Pennsylvania, physician

ASH, Lee, New York, N. Y., Librarian, Carnegie Endowment for International Peace

ASKEW, Ruth, Chicago, Illinois

BACHRACH, Dr. Samuel, Worcester, Massachusetts

BAER, Theodore F., Los Altos, California, past President of California State Branch, United World Federalists

BAILEY, Fred K., West Hartford, Connecticut, former C h a i r m a n, Greater Hartford Chapter, United World Federalists

BALLENGER, Dr. John J., Winnetka, Illinois, physician

BARNARD, Mrs. John R., Mill Valley, California, Chairman of Mill Valley Chapter, United World Federalists

BARR, Dr. Stringfellow, Princeton, New Jersey, Professor of Humanities at Rutgers University; former President of St. Johns College, Annapolis, Maryland; originator of "Great Books" curriculum; former head of Foundation for World Government; author of Let's Join the Human Race and Citizens of the World

BARRY, Mrs. Scammon, Glenview, Illinois, former Chairman, Glenview Chapter, United World Federalists

BARTER, Marjorie, Moonachie, New Jersey, member of Executive Board, Northern Valley Chapter, United World Federalists

BASSIR, Dr. Olumbe, Ibadan, Nigeria, University College

BAUM, Richard, Stonington, Connecticut

BEASLEY, Alec C., Winfield, British Columbia, Canada, farmer

BECKMAN, F. Woods, Knoxville, Tennessee, former executive of Tennessee Valley Authority; former member of Executive Council, United World Federalists

BEDFORD, Alfred, Princeton, New Jersey

207

BELL, Laird, Winnetka, Illinois, lawyer and lumber executive; Chairman of the Board of Directors, Weyerhaeuser Timber Company; member of the Board of Overseers of Harvard University; former Alternate Delegate of the United States to the General Assembly of the United Nations

BENHAM, Mrs. Maude, Versailles, Indiana

BENNETHUM, Mrs. George S., Aurora, Illinois

BENOIT, Emile, New York, N. Y., Professor of International Relations, Columbia University; former Attaché in the American embassies in London and Vienna and Senior Economist in United States Department of Labor; contributing author, *United Nations or World Government* (Wilson, 1947), and other books and articles; a founder of United World Federalists and delegate to World Association of World Federalists

BENT, David, Coral Gables, Florida

BENTLY, N. E., Syracuse, New York

BERGER, Sherna, Berkeley, California

BIRK, Peter, Princeton, New Jersey

BISHOP, Arthur, Melbourne, Australia, author; President, World Government Movement, Australian Section

BLACKWELDER, Eliot, Stanford, California, retired professor of geology; Chairman of Palo Alto Chapter of Atlantic Union Committee

BLACKWELDER, Justin, Washington, D. C., Executive Secretary, Atlantic Union Committee

BLAKE, Mildred Riorden, Dobbs Ferry, New York, former member of Executive Council, United World Federalists; former co-Chairman, New York Branch, United World Federalists

BLOCK, James, New York, N. Y., member of the Co-ordinating Council of New York Student Federalists

BLOME, Lithgow, New York, N. Y.

BLUMER, J. W., The Hague, The Netherlands

BOAL, Stewart, Winnetka, Illinois, manufacturer, President, Randolph Laboratories; President of the Conference Upon Research and Education in world government; former Chairman, North Shore Chapter, United World Federalists

BOAL, Mrs. Stewart, Winnetka, Illinois

BOARDMAN, John M., Syracuse, New York, graduate student in theoretical physics at Syracuse University; expelled from Florida State University for supporting integration, 1957; member of Committee on Elections of North American Council for a Peoples' World Constitutional Convention

BODNER, David, Middletown, Connecticut

BOFMAN, Albert, Chicago, Illinois, accountant

BOONE, Ilsley, Egg Harbor, New Jersey, publisher; Chief of Publications of the Interchurch World Movement; co-founder of the American Society for Visual Education; member of Governing Council, Commonwealth of World Citizens; Executive Director, World Government Sponsors

BORRY, Mme. Florence, Paris, France

BOURCIER, Claude L., Middlebury, Vermont, university professor; Director of Middlebury College Graduate School of French in France; Secretary of Vermont Branch, United World Federalists

BRADSHAW, J. S., Del Mar, California, oceanographer, University of California.

BRADSHAW, Mrs. J. S., Del Mar, California, Chairman of Del Mar Chapter, United World Federalists

BRAENDEL, H. G., Malvern, Pennsylvania

BRENDLIN, Marie, San Francisco, California

BRENT, Alfredo Rodrigues, Bergen, N. H., Holland, journalist; served in Netherlands Underground Resistance 1940-45; author of *Federatie van de Wereld;* member of World Council for Peoples' World Constitutional Convention

BRIGGS, Dorothy S., Adamsville, Rhode Island, member of Executive Council, United World Federalists

BROADY, Florence, Ogden Dunes, Indiana, Chairman of Motivation Research Committee, Chicago Area Council, United World Federalists

BRONEER, Carl K., Santa Barbara, California, contractor

BROWN, James R., Durham, North Carolina

BRÜCKWILDER, William M., Burns, Oregon

BRYANT, Ralph C., New Haven, Connecticut

BURTON, Lindley J., Lake Forest, Illinois, Professor of Mathematics, Lake Forest College; Chairman of Lake Forest Chapter, United World Federalists

CARPENTER, Mrs. John Alden, Chicago, Illinois

CARPENTER, Mrs. Kenneth G., West Hartford, Connecticut

CASANOVA, Mrs. José, Hamden, Connecticut

CHAKRAVARTI, Birendra Nath, Jalpaiguri, West Bengal, India, veteran of World War II, Burma Front, and of non-violent revolution against British rule in India and Portuguese rule in Goa; author, *Hinduism Triumphs;* former Honorary Treasurer of Socialist Party, Poona Branch

CHARLTON, Peter, Pasadena, California

CHARNEY, Elliott, Bethesda, Maryland

CHAZEN, Bernard, Hoboken, New Jersey

CHIPPS, Roy B., St. Louis, Missouri

CHRISTMANN, Rev. R. Frederick, Defiance, Ohio

CLARK, Mrs. Donald, Winnetka, Illinois

CLARK, Grenville, Dublin, New Hampshire, l a w y e r; co-author *World Peace Through World Law;* Vice President, United World Federalists; Consultant to United States Secretary of War Henry Stimson, 1940-1944

COHN, Dr. Heinz G., Lebanon, Pennsylvania

CONNORS, Edith Olshin, New York, N. Y., Public Relations Counsel, Olshin-Connors Agency; former Associate Editor, *Magazine Digest;* member of Executive Council, New York State Branch, United World Federalists

COOPER, Peter P., Salisbury, North Carolina, Executive Director, American Freedom Association

CORKEY, W.B.H., Charlotte, North Carolina

COSYN, Maurice M., Boitsfort, Brussels, Belgium, Secretary General, Union Fédérale

COX, William H. D., Kew Gardens, L. I., New York, aircraft pilot, United Air Lines; former executive Secretary of New Jersey Branch, United World Federalists; member of Board of Directors of the Conference Upon Research and Education in world government

CRAFTS, Robert, Jr., Cuyahoga Falls, Ohio, graduate student, Yale University; founder and former Chairman, Yale Chapter, former Chairman, National Student Committee, and member of Executive Council of United World Federalists

CRAWFORD, Arthur L., Salt Lake City, Utah, engineer, Geneva Steel Company; Secretary-Treasurer, Utah Geological Society; Director, Utah Geological and Mineralogical Survey of University of Utah; member of National Council of American Veterans Committee

CRICHTON, Andrew, Mamaroneck, New York, publishing executive, *Sports Illustrated;* former Editor, *The Federalist*

CROSBY, Caresse, Washington, D. C., Director, International Registry of World Citizens

CULLER, Mrs. George, San Francisco, California, former Chairman, Evanston (Illinois) Chapter, United World Federalists

CULP, Amos D., Goshen, Indiana

DAILEY, Louis B., Maplewood, New Jersey, lawyer; radio commentator, *World Peace Roundup;* member of Executive Council of United World Federalists; former President, First Unitarian Church of Essex County; former President, New Jersey State Branch, United World Federalists

DALTON, Pat, Evanston, Illinois, journalist, The Chicago Daily News

DANA, Mrs. George W., Portland, Oregon, Executive Secretary of Portland Chapter, United World Federalists

DAVENPORT, John H., Levittown, New York, Analyst, International Business Machines; former Instructor in Political Science, University of Miami; former Chairman, United World Federalists of Miami

DAVIS, Clare A., Oak Park, Illinois, retired civil engineer; member of Friends Committee on National Legislation; Chairman of Public Affairs Committee, Illinois State Branch, and past Chairman, Oak Park-River Forest Chapter, United World Federalists

DeBEVERE, E. A., Purley, Surrey, England, founder of Union Now, British branch of movement inspired by Clarence Streit; former member of the Executive Board, Crusade for World Government

DEHNE, Marion, Wilmette, Illinois, member of Executive Council and Chairman of Students Committee, Chicago Area of United World Federalists

DELIN, Norman, Minneapolis, Minnesota, student at University of Minnesota; Associate President of Student Federalist Club

DELIN, Stephen, Minneapolis, Minnesota, student at University of Minnesota

DENNIS, Anne P., Califon, New Jersey, past Chairman, Oldwick Chapter, United World Federalists

DENNIS, Eldon, North Little Rock, Arkansas, groundwater geologist; former Associate Professor of Geology at Texas Technological College; Chairman of North American Coun-

cil for a Peoples' World Constitutional Convention

DENTON, William Wells, Tucson, Arizona, retired professor of mathematics and dean of liberal arts college; Provisional Treasurer of North American Council for a Peoples' World Constitutional Convention

DIAMOND, Saul, Cedar Falls, Iowa

DIEHL, Valida, Escondido, California, former school teacher

DIETZGEN, Mrs. Joseph, Highland Park, Illinois

DOLE, R. W. Jr., Lima, Pennsylvania

DORR, Rev. M. Everett, Des Moines, Iowa, Minister, Trinity Methodist Church; President, Des Moines Chapter, United World Federalists; State Chairman, United States Committee for UNICEF

DOUGLASS, Harl R., Boulder, Colorado

DUNCAN, Cecil, Lamar, Colorado

DUNCAN, Mrs. Robert, St. Petersburg, Florida

EBY, Kermit, Chicago, Illinois, Professor of Social Science at the University of Chicago; Minister of Church of the Brethren; former Director of Education and Research of the Congress of Industrial Organizations (CIO)

EDSON, Col. Carroll A., Syracuse, New York, District Manager, Social Security Administration; f o r m e r Moderator, Oneida Association of Congregational Churches; former Chapter President, Reserve Officers' Association; President, Onondaga Chapter, Atlantic Union Committee

ELLIGETT, Mrs. R. T., Odessa, Florida

ERNST, Dr. Robert, Springfield, Massachusetts

ESPENSCHIED, Peter, Metuchen, New Jersey, student in astronomy, Harvard University and Research Assistant in Radio Astronomy at the Central Radio Propagation Laboratory, National Bureau of Standards, Boulder, Colorado; past member of New Jersey State Executive Council of United World Federalists and past Secretary of Harvard World Federalists

ESSLINGER, William, New York, N. Y., author, *Politics and Science*

EWBANK, John R., Southampton, Pennsylvania, patent attorney; Secretary, Society for Social Responsibility in Science; Treasurer, Philadelphia Chapter, United World Federalists; Finance Chairman, 8th Congressional District Republican Committee

FARMER, Fyke, Nashville, Tennessee, attorney; elected Delegate by Tennessee State ballot to World Constitution Assembly, G e n e v a, Switzerland, 1950

FEINGOLD, Eugene, Princeton, New Jersey, graduate student and Assistant Instructor in Department of Political Science, Princeton University; former member of National Student Council, Chairman of Brooklyn High School Area Chapter, and Chairman of Cornell University Chapter, United World Federalists

FENN, Dan H. Jr., Boston, Massachusetts, assistant Editor, *Harvard Business Review;* former Director, World Affairs Council of Boston; author *Citizens Guide to International Affairs* (Beacon)

FENNER, Frances, Afton, New York, advertising; Secretary of the New York Citizens Committee for a Peoples' World Constitutional Convention

FERBER, Mrs. Frederick, Englewood, New Jersey

FLACK, Michael J., Pittsburgh, Pennsylvania, Associate Professor in the Graduate School of Public and International Affairs of the University of Pittsburgh

FLARSHEIM, Marjorie, Wilmette, Illinois

FLEMING, Rev. Ralph L., Jr., Newport, North Carolina, Methodist Minister; former National Student Chairman of United World Federalists

FORD, J. Holmes, Los Angeles, California, Counsellor, Senior Citizens

Service Center, Los Angeles; President of Los Angeles Chapter, Atlantic Union Committee

FOSTER, Billy, Denver, Colorado

FRANK, Mrs. Murray (Virginia deConingh), Chicago, Illinois; past Chairman, Smith College Chapter, United World Federalists; former Executive Secretary of WORLD

FRANKLIN, Dr. Sidney, Cleveland, Ohio

FRANKLIN, Ward, West Ardmore, Oklahoma, retired oil executive

FRAUENGLASS, Harvey, Iowa City, Iowa, Graduate Instructor in English at State University of Iowa; member of Special United Nations Subcommittee of American Veterans Committee

FREEMAN, David N., Mill Valley, California

FRIENDLY, Joan, New York, N. Y.

FRY, A. Ruth, London, England

FUCHS, Lawrence, Weston, Massachusetts

FUTTNER, Jody, East Hartford, Connecticut

GARDNER, Gilbert, Grand Rapids, Michigan, public relations counsel; former Secretary to Lend-Lease Administrator Edward R. Stettinius, Jr.

GERNERT, M. L., Kingsport, Tennessee, industrial executive

GIDNEY, James, Shaker Heights, Ohio, statistician for the Juvenile Court of Cuyahoga County and instructor at Cleveland College; former instructor at the University of Beirut, Lebanon; member of OSS in World War II; former member of Executive Council, United World Federalists

GILCHRIST, David I., New York, N. Y., attorney; former Chairman of Greenwich Village Chapter and West Side Chapter, New York, and former Executive Director of Connecticut State Branch, United World Federalists

GILLIAM, Elsie W., Lynchburg, Virginia

GILFILLAN, S. Colum, Ph.D., Chicago, Illinois, University Professor in Social Sciences; author, *Social Implications of Technical Advance* (UNESCO); Vice-Chairman, Chicago Chapter, Atlantic Union Committee

GLASCOCK, Mrs. J. S., Salem, Oregon

GLAZER, Gabriel, Ottawa, Ontario, Canada

GLUCK, Kenneth, Elizabeth, New Jersey, lawyer and accountant; former lecturer in law, Rutgers University; former Agent, United States Internal Revenue Service; former President of Elizabeth Chapter, United World Federalists

GOODMAN, Arnold, Racine, Wisconsin, property management; President, Midwest Branch, and member of Executive Council, United World Federalists

GOODMAN, Dr. Elliot R., Providence, Rhode Island, Professor in Political Science, Brown University; author of *The Soviet Design for a World State* (Columbia, 1958)

GRANT, Rev. Gerard G., S.J., Chicago, Illinois, Assistant Professor of Philosophy, Loyola University

GRAY, Charles H., Wheatridge, Colorado

GREENE, G. W., Salisbury, North Carolina, World Government Institute, Catawaba College

GREGORY, Glenn W., Wheatridge, Colorado

GRIFALCONI, John, Cincinnati, Ohio, architect; member of Executive Council, International Registry of World Citizens; former member of Board of WORLD

HABICHT, Max, Geneva, Switzerland, lawyer; former member of Legal Section, League of Nations Secretariat; President of Swiss Peace Council

HAFLICH, Victor, Garden City, Kansas, former member of Kansas State Legislature and past President of Kansas State Committee for UNESCO

HAGEBOECK, Jack, Bettendorf, Iowa, member of Executive Council, United World Federalists

HAMLIN, Bryan, Bridgehampton, New York, lawyer; Editor-in-Chief of Suffolk County Bar Bulletin; officer of United States Air Force in World Wars I and II

HANSEN, Ellen, Denver, Colorado

HANSON, David A., Lexington, Massachusetts, past Chairman, Harvard World Federalists

HANSON, Gilbert, Minneapolis, Minnesota, member of Executive Council, United World Federalists

HANSON, Mrs. Paul, Lexington, Massachusetts, Foreign Affairs Chairman, Lexington League of Women Voters; organizer of Lexington Chapter, United World Federalists

HARDIN, George C., Philadelphia, Pennsylvania, Secretary, Friends Peace Committee

HARDY, T. W., Jr., St. Louis, Missouri

HARLESS, Richard F., Phoenix, Arizona

HARMER, Miss V. A., St. Louis, Missouri

HARRIS, Ben T., Clayton, Missouri

HARRIS, Dr. Morgan, Los Angeles, California

HASKELL, Ellery B., Reading, Pennsylvania, Associate Professor of Philosophy; teacher of American History and History of Religions; Chairman of Christian Social Progress Committee of First Baptist Church, Reading; former Chairman of Reading and Berks County Chapter, United World Federalists

HASSELFELDT, Ernest C., Chicago, Illinois

HASTINGS, Courtland, New York, N. Y., member of Executive Council and past Chairman of New York State Branch, United World Federalists

HAYS, Howard K., Ambler, Pennsylvania

HAYWOOD, Charles M., Owego, New York

HENRY, Gerald B., Buffalo, New York

HENSEL, Donald, Denver, Colorado, university administrator and teacher; former President, Morgan County Chapter, United World Federalists

HERBERT, Frederick, Kansas City, Missouri; service in World War I as Sergeant of Artillery in German Army

HERTZ, Gerhard, Hamburg, Germany, Institut für Physikalische Chemie

HESS, F. Eugene, South Bend, Indiana, social worker; President, Indiana Visitors' Association; former member of Executive Council, United World Federalists

HESTOFT, Svend-Aage, Hellerup, Denmark

HIGGINS, Carter C., North Brookfield, Massachusetts, member of Executive Council, United World Federalists

HIGGINS, Donald, New York, N. Y., former Field Director, New York Branch, United World Federalists

HILL, David, Weston, Connecticut, nuclear physicist

HILLER, Dale, Wilmington, Delaware, research chemist; Education Chairman, Wilmington Chapter, member of Executive Council, Atlantic Region, past Vice-President of Student Division and former member of Executive Councils, Ohio Branch and Iowa Branch, United World Federalists

HOFFMAN, Walter F., Wayne, New Jersey, Chairman of Passaic County Chapter of United World Federalists

HOISINGTON, Harland W., Jr., Princeton, New Jersey

HOLABIRD, Christopher, Chicago, Illinois

HOLT, George, Woodstock, Connecticut, Executive Vice-President, United World Federalists; newspaper columnist; former Rhodes Scholar; war service as Lieutenant Commander in United States Navy; former member of Staff of League of Nations and of Governor Chester Bowles of Connecticut

HOLT, John C., Boston, Massachusetts, former Executive Director of New York State Branch, United World Federalists

HOSKINS, William, Jacksonville, Florida

HUDSON, Mrs. Charles J., West Boylston, Massachusetts, Chairman of Worcester League of Women Voters; Chairman of Worcester Chapter, United World Federalists

HUNT, Mrs. Walter, Jr., Raleigh, North Carolina

HUTCHINSON, Dr. Martin T., New Brunswick, New Jersey, agricultural research and teaching, Department of Entomology, Rutgers University; Public Affairs Chairman, New Jersey State Branch, past State President, member of Executive Council and National Education Chairman of United World Federalists

HYDE, Mrs. Ralph U., Washington, D. C.

INDERLIED, Mrs. Helen T., Binghamton, New York, retired school teacher; member of Board of Governors, American Civic Association

ISBRÜCKER, Mrs. Julia, The Hague, The Netherlands

ISELY, Philip, Lakewood, Colorado, President of The Builders Foundation; Executive Secretary of Committee on Elections and former Secretary of North American Council for a Peoples' World Constitutional Convention

JACCARD, Dr. h.c. René, Unitarian Church, Geneva, Switzerland

JACK, Dr. Homer, Evanston, Illinois, Minister, The Unitarian Church of Evanston; author of *The Gandhi Reader* (Indiana University Press, 1956) *To Albert Schweitzer, Bandung* and other pamphlets; member of Board of Directors, *Toward Freedom*

JESPERSEN, H. Koefoed, Copenhagen, Denmark

JOCHANAN, P. Scott, New York, N. Y., Editorial Assistant, *Time*, Inc.

JOERGENSEN, Aage, Copenhagen, Denmark

JOHNSON, Iris, Washington, D. C.

JOHNSON, Richard B., Sonoma, California, writer and former Social Science teacher; Editor *The Sphere;* former Chairman, Seattle Research Group on World Federation and Secretary, Berkeley Chapter and Northern California Branch, United World Federalists

JONAS, Gilbert, New York, N. Y., Secretary, Newcomb-Oram International Corporation; past Chairman, WORLD

JONES, C. Myron, Chicago, Illinois, member of Executive Council of Chicago Area and past Chairman of Near North Side Chapter, United World Federalists

JOSSLIN, William L., Portland, Oregon

JOYCE, James Avery, London, England, Professor of International Law, member of the Council of World Association of World Federalists; author of *Revolution on East River* (Schuman, 1956), *World in the Making* (1953)

JUDSON, David, Charlotte, North Carolina, contractor; Chairman of International Affairs Council; past chapter Chairman and former member of Executive Council, United World Federalists

KADANE, Joseph B., Cambridge, Massachusetts, student; President of Harvard World Federalists

KAHN, Warren J., Jamaica, New York, high school teacher of social studies; Vice President of New York Teachers' Guild, AFL-CIO; Army training in Chinese language and service in India; former Chairman, World Government Society, London School of Economics; former Chairman of Jackson Heights, L. I., Chapter and former member of New York State Executive Council, United World Federalists

KAHN, Irene (Mrs. Warren J.), Jamaica, New York, Chairman, Jamaica, L. I., Chapter of United World Federalists

KAPLAN, Cyril, Whitestone, New York

KAYE, Alvin, Philadelphia, Pennsylvania, Department of Zoology, University of Pennsylvania

KEYS, Donald F., New York, N. Y., Executive Director, World Good Will; former Field Secretary, California State Branch, United World Federalists

KIEFER, Durand, Del Mar, California

KLAUS, Erwin H., Fresno, California, grain and feed executive; Chairman of Special United Nations Subcommittee, American Veterans Committee

KNAP, Marcus, Amsterdam, The Netherlands, dentist; former Professor at University of Indonesia; Netherlands Delegate to Parliament of Commonwealth of World Citizens

KNAPP, C. W., Eugene, Oregon

KORNHAUSER, Richard, Escondido, California

KRABBE, Dipl. Pol. Günter, Stuttgart, Germany, Präsident, Internationaler Studentenbund-Studentenbewegung für übernationale Föderation (ISSF)

KRONISCH, Myron W., Livingston, New Jersey

KURTZ, Kenneth, Weston, West Virginia, news broadcaster; past chairman, WORLD

LAIBLIN, Jürg, Nurnberg, Germany, economics student

LAPTAD, Evadne M., Lawrence, Kansas, social worker; President, Douglas County Health Council; service overseas in American Red Cross in World Wars I and II

LARMER, Forrest, Muscatine, Iowa, past Chairman of Muscatine Chapter, United World Federalists

LASLEY, Jack, Chapel Hill, North Carolina, attorney

LAWSON, A. V., Atlanta, Georgia, Reference Librarian, Atlanta Public Library

LEHMER, Mrs. D. N., Berkeley, California

LENTZ, Dr. Theodore F., St. Louis, Missouri, Professor at Washington University; Director, Peace Study

Institute; author of *Towards a Science of Peace*

LEUTZINGER, Ted R., Los Angeles, California

LeVINESS, W. Thetford, Santa Fe, New Mexico, Librarian, New Mexico Department of Public Welfare

LEWIS, George, II, Tallahassee, Florida, banking; President of Tallahassee Chapter and past President of Florida State Branch, United World Federalists

LINEWEAVER, J o h n, Levittown, New York, biology teacher, Wheatley School, Old Westbury, New York

LIVINGSTON, Richard, Oak Park, Illinois, Chairman, Chicago Area Council, United World Federalists

LLOYD, Georgia (Mrs. Paul Berndt), Glencoe, Illinois, co-author of *Searchlight on Peace Plans* (Dutton, 1944)

LLOYD, William Bross, Jr., Winnetka, Illinois, Editor of *Toward Freedom;* a Director of Conference Upon Research and Education in world government; author, *Town Meeting for America*, and *Waging Peace: the Swiss Experience* (1958); former Executive Secretary, Campaign for World Government

LOEWENTHAL, Dr. Ernst L., Nottingham, England, physician; President of the Nottingham Business and Professional Men's Council for World Government and Member of the Council of the World Association of World Federalists

LOFQUIST, H. V., Bessemer, Alabama

LOGUE, John J., New York, N. Y.; Department of Political Philosophy, Fordham University; former Chairman of United Nations Charter Revision Subcommittee of the Catholic Association of International Peace; former member of the Executive Council, United World Federalists; former member of the Board of WORLD

LOMBARDI, Ralph E., Amsterdam, Holland, Secretary General of the World Association of World Federalists; radio commentator and author; former University instructor and assistant professor in political science, history and English; former education co-ordinator with Third United States Air Force

LOOS, A. William, New York, N. Y., Executive Director, The Church Peace Union

LOVELACE, Denis, Amsterdam, The Netherlands, Secretary G e n e r a l, Young World Federalists

MACK, Robert T., Jr., Millbrae Highlands, California, member of Special United Nations Subcommittee, American Veterans Committee; author of *Raising the World Standard of Living* (New York, Citadel, 1953)

MADEC, R., Cauderan (Gironde), France, Secrétaire Général, Ligue des Citoyens du Monde

MALM, Harry, Chicago, Illinois, lawyer, member of Board of Directors of the Conference Upon Research and Education in world government; past Chairman of Near North Side Chapter, United World Federalists

MANN, Dr. Lothar, Horrem bez. Köln, Germany

MARK, Edward B. W., La Mesa, California, retired teacher of high school science; member of the Civic Affairs Commission of the San Diego Council of Churches

MARAN, Rita, New York, N. Y.

MASON, George Allen, Kenilworth, Illinois, attorney, Sears Roebuck and Company; Vice-President, Illinois Branch, and former Chairman of North Shore Chapter, United World Federalists

MATHEWS, John A., Silver Springs, Maryland, Lieutenant C o l o n e l, United States Air Force; author, *Logistical Aspects of Atlantic Union;* a Director of Atlantic Union Committee; former Chairman of Washington Chapter, A t l a n t i c Union Committee; former International Relations Chairman, Virginia Congress of Parents and Teachers

MAYER, Rev. Theodore, Steubenville, Ohio

MEAD, Waldo B., Buffalo, New York, Associate Pastor of Asbury Delaware Church; former Managing Editor of *World Frontiers*

MEARNS, J. B., Berkeley, California

MELCHIOR, Charles, B r o o m a l l, Pennsylvania

MENUHIN, Yehudi, Los Gatos, California, concert violinist

MEREDITH, Christopher, Stanmore, Middlesex, England

MERRITT, Oscar K., Mount Airy, North C a r o l i n a, manufacturer, President of Renfrou Hosiery Mills; founder of high school world peace study and speaking program

MEYER, Mike, Princeton, New Jersey, advertising executive

MILLARD, Elizabeth Boynton (Mrs. Everett Lee, Sr.), Highland Park, Illinois; a principal contributor of funds to meet deficits of CURE's letter of discussion ONE WORLD, 1953-1959

MILLARD, Everett Lee, Highland Park, I l l i n o i s, Editor, *ONE WORLD;* Executive Director, Conference Upon Research and Education in world g o v e r n m e n t (CURE); Secretary, Special United Nations Subcommittee of American Veterans Committee; former member of Board of Illinois State Branch, United World Federalists; service as Lieutenant Commander in United States Navy, World War II

MILLARD, Malcolm, Carmel, California, lawyer; Chairman of Monterey Institute of Foreign Studies; service as Lieutenant in United States Navy, World War II; former member of Board, Conference Upon Research and Education in world government

MILLARD, Mary Hyde (Mrs. Everett Lee), Highland Park, Illinois

MILLER, Carl S., West Somerville, Massachusetts

MILLER, Frank, Quincy, Illinois, former Chairman of the National Board of WORLD

MILLIGEN, Ralph, Rochester, New York

MOECKLY, Floyd J., Des Moines, Iowa, Manager of National Finance Company, Corporal in 6th U. S. Field Artillery, 1st Division, with 21 months World War I service in France; Chairman of World Peace Education Committee, T r i n i t y Methodist Church; an organizer and Board member of Goodwill Industries; former President of Des Moines Chapter and member of Executive Council of Midwest Region, United World Federalists

MONTAGUE, Leroy, Chicago, Illinois, Co-Editor of *Federalist Opinion*

MOORE, Rev. Philip S., C.S.C., Notre Dame, Indiana, Vice-President for Academic Affairs, University of Notre Dame; Editor of *Publications in Medieval Studies*

MOORE, Miss Sarah Hill, Fayetteville, North Carolina, housing executive; Secretary, American Freedom Association

MOSTEK, Raymond, Chicago, Illinois

MULLER, Professor Philippe L., Neuchâtel, Switzerland

MUNGER, Mrs. T. T., Portland, Oregon

MYERS, Robert, Quincy, Illinois

MYGATT, Tracy D., Brewster, New York, New York Secretary of Campaign for World Government; member of National Advisory Committee, War Resisters' League; author of *The Sword of the Samurai* (Century)

McALLISTER, Gilbert, London, England, correspondent, author and editor; Secretary General, World Association of Parliamentarians for World Government; former Member of Parliament (Labour, Rutherford Glen Division of Lanarkshire) 1945-1951; former Chairman of British Parliamentary Group for World Government

McCARTHY, Michael V., Jr., Chicago, Illinois

McILVAINE, Henry C., Jr., San Diego, California, Captain USNR

(Ret.); commissioned service in World Wars I and II; member of Board of Directors, San Diego Chapter, American Association for the United Nations; former Chairman West Side Chapter (N.Y.), Le Mesa Chapter (California) and San Diego Area Council of United World Federalists

McINARRIE, Mrs. Irvine, Minneapolis, Minnesota

McKEE, Josephine, Indianapolis, Indiana

McLANE, Robert, Tahoe City, California

McMILLEN, Mrs. Denise, Zuider Paare, Cape Province, Union of South Africa

NAKAMURA, T., Kameoka, Kyoto-Fu, Japan

NASH, Hugh, New York, N. Y., staff member, *Architectural Forum*

NASH, Dr. Vernon, Santa Barbara, California, writer and lecturer; over 2500 speaking engagements in every state, Canada and Mexico; founded first school of journalism in Asia at Yenching University, Peking; member of Executive Council, a founder and former National Vice-President of United World Federalists; author of *The World Must Be Governed* (Harper's) and several pamphlets

NIELSEN, Knud, Alleröd, Denmark

O'CONNELL, Richard M., Ann Arbor, Michigan, Department of Psychology, University of Michigan

OGILVY, Stewart M., New York, N. Y., staff member of *Fortune;* former Associate Editor, *World Government News*

OKIE, Richardson B., St. Paul, Minnesota

ONG, Richard M., Washington, D. C., graduate student in Department of Government, Georgetown University, Washington, D. C.

ORMES, Merrill, Gary, Indiana, sales and public relations counsellor; member of Chicago Area Council, United World Federalists

OSBORN, Mrs. Chase S., Poulan, Worth County, Georgia

OSBORN, Earl D., New York, N. Y., President, Institute for International Order; member of Executive Council, United World Federalists

PAPIN, Dr. Joseph, South Bend, Indiana, Professor of Religion, University of Notre Dame; former President of Middle European Federal Association

PARMELEE, J. Foster, New York, N. Y.

PARMELEE, Professor Maurice, Ft. Pierce, Florida

PARSONS, Neil, Dallas, Texas, District Manager for construction equipment distributor; former President, Iowa State College Chapter, and former Executive Director for Iowa, United World Federalists

PAVLO, Hattie May, Las Vegas, Nevada, Women for Union of the Free

PEPPER, Claude E., Tallahassee, Florida, lawyer; former United States Senator from Florida

PERRY, Mrs. R. J., Lachine, P. Q., Canada, past Chairman, World Federalists of Canada

PETERSON, Johanna S., Boston, Massachusetts, teacher and translator, Department of Translations, Christian Science Monitor; former Lecturer at Finnish University, Turku, Finland; former Secretary and Treasurer, Woodstock (Vt.) Chapter, United World Federalists

PETERSON, Walter J., Detroit, Michigan

PICKARD, Clarence, Indianola, Iowa, retired educator and farmer; Associate Professor of Agricultural Economics; former President of Adult Education Council, Indianola; member of Executive Council, Midwest Region, United World Federalists

PIERCE, Charles, Augusta, Maine

PITMAN, Hon. Isaac James, London, England, Member of Parliament (Conservative, Bath) since 1945; Chairman of Sir Isaac Pitman and Sons, Publishers, and a director of other corporations; former football, skiing, track and boxing blue; war service as Squadron Leader in Royal

Air Force; former Director of the Bank of England

PLATT, Stanley K., Minneapolis, Minnesota, investment adviser; Vice-Chairman, Board of Directors, World Affairs Center, University of Minnesota; former Chairman of Minneapolis Chapter, Chairman of Minnesota State Branch, and member of Executive Council of United World Federalists

POLKA, L. Brayton, Cambridge, Massachusetts

POST, Eleanor, Brooklyn, New York

POTTER, Neal, Chevy Chase, Maryland, economist; former Associate Professor of Economics at Washington State College; Chairman, Washington, (D. C.) Branch, former President and former Field Director of Washington State Branch, United World Federalists

POTTS, Col. R. Frazier, Miami, Florida, advertising executive; Commander, 9187th Air Reserve Group, United States Air Force; former United States Foreign Service officer and former banker in the United States, Europe and South America; co-founder of Federal Union and past Chairman of New York City Chapter; co-founder of Miami Chapter of United World Federalists; member of Board of Directors, Greater Miami Chapter, American Civil Liberties Union

PRICE, Dr. Charles C., Lansdowne, Pennsylvania, Head of the Department of Chemistry, University of Pennsylvania; Chairman, Federation of American Scientists; former member of United States Office of Scientific Research and of National Research Council; First Vice-President and Chairman of Public Affairs Committee, United World Federalists

PRICE, Rev. Willy, Notre Dame, Indiana, University of Notre Dame

PUGH, Robert, Ramona, California

PURVIS, Harry, Northport, New York

PUTNAM, Mrs. John B., Bratenahl, Cleveland, Ohio

RABER, Sam, Beverly Hills, California; Vice-President California Branch and Member of Executive Council, United World Federalists

RAGAN, Sue, Avondale Estates, Georgia

READ, Thane, Tempe, Arizona, economist; Chairman of Committee on Elections of North American Council for Peoples' World Constitutional Convention

REFIOR, Everett L., Whitewater, Wisconsin, Assistant Professor of Economics at Wisconsin State College; former Vice-President, Iowa State University Chapter, United World Federalists

RENO, Robert H., Concord, New Hampshire, lawyer; former member of Federal Bureau of Investigation

RICHARDS, Howard C., Redlands, California, law student, Stanford University; Western Area Student Chairman, United World Federalists; organizer and Chairman of first Model United Nations on East Coast; past Chairman, Yale Student Federalists

RINGER, Mrs. Fritz K. (Mary Master), Montclair, New Jersey, Administrative Assistant of New England Region, United World Federalists

RIORDEN, Mrs. Shane, Williamstown, Massachusetts; former Secretary General of Young World Federalists; former Executive Director of WORLD; former member of Executive Council of United World Federalists

ROALSON, J. E., Franklin Park, Illinois, Leyden Community High School

ROBERSON, Mary E., Corvallis, Oregon

ROBERTSON, T. E., Jr., Longmont, Colorado, former member of Mutual Security Agency in Formosa; former Chairman of Student Division, United World Federalists

RODEWALD, Eliza, St. Louis, Missouri

ROLOFF, Paul, Columbus, Ohio, former Executive Director, Ohio Branch, United World Federalists

RØNN, Erik S., Gentofte, Denmark

ROOT, Mrs. John W., Chicago, Illinois, past President of Illinois State Branch and former member of Executive Council, United World Federalists

ROPER, Elmo, New York, N. Y., public opinion analyst; President of Atlantic Union Committee

ROSENFELD, George, Berea, Ohio

ROSS, Carl A., Grass Valley, California, retired lawyer; author of several pamphlets

RUCKMAN, Clyde E., Seal Beach, California

RYDER, John, Boonton, New Jersey, high school teacher; member of Executive Council of New Jersey State Branch, United World Federalists

SANDBERG, Allen L., Riverside, Illinois, Assistant Village Manager

SAVARY, Jacques, Paris, France, Secretary General, World Council for Peoples' World Constitutional Convention

SAXTON, Dr. George, Hinsdale, Illinois

SCARRITT, James, Kansas City, Missouri, graduate student of political science, Woodrow Wilson School, Princeton University; former Chairman of Princeton University Chapter, United World Federalists

SCHILPP, Paul A., Glenview, Illinois, Professor of Philosophy, Northwestern University; President of the American Philosophical Society; Editor of the Library of Living Philosophers

SCHLAIN, Mrs. Harold D., Philadelphia, Pennsylvania, member of Executive Board, and Chairman of Organization Liaison Committee, Philadelphia Area Council, and former Chairman of Germantown-Chestnut Hill Chapter, United World Federalists; former leader of Great Books discussion group

SCHMALT, Karl, Weinheim a.d.B., West Germany, architect and Jugo Liaison Officer of Westdeutsche Zeitung; Weltföderalisten Kreisgruppe Mannheim

SCHMIDT, A. W., Pittsburgh, Pennsylvania

SCHMIEDESKAMP, Mrs. Carl, Quincy, Illinois

SCHNEEBERG, Boris, Binghamton, New York

SCHNEIDER, John W., Bay Shore, L. I., New York, accountant; Treasurer, New York State Branch, United World Federalists

SCHOENTHAL, Val L., Des Moines, Iowa

SCHULTZ, L. H., Batavia, New York, President of Blue Bus Lines; President, Genessee Memorial Hospital; former Chairman, Action Committee, Federal Union; Chairman of American delegation at first Congress of World Movement for World Federal Government at Montreaux, Switzerland, 1947, and former Treasurer of World Movement for World Federal Government

SCHWARZ, William H., Minneapolis, Minnesota

SCOTT, David, Wallowa, Oregon

SEAVER, Ben, San Francisco, California

SEILER, Charles, Northbrook, Illinois, newspaper advertising executive, the St. Louis *Post-Dispatch;* Chairman, North Shore Chapter, United World Federalists

SEMLING, Harold V., Jr., Washington, D. C., trade association public relations executive; lecturer in Government Public Relations at American University; former member of National Board, Americans for Democratic Action; former Student Chairman, Washington (D. C.) Chapter of United World Federalists

SHAW, Rev. Rodney, Oconomowoc, Wisconsin, Regional Field Director, Midwest Branch, United World Federalists; member of Board of Directors, Wisconsin Branch, American Association for the United Nations; former Southwestern Golden Gloves boxing champion; service as Chaplain, United States Army, during World War II

SHEA, George E., Jr., New York, N. Y.

SHELDON, Horace, Yonkers, New York

SHULER, Joy, Philadelphia, Pennsylvania

SIBLEY, Hiram Watson, Chicago, Illinois, Secretary of Council on Planning, Financing and Prepayment of the American Hospital Association; Trustee of Anatolia College, Thessaloniki, Greece; former member of United Nations Relief and Rehabilitation Administration (UNRRA) in Greece; former Director of Program Development, Yale-New Haven Medical Center and Assistant Professor of Public Health Administration

SIECK, Mrs. Herbert, Winnetka, Illinois, member of Chicago Area Council, United World Federalists

SINGER, Dr. J. David, Ann Arbor, Michigan, member of the Department of Political Science at the University of Michigan; former visiting Ford Fellow in International Relations in Harvard University

SMEDLEY, Frederick, Brooklyn, New York

SMITH, Mrs. Albert S., Winnetka, Illinois

SMITH, Gilbert K., New York, N. Y.

SMITH, Lewis F., La Mesa, California

SMITH, Mrs. P. R., Alameda, New Mexico

SMITH, Perry Dunlap, Winnetka, Illinois, Professor of Education, Roosevelt College; former headmaster, North Shore Country Day School; service in France as Captain of Artillery, United States Army, during World War I

SMITH, Reed, Berea, Ohio, Professor of Political Science, Baldwin Wallace College

SMITH, Taylor J., Avon, Ohio, past Chairman, Harvard World Federalists and Editor of the *Harvard World Federalist*

SMOYEI, Mrs. Stanley, Princeton, New Jersey

SOHN, Louis B., Cambridge, Massachusetts, Professor of Law, Harvard University Law School; co-author of *World Peace through World Law*; former Legal Officer, Secretariat of the United Nations

SOLA, Renzo, Venice, Italy, Professor of English Language and Literature; Italian Delegate to Parliament of Commonwealth of World Citizens

SPARLING, Dr. Edward J., Chicago, Illinois, President of Roosevelt College

SPRINGER, Robert, Worcester, Massachusetts

STANLEY, C. Max, Muscatine, Iowa, President, S t a n l e y Engineering Company; member of Executive Council and past national President of United World Federalists

STANLEY, David, Muscatine, Iowa, lawyer; State Representative (Republican); former member of Executive Council, United World Federalists

STANLEY, Harry E., West Chester, Pennsylvania, research supervisor; Chairman of Chester County Chapter, Atlantic Union Committee

STARK, Bruce, Eugene, Oregon

STEEN, Julian J., Chicago, Illinois, Dean, Academy of Languages; former member of Faculty of Languages, University of Pittsburgh and University of South Dakota; Chairman of Chicago Chapter, Atlantic Union Committee

STEIER, Arthur, New York, N. Y., member of co-ordinating Council, New York Student Federalists

STICKNEY, David, Lake Forest, Illinois, Manager of Professional Relations, Bauer and Black; Member of Board, Illinois-Chicago Chapter, American Association for the United Nations

STILLIANS, Dr. A. W., Chicago, Illinois, physician; Professor Emeritus of Dermatology and for 21 years head of Department of Dermatology at Northwestern University; member of Board of Directors of the Conference Upon Research and Education in world government

STUART, Robert, Chicago, Illinois, Vice-President of National Can Corporation; Vice-President of Illinois State Branch, and member of Executive Council, United World Federalists

SUITS, Hollis E., St. Louis, Missouri

SURR, John V., Redlands, California, student, Yale University; New England Student Chairman and past President of Yale University Chapter of United World Federalists

SWENSON, Adrienne S., Manhattan Beach, California

SWETT, Dr. Norris P., Bloomfield, Connecticut

TAKARO, Dr. Timothy, Oteen, North Carolina, physician

TAYLOR, Mrs. William H., Portland, Oregon

TEMPLE, Mary N., (Mrs. Edward Holmgren), Chicago, Illinois, American Friends Service Committee; former Field Director, Midwest Branch, United World Federalists; former Executive Director, Conference Upon Research and Education in world government

TEMPLIN, Paul, San Francisco, California

TEMPLIN, Ralph, Cedarville, Ohio, Professor of Sociology, Central State College

TEW, E. S., London, England

THROCKMORTON, Mrs. Edgerton, Dundee, Illinois, former Chairman, Barrington Chapter, United World Federalists; former member of Board of Directors of the Conference Upon Research and Education in world government

THYGESON, Fritjof, Berkeley, California, graduate student of political science at the University of California, past National Chairman, Young Peoples' Socialist League; past National Vice-Chairman of Student Division and member of Executive Council, United World Federalists; former member of board, WORLD

TIFFANY, Mrs. Albert, Geneseo, Illinois

TIELE-RANEY, Mrs. Clyde L., The Hague, The Netherlands

TOBIN, Irving, Elizabeth, New Jersey

TROPE, Sally Hammond, New York, N. Y., journalist, *The New York Post*; former editor of weekly newspapers in Winter Park, Florida and Watch Hill, Rhode Island, founder and former Chairman of four chapters and member of Executive Council, New York State Branch, United World Federalists

TURNER, Glenn P., Middleton, Wisconsin, retired lawyer; former member of the Wisconsin State Assembly; Director of Esperanto Library; member of School Board; instructor in United States Air Corps radio school, Truax Field, for three years during World War II

UNWIN, Colin, Perth, Western Australia

VALIMONT, Robert W., Doylestown, Pennsylvania

VANMETER, Kezia, Poughkeepsie, New York, student, Vassar College

VOORHEES, Koert, Cedar Falls, Iowa, manufacturer; President of Universal Hoist Company; past member of Executive Council, United World Federalists

VOORHIS, Jerry, Winnetka, Illinois, Executive Director, Co-operative League of America; member of Executive Council, United World Federalists; former United States Representative from California

WADLOW, René, Twin Lakes, Far Hills, New Jersey, graduate student; member of Board of Directors of the Conference Upon Research and Education in world government; former Chairman, Young Adult Council, National Social Welfare Assembly; former member of Executive Council, United World Federalists

WAGNER, Robert J., Feasterville, Pennsylvania

WAGNER, W. J., Notre Dame, Indiana, Associate Professor of Law, University of Notre Dame; Vice President, Mid - Lakes Branch,

United World Federalists; former President, Association for Central European Co-operation; author, *Les Libertés de l'Air* (Paris)

WALKER, J. W., Johnson City, New York, insurance salesman; former junior high school teacher; two years active duty as Lieutenant, United States Naval Reserve during World War II; former Chairman, New York Citizens Committee for a Peoples' World Constitutional Convention

WANG, Mrs. Arthur, (Mary Ellen Mackay), New York, N. Y.

WASSERMAN, William J., Seattle, Washington

WATERS, William, Hilton, New York

WAYMACK, W. W., Adel, Iowa, former Editor of the Des Moines Register and Tribune; winner of the Pulitzer Prize for Editorial Excellence; former member, United States Atomic Energy Commission

WEBB, M. A., San Antonio, Texas

WEBER, Carl E., Portland, Oregon, past President of Seattle Chapter, United World Federalists

WEBER, Richard, Summit, New Jersey

WEBSTER, David J., London, England, news analyst, British Broadcasting Corporation; former Secretary-General, Young World Federalists

WECKER, Franz Theodor, Lübeck, Germany, importer, proprietor of wholesale fruit business and world traveller with 17 years' residence in Caracas, Venezuela; Member of Kaufmannschaft zu Lübeck and of World Association of World Federalists, German Branch

WEIK, Mary Hays, Cincinnati, Ohio, Director, American Registry of World Citizens; member of World Administrative Council, International Registry of World Citizens; Editor, *World Citizens*; author, World Community Pamphlets; former Chairman, Action Committee for Peace, United World Federalists of New York City

WEIL, Frank E. G., New York, N. Y., attorney; member of Special United Nations Subcommittee, American Veterans Committee

WELCH, Mrs. Rachel, Georgetown, D. C., writer; former naval architect

WHEELER, William A., Rochester, New York, adjuster; veteran of three years in European Theatre, World War II; Treasurer, New York State Branch and former Chairman, Genesee Council, United World Federalists

WHEELWRIGHT, Robert, Wilmington, Delaware, past President United World Federalists of Delaware

WHITNEY, Byrl A., Kensington, Maryland, Director of Education and Research, Brotherhood of Railway Trainmen; former legal advisor on foreign law, United States Department of State; author of *Parliamentary Guide* and many magazine articles; former member of Executive Council, United World Federalists

WILDER, Erskine, Jr., Dundee, Illinois, Vice-President, Falley Petroleum Company

WILLIAMS, John R., Lakewood, Ohio, lawyer; lecturer in World Law at Western Reserve University; Chairman of World Affairs Committee, Cuyahoga County Bar Association; past Chairman, International Relations Committee, Cleveland Bar Association; Secretary, North East Ohio Board of World Peace of the Methodist Church

WILLIAMS, Stillman P., Lexington, Massachusetts, Director of World Order Library; member of Special United Nations Subcommittee, American Veterans Committee

WILSON, Charles Carrol, Danville, Illinois, Managing Editor, *Taxpayer-Consumer Research Reports;* former President, Calumet Life Underwriters' Association; former President, Landlords and Property Owners Association

222

WINIKER, Norman, Levittown, New York

WOLF, Paul, Cresskill, New Jersey

WOLFF, Edward, Hyattsville, Maryland, electronics engineer, Maryland Electronics Manufacturing Corporation; former President, University of Illinois Chapter, United World Federalists; former President, Washington (D. C.) Chapter, WORLD

WRAY, Llew H., Ridgewood, New Jersey

WRIGHT, Quincy, Charlottesville, Virginia, Professor of Political Science at the University of Virginia; Professor Emeritus of Political Science, University of Chicago; member of the Board of Carnegie Endowment for International Peace; author, *A Study of War, Problems of Stability and Progress in International Relations* (Berkeley, 1954) and other works

WYNNER, Edith, New York, N. Y., writer and lecturer; former New York Secretary of Campaign for World Government; former Vice-President of World Movement for World Federal Government; co-author of *Searchlight on Peace Plans* (Dutton, 1944); author of several pamphlets.

Libraries containing bound volumes of CURE debates published in *One World*

BELGIUM

Brussels — Union of International Associations

ENGLAND

London — The British Museum

GERMANY

(West) Berlin — Deutsche Hochschule Für Politik

INDIA

Jalpaiguri (West Bengal) — A. C. College

NETHERLANDS

Amsterdam — World Association of World Federalists
The Hague — The Peace Palace

UNITED STATES

Atlanta, Georgia — Carnegie Library
Atlanta, Georgia — Public Library
Bloomington, Indiana — University of Indiana
Bluffton, Ohio — Musselman Library
Cambridge, Massachusetts — Harvard University Library
Chicago, Illinois — Joint Reference Library
Chicago, Illinois — University of Chicago
Concord, Massachusetts — Public Library
Escondido, California — City Library
Hartford, Connecticut — Connecticut State Library
Hartford, Connecticut — Hartford City Library
Indianola, Iowa — Simpson College
Kearny, New Jersey — Public Library
Little Ferry, New Jersey — Public Library
New York, N. Y. — Public Library
New York, N. Y. — United Nations
Philadelphia, Pennsylvania — Free Library (Logan Square Branch)
Philadelphia, Pennsylvania — Free Library (Oak Lane Branch)
Poughkeepsie, New York — Vassar College
Rochester, New York — Public Library
Rochester, New York — Rundel Memorial Library
Salisbury, North Carolina — Catawaba College
Santa Monica, California — Public Library
Tallahassee, Florida — Florida State University
Washington, D. C. — Library of Congress
West Hartford, Connecticut — West Hartford Town Library